CW01346861

Return of the Prodigal

SOUTH AFRICA'S CRICKETING COMEBACK

COLIN BRYDEN

Jonty Rhodes dives to run out Inzamam-ul-Haq, one of the enduring images of South Africa's World Cup campaign.

Return of the Prodigal

SOUTH AFRICA'S CRICKETING COMEBACK

COLIN BRYDEN

Sunday Times with Jonathan Ball Publishers

JOHANNESBURG

PHOTOGRAPHIC ACKNOWLEDGEMENTS

All photographs used in both the photographic illustration sections were supplied by the South African Sports Illustrated Agency, with the exception of the photograph of Jonty Rhodes with autograph hunting fans at Jan Smuts Airport, which was supplied by courtesy of the Sunday Times.

SASI = South African Sports Illustrated Agency

Title page	Jim Fenwick (Australia)
Page	
8	SASI
10	SASI
12	SASI
14	Associated Press Wire Service
16	Sunday Times
19	Times Media Library
20	Sunday Times
22	Sunday Times
24	Times Media Library
26	SASI
29	Times Media Library
32	SASI
34	Times Media Library
36	United Cricket Board
38	SASI
40	SASI
42	SASI
45	SASI
46	Sunday Times
48	SASI
50	SASI
53	SASI
60	SASI
62	SASI
64	Business Day
67	SASI
70	Times Media Library
72	Sunday Times
73	SASI
76	Sunday Times
77	SASI
80	SASI
81	SASI
86	SASI
88	Times Media Library
92	SASI
96	SASI
99	SASI
103	Times Media Libary
104	Sunday Times
108	Sunday Times
110	Sporting Pictures (UK) Ltd
114	SASI
116	Times Media Library
118	SASI
122	Sunday Times
126	SASI
129	SASI
132	Sunday Times
134	SASI
135	Times Media Library
136	SASI
141	SASI
143	SASI
146	SASI
152	SASI
159	Sporting Pictures (UK) Ltd
160	SASI
163	SASI
166	SASI
169	SASI
170	Times Media Library
173	SASI
174	SASI
182	SASI
185	SASI
186	Sporting Pictures (UK) Ltd
188	SASI
190	SASI
193	SASI
194	Sporting Pictures (UK) Ltd
197	SASI

All rights reserved. No part of this publication may be reproduced or transmitted, in any form or by any means, without permission from the publishers.

© Text – Colin Bryden 1992
© Photography – see Photographic Acknowledgements

First published in 1992 by
Sunday Times and
Jonathan Ball Publishers
P O Box 2105
Parklands
2121

ISBN 0 947464 58 1

Cover design and text layout by Michael Barnett

Cover photograph by courtesy of Syndication International

Typesetting and reproduction by Book Productions, Pretoria

Reproduction of cover and illustration sections by Adcolour, Johannesburg

Printed and bound by The Penrose Press, Johannesburg

CONTENTS

	FOREWORD	
CHAPTER ONE	TRIUMPH OUT OF TRAGEDY	9
CHAPTER TWO	THE LONG AND WINDING ROAD	15
CHAPTER THREE	FROM GATTING TO UNITY	25
CHAPTER FOUR	THE MAGICAL MYSTERY TOUR	41
CHAPTER FIVE	THE SELECTION BOMBSHELL	61
CHAPTER SIX	THE WARM-UP MATCHES	71
CHAPTER SEVEN	THE IMPOSSIBLE DREAM COMES TRUE	87
CHAPTER EIGHT	DISASTER AND TRIUMPH IN NEW ZEALAND	97
CHAPTER NINE	ON THE VERGE OF THE SEMI-FINALS	115
CHAPTER TEN	INTO THE HOME STRAIGHT	133
CHAPTER ELEVEN	REFLECTIONS ... AND THE FINAL	153
CHAPTER TWELVE	CARIBBEAN SUNSET	167
CHAPTER THIRTEEN	THE ULTIMATE CHALLENGE	183
	SOUTH AFRICAN INTERNATIONAL CRICKET RECORDS	202
	INDEX	205

FOREWORD

The 1991/92 season has been a special time for South African cricket.

The unexpected nature of our return to international cricket and the remarkable happenings that followed, made it probably the most eventful season in our history.

The tours of India and the West Indies were historic as was our participation in the World Cup.

Colin Bryden has been involved in South African cricket through these momentous times and there is probably no-one better equipped to comment on both the political and cricket aspects of our return to international cricket.

Having been on all three tours with the South African team he is able to give a first-hand objective account.

Although South Africa did well in cricket terms considering the years of isolation, the tours have taught us that much hard work remains to be done.

South African cricket journalists have also suffered with isolation but Colin Bryden is a cricket writer more than capable of holding his own in the international scene.

KEPLER WESSELS
Port Elizabeth
13 May 1992

8

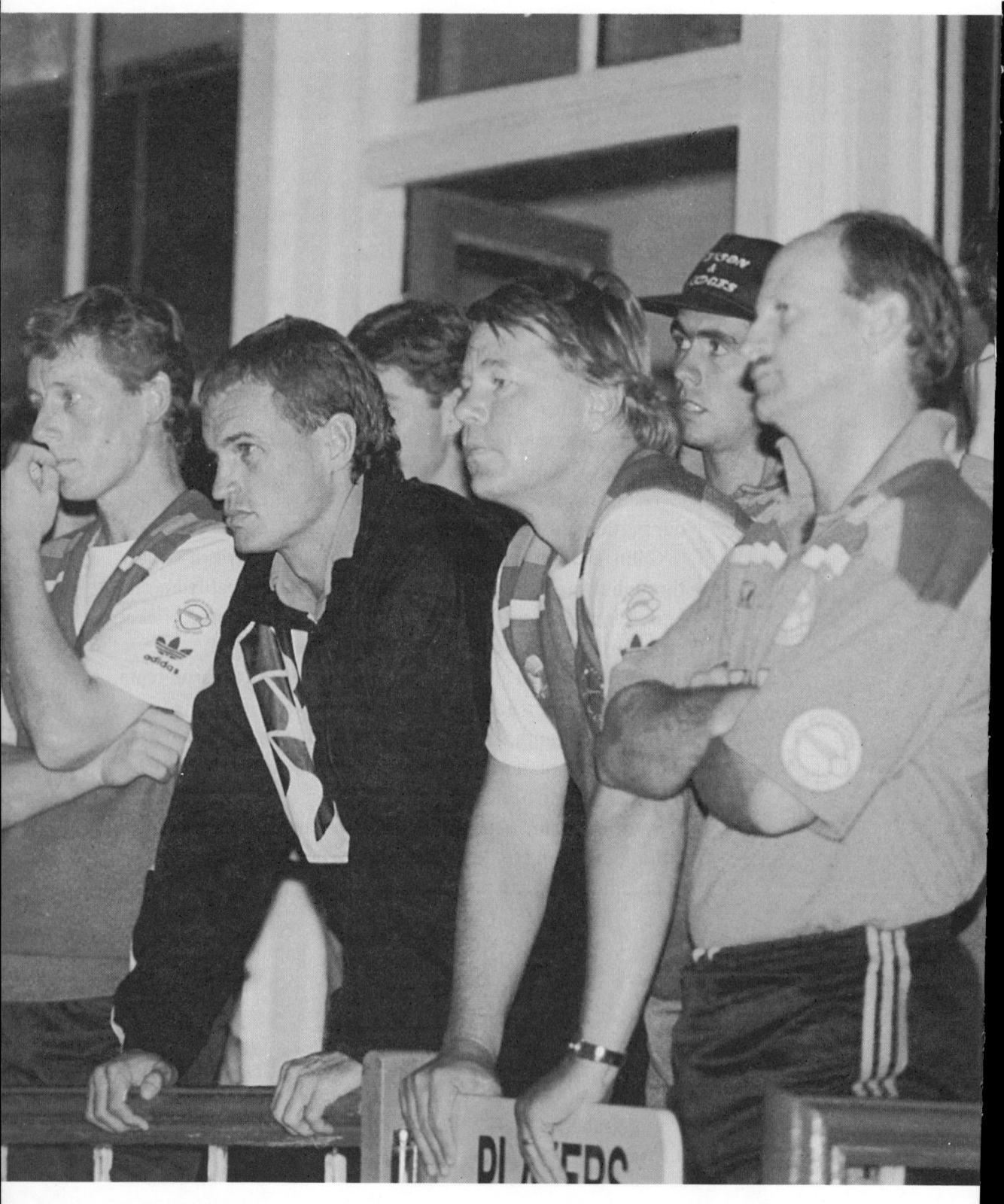

Agony on the balcony as the South African players watch the last moments of the World Cup semi-final in Sydney.

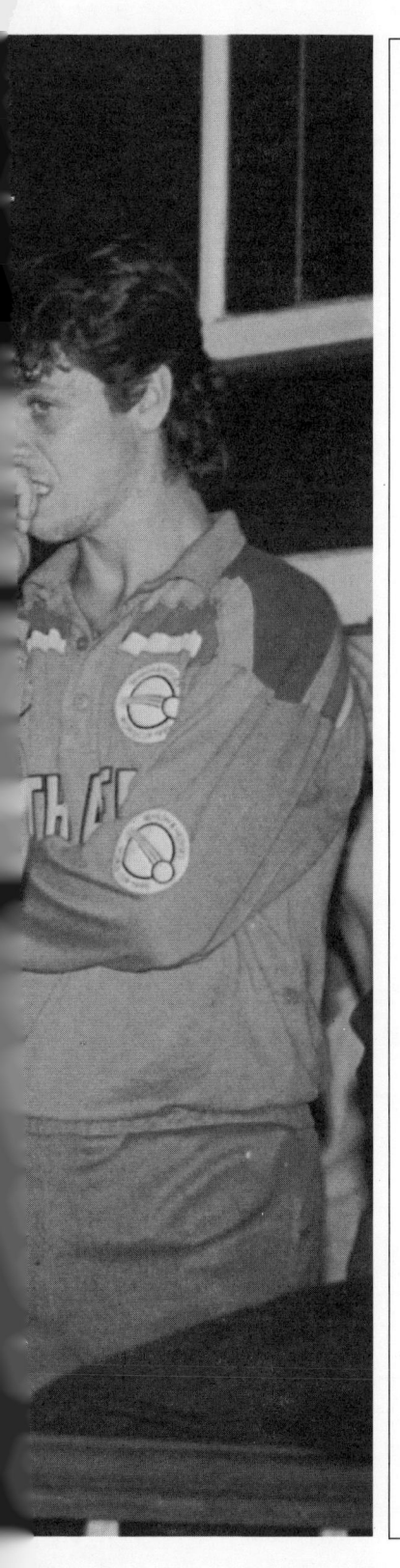

CHAPTER ONE

TRIUMPH OUT OF TRAGEDY

South Africa stood on the brink of one of its greatest sporting triumphs. Twenty-two runs were needed off 13 balls for a win over England and a place in the World Cup cricket final.

For a country banished from the world cricket stage for 22 years this would be no ordinary sporting victory. It would mark the end of a long and painful road, of years of hopelessness and, more recently, a year of dramatic change.

As the drama built up for 28 410 spectators at the Sydney Cricket Ground and for millions of South Africans watching on television, so did a steady drizzle, which had been falling for several minutes. The slanting rain was etched against the dazzling floodlights and dripping down Brian McMillan's face as he squared up to Chris Lewis, carrying his nation's hopes. The umpires conferred.

The South African batsmen were asked whether they were prepared to carry on. They were. The same question was asked of Graham Gooch, the England captain. He threw it back at the umpires. What do you think? he asked. The answer, sadly for South Africa, had to be that conditions were no longer suitable for play.

The players left the field to a chorus of boos. The crowd would be denied an exciting finish; South Africa the opportunity to score those 22 runs, just one for each long year of isolation.

In an atmosphere of farce, they returned to the field, to face only one ball. The giant electronic scoreboard proclaimed that 22 runs were needed. In fact, under the formula governing interrupted games, it was only 21, but it didn't matter. England

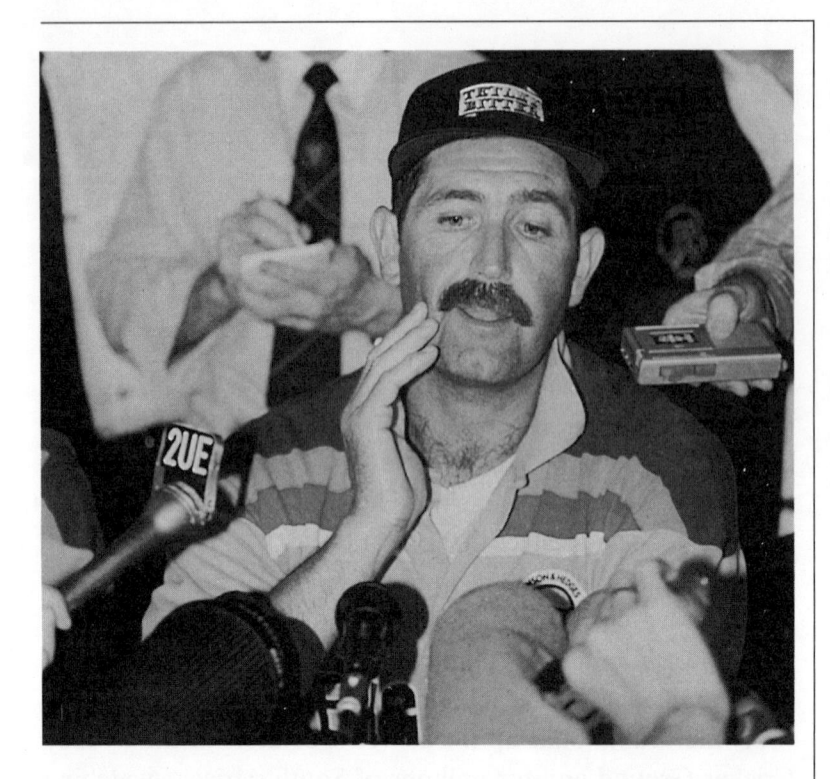

England captain Graham Gooch ... 'an unsatisfactory finish'.

would be the winners. McMillan tapped the ball to the on-side, took a single, and then he and Dave Richardson shook hands with sympathetic England players. South Africa were out of the World Cup.

It was a moment of numbing disappointment but the South African players turned their exit into a glorious, emotional farewell. They went on to the field to congratulate the Englishmen, then jogged around the ground to wave farewell to a wildly cheering crowd – one that had booed them barely four hours earlier for bowling only 45 overs in the time allotted for 50. It was a time for tears and unabashed emotion, an end to the most dramatic chapter in South Africa's sporting history.

The World Cup saga had captured the imagination of South Africa. People with no previous interest in the game had become instant experts. Because this was the first sporting team to represent a South Africa of negotiation and conciliation, the enthusiasm crossed all barriers. Afrikaner farmers in the northern Transvaal and young radical politicians of the ANC followed the matches with equal passion.

From the time that South Africa were admitted to the 1992 World Cup the tour had a significance beyond cricket. The fact that it coincided with a referendum on President F W de Klerk's reform process heightened the intensity of interest in the cricket. As campaigners for a yes vote pointed out, future tours would be doomed if the white electorate put the brakes on political change – and when the voters gave a resounding yes to reform it was suggested by at least one columnist that South Africa's win over India two days earlier to secure a place in the semi-finals had influenced voters to see the positive, optimistic face of change.

Amid such momentous events, the players could scarcely avoid feeling burdened with an extra sense of responsibility. For seven weeks, 14 young men had been under a relentless spotlight. Every ball, every stroke played, was subject to the scrutiny and discussion of a nation at last united behind a sporting team. The pressure could hardly have been greater, yet the players had exceeded all expectations by reaching the semi-finals, taking their place among the elite of the nine competing nations. They had won five of their eight matches and had beaten such established Test nations as Australia, West Indies, Pakistan and India.

Perhaps it was an intuitive understanding of the significance of the events of preceding decades that prompted Kepler Wessels and his players to make the supreme sporting gesture of congratulating the English team in public, when, minutes earlier, some of the players had wept tears of anguish and anger as the realisation of the illogicality and inflexibility of the rules sank in.

Later, at a chaotic press conference, speaking without a microphone against the hubbub of the adjacent SCG Members bar, Wessels had swiftly come to terms with the situation. He was disappointed with the way South Africa had lost but he had no complaints about the conduct of the umpires and Graham Gooch. If he had been Gooch, with his bowlers having to control a wet ball and fielders liable to slip on the greasy turf, he too would have put the onus on the umpires to make the decision.

Mike Procter commiserates with Brian McMillan after the semi-final.

Most of all, though, Wessels was proud of his team who had done so well in reaching the last four.

The villain of the piece was the rulebook. There had been controversy throughout the World Cup about the rules governing rain-interrupted matches.

The rules in this most-marketed competition in cricket history were designed with television in mind. The Channel Nine organisation has immense influence on cricket in Australia. As a commercial broadcasting organisation, Channel Nine is happy to capitalise on the drawing power of cricket – but not at the expense of the next programme. There was, therefore, no provision for an extension of time for the team batting second. Any interruption caused overs to be deducted at a rate of 14 to the hour.

In the event of an interruption, the revised target for the batting team was set according to the highest-scoring equivalent overs of their opponents. According to this formula, the

South African innings was to be reduced to 43 overs and the England score adjusted from 252 off 45 overs to 251 off 43, a difference of only one run.

Although one would not have dared mention it to a South African supporter in the heat of the controversy, it is likely that if rain had not stopped play South Africa would have failed to score the required runs. If anything England were favourites, although McMillan and Richardson had scored 10 runs off the first five balls of Lewis's over and were in relentless form. McMillan in particular had been one of the stars of the World Cup and had shown himself to be a supreme competitor.

Mike Procter, the South African coach, said afterwards he felt confident simply because McMillan was still at the crease. 'On a big field like the SCG it is relatively easy to chip the ball between the inner and outer rings of fielders and take twos instead of ones.'

One mistake by either batsman, or a brilliant piece of bowling or fielding, would probably have dashed South Africa's hopes, although the batsmen still in the pavilion, Richard Snell, Meyrick Pringle and Allan Donald, were all prepared to have a full tilt at glory.

What Gooch described as 'an unsatisfactory finish to a great game of cricket' meant that the world would never know who would have won if the rules had allowed for even 10 extra minutes of play.

England went on to play Pakistan in the final in front of 87 182 spectators in Melbourne three days later. Pakistan, beaten twice by South Africa in the space of the previous five weeks, carried off the crystal trophy. It was, however, a much-improved Pakistan team, who had come through to win their last five matches after a poor start to the tournament.

To claim that South Africa were robbed of the World Cup is an emotional reaction. Although the rules were unsatisfactory they applied to all teams and had been approved by the competing nations.

Emotion, though, is understandable. After many years in the wilderness the cricket tour held South Africa spellbound. It was an unforgettable period in the country's history.

Back at Lord's. Krish Mackerdhuj, Geoff Dakin, Ali Bacher and Steve Tshwete after the UCB was admitted to the ICC.

CHAPTER TWO

THE LONG AND WINDING ROAD

Colin Cowdrey's voice came across a telephone link-up from Sharjah in the United Arab Emirates. 'I am delighted to announce that South Africa has been invited to play in the 1992 Benson and Hedges World Cup,' said the president of the International Cricket Council.

It was October 23, 1991. South Africa's time in the cricket wilderness was over.

In a Sandton hotel, where an audience of more than 100 cricket officials, journalists and sponsors had been anxiously chewing on snacks and making small talk for more than two hours, there was jubilation as Cowdrey's announcement came across a specially set-up speaker system. Although there had been great optimism, there had also been concern that the invitation might be blocked by cricket powers such as Pakistan and the West Indies, both of which had expressed reservations before the meeting. As it turned out, no vote was necessary: it was obvious that most of the ICC members in Sharjah wanted South Africa back.

Among those who celebrated most loudly were two young officials from the National Olympic and Sports Congress (NOSC), Moss Mashishi and Dan Moyo. Their organisation was the sports arm of the African National Congress (ANC) and their broad smiles on this Wednesday night were an indication of just how far-reaching had been the changes in South Africa, and particularly in cricket, since the upheavals of Mike Gatting's rebel English tour which had ended only 20 months before.

Another celebrant in Sandton was Khaya Majola, the

former star allrounder of the South African Cricket Board (SACB), which had been on the other side of a great political divide from the 'establishment' South African Cricket Union (SACU). Majola had once been quoted as saying that SACU should stay out of the townships of his home town of Port Elizabeth or risk violence.

The same Majola was now the development director of the United Cricket Board (UCB), working in an office next to that of Dr Ali Bacher, managing director of the UCB, at the board's headquarters in the gardens of the Wanderers Club in the wealthy northern suburbs of Johannesburg.

On this night, though, Dr Bacher was in Sharjah with a UCB delegation which also included president Geoff Dakin, vice-president Krish Mackerdhuj and management committee member Percy Sonn. As they took turns to come on to the line to Sandton they all expressed their delight. Dakin invited the folks back home to raise their glasses. Because Sharjah was 'dry', he said, his delegation would celebrate with a large jug of water. Mackerdhuj, the former president of the SACB and next president of UCB, reflected that for the first time all South African cricket lovers would be able to support a national team; Sonn, a livewire advocate from Cape Town and another former leading luminary of the SACB, said he hoped to be cheering South Africa all the way to victory in the World Cup.

Questions from journalists were relayed up the line to Sharjah and answered before one of the most remarkable press conferences staged in South Africa came to an end. Jimmy Cook, the most recent Springbok captain and recently returned from a third successive prolific season in England, was invited to the podium and cracked open a bottle of South African sparkling wine. In a typically modest speech he said the World Cup would be a tremendous opportunity 'for those chaps picked'. They were prophetic words, because Cook was to be at the centre of an extraordinary selection controversy and would not make the trip to Australia and New Zealand.

Acceptance in the World Cup brought to an end more than 20 years of isolation brought about because of apartheid.

GEOFFREY DAKIN was born in Port Elizabeth on August 13, 1935, and has spent his life in the Eastern Cape's 'Friendly City'. He was educated at Grey High School and represented Eastern Province Schools between 1952 and 1954, being selected for South African Schools in 1954. An opening batsman, he made his first-class debut for Eastern Province in the 1952/53 season and played in 59 matches until the 1962/63 season with 165 against Western Province being the highest of four centuries.

Geoff Dakin entered administration in 1969 when he became a board member of the Eastern Province Cricket Union and served two terms as president of the South African Cricket Union, from 1984 to 1986 and 1989 to 1991, before being unanimously elected as the inaugural president of the United Cricket Board on June 29, 1991, and was at Lord's 12 days later when South Africa was admitted as a full member of the International Cricket Council.

He is managing director of an agency business in Port Elizabeth.

South Africa was a founder member of the Imperial Cricket Conference in 1909 together with England and Australia and had been playing Test cricket against both these countries since 1888/89. But membership was automatically forfeited in 1961 when South Africa left the Commonwealth. Although the South African Cricket Association applied for a change to the rules to allow full membership to continue, this was blocked by the West Indies, Pakistan and India.

The statement of the Pakistan Cricket Board of Control at the time was to set the tone for future negotiations: 'Unless South Africa is prepared to play such (Test) matches exactly on equal terms with Pakistan, India and the West Indies – coloured members of the Conference – in accordance with the requirements of equality in cricket, no country should play matches of Test status, whether official or unofficial, against South Africa.'

Remarkably, South African newspaper clippings of the time reveal that Pakistan's stance was regarded as unreasonable and 'political'.

The Nationalist government, elected in 1948, was at its most intransigent and was still busily tightening up its apartheid legislation to outlaw social contact between black and white. As C O Medworth, a leading sports journalist, wrote: 'There is precious little chance for some time to come of South Africa's changing her views on the playing of mixed sport. That is Government decree and there it must remain. There is absolutely nothing that cricketers or cricket legislators can do about it, try as they would. Springbok teams would only too gladly visit the West Indies, India and Pakistan – if they would have us. But the trouble is that we could not reciprocate without causing our guests some embarrassment on the social side and in the matter of accommodation.'

It should be noted that there had been no Test matches against the 'coloured' countries before 1948 either.

Test matches continued to be played by South Africa until 1970. The ICC decided that such matches should be 'unofficial' but they have been included in all major statistical records. However, even as the Springboks were reaching their greatest heights, with successive series victories in England in 1965 and at home against Australia in 1966/67 and 1969/70, the noose on international contact was tightening.

In 1965, when the Imperial Cricket Conference became the International Cricket Conference and admitted non-Commonwealth members, South Africa remained excluded. But the greatest blow to South Africa's credibility as a Test cricket country came in 1968 with the infamous Basil d'Oliveira incident.

The Cape Town-born coloured player had become an England cricketer and there was much speculation about his chances of being selected for the scheduled 1968/69 MCC tour of South Africa. D'Oliveira had been dropped from the England side during the series against Australia, but was recalled because of an injury to Roger Prideaux and scored 158 in the final Test at the Oval. It therefore came as a shock when he was omitted from the touring party. Nineteen members of the MCC resigned in protest and there was an outcry from British political and labour leaders. Then came another bombshell. Tom Cartwright withdrew from the team because of injury and D'Oliveira was included. John Vorster, the South African Prime Minister, thundered at a National Party congress in Bloemfontein: 'It is the team of the anti-apartheid movement. We are not prepared to accept a team thrust upon us – it is a team of people who don't care about sports relations at all.' The MCC immediately responded that if the chosen team was not acceptable to South Africa, the tour would be called off. Within a week, after the SACA had regretfully confirmed that the team was not acceptable, the MCC carried out its threat.

Yet MCC went ahead with plans for a South African tour of England in 1970. By this time the anti-apartheid movement was at its strongest and a South African rugby tour of England in 1969/70 was turned into a nightmare for the touring party by relentless demonstrations. Following intervention by the British Home Secretary, James Callaghan, who requested that the cricket tour be cancelled on the grounds of broad public safety, the MCC withdrew its invitation.

The planned 1971/72 tour of Australia was similarly can-

Basil d'Oliveira, son Damian and wife Naomi at Buckingham Palace when he received the OBE in 1969.

celled because of concern about protests. Sir Donald Bradman, chairman of the Australian board, ended a Press statement with the earnest hope 'that the South African Government will, in the near future, so relax its laws that the cricketers of South Africa may once again take their place as full participants in the international field.'

The mounting pressure forced South African cricketers and their administrators to 'look in the mirror', as a future president of SACU, Joe Pamensky, was to say in retrospect.

With the prospects of the 1971/72 tour diminishing, the SACA asked the government for permission to include two black players, chosen from their own trials, in the official touring party. When this was rejected in April 1971, the country's leading players staged a walk-off at Newlands where Transvaal, the Currie Cup champions, were playing a Rest of South Africa team in what amounted to a final trial before the selection of the team for Australia. They handed a statement to the Press supporting SACA's application. The players also stated their support for merit selection, although as Hassan Howa of the rival SA Cricket Board of Control (Sacboc) quickly pointed out, there was a degree of hypocrisy about SACA's wish to include two black players regardless of merit.

It was against this background that protracted negotiations for unity in South African cricket resulted in the formation of the South African Cricket Union (SACU) in September 1977, with SACA and Sacboc joining forces with the SA African Cricket Board. A nine-man motivating committee, consisting of three members each from the three controlling bodies, had held frequent meetings during 1976. They also met regularly with the Minister of Sport, Dr Piet Koornhof, who announced a new sports policy on September 23 which enabled mixed cricket at club level to be played in the 1976/77 season. However, even before the inauguration of the SACU, with Rashid Varachia of Sacboc as the first president, cracks had appeared in the structure of unity. Hundreds of mixed club matches were played, but there were also numerous problems due to misunderstandings and, in some cases, contradictory statements by government officials. The root cause of this was an official policy which, while allowing cricketers of various race groups to play against each other, did not allow mixing within a club – although some players did cross the colour line in joining clubs. In addition, Hassan Howa, Varachia's arch-rival in Sacboc, was mobilising increasing support for a policy of 'no normal sport in an abnormal society'. Even as the SACU was formed, dissident Sacboc members were establishing the SA Cricket Board, which was to take the place of Sacboc as a cricket body opposed to the SACU.

The SACU several times tried to gain admission to the ICC, but without success. They were buoyed by the finding of an ICC commission in 1979 that the SACU was the effective controlling body of cricket in South Africa, but the credibility of the finding was undermined by the refusal of the black Test nations to participate in the commission. The report was simply shelved.

During the lengthening isolation years, the last remaining official international tours on South Africa's schedule, including a 1975 tour of England, were called off. The gap in fixtures enabled England to host the inaugural World Cup,

JOSEPH PAMENSKY, born in Port Elizabeth on July 21, 1930, and educated at Grey High School, has been involved in cricket administration since the age of 19. He played a key role in the negotiations which led to the formation of the SA Cricket Union in 1977.

Joe Pamensky became acting president of the South African Cricket Union when his close friend Rashid Varachia died in office on February 11, 1981. He was formally elected president in 1982 and served until 1984, when he stepped down to become vice-president. He was elected to a second term as president between 1986 and 1989 before retiring from active administration at national level, although remaining an influential figure within cricket. He received the State President's Sports Merit award in 1984 and was honoured as Transvaal cricket administrator of the century when the Transvaal Cricket Council celebrated its centenary in 1990. Managing director of his own financial services company, he was South African Chartered Accountant of the Year in 1984.

thereby establishing limited overs cricket as a major feature on the international calendar. Variety, and a modicum of international competition, was supplied to the domestic scene by a succession of touring teams, including several Derrick Robins XIs and, during unity negotiations, a particularly strong International Wanderers XI in 1975/76 which included Ian and Greg Chappell, Dennis Lillee, Max Walker, Glenn Turner, Mike Denness and Derek Underwood. In the spirit of rapprochement, the South African XIs that opposed the Wanderers included Sacboc players, and in the last of three matches Baboo Ebrahim, a leftarm spinner from Sacboc, took six wickets in the final innings to secure a victory for his team.

Robins XI and International Wanderers tours were no substitute for Test matches, nor could Springbok colours be awarded for matches against such tourists. As 12 years went by with no award of national colours, the SACU were well aware of the frustration of their players. It was therefore not surprising that when a private entrepreneur, Peter Cooke, of Johannesburg, offered them a deal involving a near Test strength English team the SACU were ready to bite. Thus, in March 1982, the era of rebel Tests began.

It was generally accepted that Geoffrey Boycott, one of the world's finest opening batsmen, was the man most instrumental in helping Cooke put together the tour. But captaincy was not part of the deal. Instead Graham Gooch was voted skipper by his fellow players soon after the team's arrival in South Africa, and the tour has been known ever since as the Gooch tour.

Springbok colours were awarded for the first time since 1970. Although the rebel tours were still no substitute for the real thing, it was an emotional time. Certainly the pride displayed by the new Springboks was immense. The sponsors, South African Breweries, held a cocktail party on the eve of the first one-day international in Port Elizabeth and the South African players, even the most hard-bitten veterans, wore their Springbok ties and their blazers with the badge of a springbok head, with an almost palpable sense of accomplishment. The next day, when they walked out to field, they re-

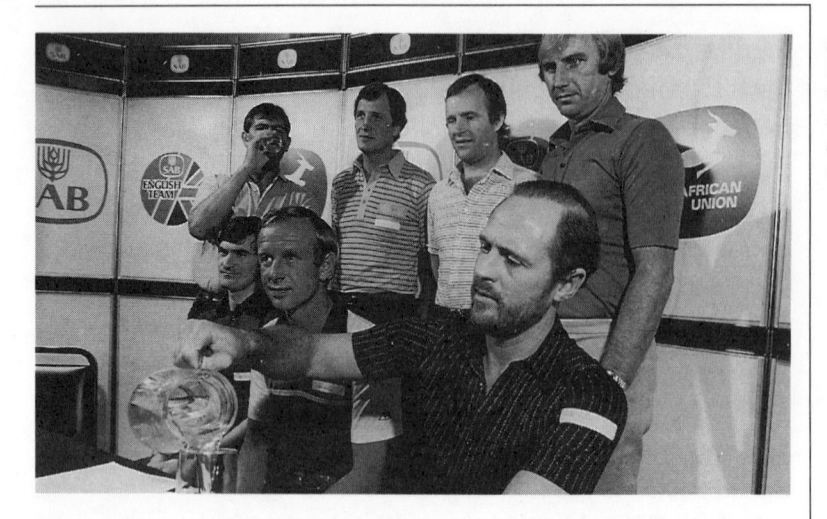

Arrival of the 1982 English team. Standing, from left: Graham Gooch, John Emburey, Dennis Amiss and John Lever. Sitting, Alan Knott, Derek Underwood and Geoff Boycott.

ceived a standing ovation from a capacity crowd. Many a tear was shed.

For Vintcent van der Bijl and Clive Rice it must have been a particularly poignant moment. Both had been selected for the cancelled 1971/72 of Australia 10 years earlier and must have despaired of ever wearing the green and gold cap. That Rice was still a contender when South Africa returned to official international cricket almost another decade later says much for his durability. Other players who had been selected for the cancelled tours of England or Australia never did win their colours – Gary Watson, Peter de Vaal, Hylton Ackerman, Anthony 'Dassie' Biggs and Arthur Short. There were many others who were selected for what were the strongest possible national teams of their day against Robins or Wanderers XIs who also missed out.

The rebel era did at least mean recognition for individuals who in other countries would have reaped a large harvest of Test caps, but the games were still not an adequate substitute for genuine Test matches. Throughout the rebel era limited overs matches drew large crowds but 'Tests' were generally played before small audiences.

After the Englishmen came a team of Sri Lankans, a cheerful and enthusiastic group of young men led by the country's first Test captain, Bandula Warnapura. Although the Sri Lankans provided some entertaining batting their bowling was hopelessly inadequate. It was a different matter, though, when a West Indian team under Lawrence Rowe came later in the same 1982/83 season. With their fast bowling and cavalier approach to the game, the West Indians were immensely popular visitors during two tours in successive seasons. On their second tour Rowe's men became the only rebel team to beat South Africa in a series, and they did it in both the one-day and 'Test' matches.

Kim Hughes led a combative Australian team on two tours in the 1985/86 and 1986/87 seasons and South Africans were content that their cricket was in reasonable shape as South Africa won hard-fought series on both tours.

Throughout these tours there had been only minor political disruption. There were strikes at SA Breweries as workers protested at vast amounts of money being spent on cricketers instead of their wages and SAB decided to restrict their sponsorship activities to local events after an aborted tour by a team of English soccer players later in 1982. There were isolated placard wavers in South Africa and there were protests from abroad. At Newlands there was an attempt to sabotage the pitch by pouring oil on the grass. This particular incident was dismissed with contemptuous glee by Western Province officials. 'They obviously know nothing about cricket,' said one official, 'because they didn't pour the oil anywhere near where a decent bowler would be aiming for.' The visiting cricketers themselves were hardest hit, although they collected substantial fees in compensation. The Englishmen were barred from Test cricket for three years, the Sri Lankans from any cricket in their own country for 25 years, and the West Indians for life. The Australians received a two-year ban for domestic cricket and could not play in Test matches for three years.

The rebel tour era had settled into a pattern. The cricket was reasonable, the protests relatively mild. For the players, it was simply an equation in which guaranteed rewards were weighed against potential penalties. The pattern was about to be broken in the most dramatic fashion, however, and the rebel era would come to an end with a tour by an English team led by the former England captain, Mike Gatting.

Protesters outside the ground in Kimberley at the start of the 1990 English tour.

CHAPTER THREE

FROM GATTING TO UNITY

Cricket officials had come to regard the opponents of rebel tours as vociferous but few in numbers and poorly organised. Their direction had come from the South African Council on Sport (SACOS), which traditionally drew its support mainly from the Cape Town area, with lesser backing in Natal, the Eastern Cape and Johannesburg. SACOS, while advocating nonracialism in sport, was made up largely of coloured and Indian members and was therefore hardly representative of South African society as a whole.

The formation of a new, politically motivated sporting body, the National Sports Congress (NSC), later to be renamed the National Olympic and Sports Congress (NOSC), had gone relatively unnoticed. In researching the origins of the NSC, I found only the scantiest mentions in the 'establishment' media. Yet there should have been more awareness. Liq Nosarka, a board member of the Transvaal Cricket Council, had told the board as early as 1988 that it would be worth while to keep tabs on and enter into dialogue with the new organisation. And, with the African National Congress a banned organisation, the NSC's links with the ANC were not immediately apparent. There was thus no great concern when, soon after the announcement that Mike Gatting would lead an English team to South Africa, the NSC, through its publicity secretary Krish Naidoo, announced the NSC would mobilise mass opposition and stop the tour.

The demonstrations started on January 19, 1990, several hours before the team arrived at Jan Smuts airport. It was the NSC's first test of strength and they were not found wanting in organisational powers. Busloads of demonstrators were at the airport, but the flight had been delayed by a bomb scare in London. A mass demonstration was broken up by police with dogs. It was an illegal gathering near an airport building. By the time the players emerged, the only demonstrators were white and they loudly welcomed the tourists. The police did not prevent this gesture of support.

From the start it was an altogether tougher and harder atmosphere than during the first English rebel tour in 1982. This extended to the media coverage. I was employed as a public relations consultant during the entire rebel era, and was appointed as the SACU's media liaison officer on all the tours. 1982 had been a challenge as there was a large British media contingent. With relatively minor exceptions, however, their attitudes towards news were in the best British traditions of truth-seeking and fairness. The 1990 contingent was dominated by a tabloid 'hit squad' whose appreciation of the evolving political situation in South Africa appeared to be non-existent, but who displayed a remarkable inventiveness in portraying events to their readers. The arrival provided several examples. Virtually all the British media were aware the team flight was late and sensibly enough delayed their departure to the airport. Some three hours after the demonstrations mentioned earlier had ended, I encountered the core of the tabloid squad seeking directions to Jan Smuts. We drove out in convoy. There the journalists pieced together the earlier events. But Paul Weaver of *Today* went further. He wrote a lurid eyewitness account which described how blood was still damp on the steps when Gatting's men arrived after 'violence which left me weak and nauseous'. He then described in graphic terms the viciousness of the dogs, the brutality of the police and their physical resemblance to young Nazis. In more than one way battle lines had been drawn.

Weaver was later deported by a government still conditioned to bring out the big stick against hostile media. This was despite pleas by Ali Bacher to take no action as Weaver had by then been effectively discredited by the distribution of copies of his 'eyewitness' account and had become a rather

AARON 'Ali' BACHER captained South Africa in the country's last four official Tests against Australia in 1970 and led his team to a clean sweep of victories. Although regarded as one of the finest cricket captains produced by South Africa, he has earned an even more formidable reputation as an administrator. Born in Roodepoort, Transvaal, on May 24, 1942, and educated at King Edward VII School and Wits University, he made his first class debut at the age of 17 and was appointed captain of Transvaal at 21. He played in 12 Tests, including four as captain, and had a highest score of 73 against Australia in 1970.

He gave up a medical practice to enter the world of business and was chairman of the Transvaal Cricket Council when fellow board members persuaded him to enter cricket administration on a full-time basis as TCC director of cricket in 1981, a position which was upgraded to managing director the following year. He was appointed managing director of the South African Cricket Union in 1986.

pathetic and isolated figure on tour. Furthermore, the editor of *Today* had agreed to publish a full-page article by Dr Bacher giving his side of the tour story. This offer, not surprisingly, was withdrawn when Weaver was evicted and, again not surprisingly, Weaver was given an undeserved boost in credibility as a victim of government suppression.

Back at the start of the tour, however, there were further demonstrations at the team's hotel and stoppages by hotel workers supporting the anti-tour movement. It was with a sense of relief that the tour party headed for the small northern Cape diamond mining centre of Kimberley. The first match had been switched at the last minute from East London, an ANC stronghold where it was feared demonstrations could get out of control. Recalling the change, an NSC official reflected wistfully on what might have been. 'It would have been the biggest demonstration this country has ever seen. We were so disappointed when they moved the match to Kimberley.'

The NSC was equal to the challenge, however. The team arrived to find hundreds of chanting demonstrators across the road from their hotel. Gatting agreed to accept a petition and was told by NSC official Bill Jardine: 'You are not welcome here.'

When the three-day match against a Bowl (minor) provinces team started at the De Beers Country Club the next day it seemed an ordinary Kimberley cricket day. The sun beat down and a handful of spectators watched the start of play. The only unusual aspect was the large contingent of some 40 journalists, half of them from Britain. Midway through the morning a small NSC delegation arrived at the ground asking for Ali Bacher. Their spokesman, Krish Naidoo, a Johannesburg lawyer who was the best-known of the fledgeling NSC organisation, told Dr Bacher: 'The police are stopping our people from demonstrating.' I accompanied Dr Bacher in a journalist's car and, some two or three kilometres from the ground, we encountered a line of police blocking several thousand marchers in a quiet residential area.

This was the start of a drama which took up the rest of the day. Dr Bacher told the police he had no objection to the demonstrators marching to the ground, but he was informed that it was an unlawful demonstration. In order to be legal, a demonstration had to be approved by the Chief Magistrate. Dr Bacher telephoned the Minister in charge of sport, Gerrit Viljoen, from a nearby house. He was told it was a police matter so he contacted Adriaan Vlok, the police minister, who told him that permission was essential. Neither minister was immediately available and it took more than an hour to establish contact. Outside, the midday sun was raising temperatures. 'The people are getting angry,' said Naidoo. A yellow police van pulled up to join an already strong contingent of uniformed men. Out jumped half a dozen men, cocking what turned out to be teargas guns. A murmur came from the crowd. Dr Bacher stepped in front of the policemen and appealed to the officer in charge: 'Move these men away, they are being provocative.' In one of the day's few humorous moments, the officer ordered a group of about a dozen journalists to move back. 'Not the journalists, the police,' said Dr Bacher. Clearly reluctantly, the officer ordered his men to take a less aggressive stance.

Later, I recounted the events to Allister Sparks, former editor of the liberal *Rand Daily Mail*, which had run out of advertising and managerial support at the very time it uncovered the massive Information Department scandal of the late 1970s. Sparks, now a correspondent for several major foreign publications, said he had reported on hundreds of demonstrations. 'In nearly every incident where there has been violence, it has been the result of police provocation,' he said. For a rookie in such matters, the experience of Kimberley offered nothing to contradict his view.

Dr Bacher, meanwhile, had explained the government's position to Naidoo. He told Naidoo he had no objection to a demonstration outside the ground provided it was peaceful. Would Naidoo agree to this? After some thought, Naidoo agreed. Dr Bacher then explained that he personally would seek permission for a demonstration to be held. Naidoo said this would be acceptable. So, with the demonstrators still massed at the barricades and Gatting scoring a half-century at De

Anti-tour protesters picket Mike Gatting and his team.

Beers, Dr Bacher went to the Chief Magistrate and encountered a reluctant official who told him he also needed the approval of the Town Clerk. After several hours of going backwards and forwards, he emerged triumphantly with permission for the NSC to stage a peaceful demonstration in a designated area outside the perimeter fence of the ground.

More than a year later, Mthobi Tyamzashe, secretary-general of the NSC, said this initiative by Dr Bacher had been a masterstroke. 'He took the wind out of our sails, because now we couldn't get angry about being refused the right to demonstrate. Although now we are good friends, at that time we regarded Ali as the devil because he was so cunning.'

The next day the game resumed peacefully. Late in the morning the first minibuses started to arrive. Soon several thousand demonstrators were massed on the other side of a wire fence. In a country where legal demonstrations were a new phenomenon, the arrival of the protestors quickly proved a rival attraction to the cricket and hundreds of spectators lined up inside the fence watching – and trading insults with – those outside. Local cricket officials and the ubiquitous Dr Bacher had to ask spectators to go back to watching cricket and respect the right of the demonstrators to make their case. Reason prevailed; apart from an isolated incident when a white spectator threw a bottle across the fence, cricket was played and the demonstrators were able to sing and toyi-toyi their objections.

The pattern had been set although there was to be a prime example of English tabloid collaboration after the match. After his side had wrapped up a comfortable win, Gatting gave a press conference during which he dealt at length with different aspects of the cricket. Only one question came from the English contingent. The following is a direct transcript from a tape recording of the press conference. Question: 'Have you any view on the distractions which you know about now which happened off the field?' Mike Gatting: 'As far as I'm concerned there were a few people singing and dancing and that was it. I didn't know of anything else happening, we were more concerned with playing cricket and that was it.'

On a tour during which political sensitivities had to be a high priority at all times it might not have been the most sensible reply. But in the context of a press conference during which all the previous discussions had been about batsmen, bowlers and cricket matters it probably was an accurate reflection of events from a cricketer's point of view. It should be pointed out that Gatting, who at all times in South Africa came across as an unusually sincere and honest individual, had several times publicly supported the right of protest. He certainly did not deserve the savaging he received in the tabloids in London the next day. 'Flaming Insult', screamed a banner headline in the *Daily Mirror*. Reporter John Jackson wrote: 'Rebel cricketer Mike Gatting sparked new fury yesterday with ANOTHER insulting blunder. He dismissed violent black protest against his hated South African tour as "a few people singing and dancing".' The story quoted 'outraged' anti-apartheid leaders who branded Gatting 'stupid and insensitive'.

Other tabloids tore into Gatting in a similar manner. The serious newspapers were also critical. Two points should be made: There were no follow-up questions after the 'singing and dancing' remark (Gatting would surely have made some conciliatory comments which would have diluted the story) and the English journalists went into a lengthy huddle immediately after the conference before writing their amazingly similar reports. Late that Sunday evening, sounds of merriment wafted up the central well of the Kimberley Sun as English journalists celebrated what they knew would be a story which would receive a 'good play' the next morning.

The fact was, though, that the tour was rapidly becoming unworkable. For the first time, a political organisation had mobilised mass support against a cricket tour. While the tour itself was not a major concern issue for most of the people who demonstrated, dissatisfaction with the apartheid system had boiled over into an identifiable issue. If the NSC could put together such an effective show of strength in little Kimberley the possibilities for other centres were frightening.

The tour limped on to Bloemfontein and Pietermaritzburg, with further massive demonstrations. In Pietermaritzburg, where estimates of the number of marchers were as high as 10 000, Gatting was persuaded to accept a petition during a break in play. Then the organisers said the crowd wanted to see him accept it on a makeshift platform on the back of a truck some 100 metres from the entrance to the Jan Smuts Stadium. The organisers guaranteed the safety of the SACU and tour party, but it was nevertheless a tense walk through a corridor of chanting people. A feature of the demonstrations in all centres was the tight control exercised by marshals and once again they did a good job, although a few missiles were thrown on the way back. A television cameraman was bloodied by a stone.

An extra dimension was introduced into the situation between the Bloemfontein and Pietermaritzburg matches when President F W de Klerk made his Opening of Parliament speech on Friday, February 2. He announced major reforms including the unbanning of organisations such as the ANC and the imminent release of Nelson Mandela. In this torrent of change the cricket tour was becoming increasingly irrelevant.

The first 'Test' was played at the Wanderers in Johannesburg behind a huge security cordon. Police helicopters hovered overhead, while bright yellow police vehicles and dozens of policemen were all about the ground and its surrounds. With permission for a march from central Johannesburg having been refused the demonstrations were relatively minor, but it was no atmosphere in which to play a cricket match.

The match itself was a disappointment, with South Africa winning within three days because of some excellent fast bowling by Allan Donald and Richard Snell on a helpful pitch.

The 'Test' was therefore all over when Ali Bacher met the NSC's Krish Naidoo on the Sunday which had been planned as the rest day.

After a long meeting and much haggling. Dr Bacher agreed that the tour should be curtailed. In return Naidoo guaranteed the NSC would stop demonstrating. Instead of a second 'Test' in Cape Town, followed by six limited overs internationals and a special match to commemorate the centenary of Transvaal cricket, the tour was reduced to four limited overs matches. True to their word, the NSC pulled the plug on the demonstrators and the matches were played in good spirit before capacity crowds. There were two major highlights – a brilliant century off 49 balls (eight sixes, eight fours) by Adrian Kuiper in Bloemfontein, and South Africa's first 'Mexican Wave', performed during the last match of the tour at the Wanderers.

Having come to an agreement, Dr Bacher informed his

MICHAEL GATTING, born in Kingsbury, England, on June 6, 1957, found himself at the centre of a political storm when he captained a 'rebel' English team to South Africa in January 1990.

A professional cricketer, he had played for Middlesex as a hard-hitting middle-order batsman since 1975 and had been selected for England two years later for the first of 68 Tests. He was appointed captain of Middlesex in 1983 and was made England captain in 1986. He scored 3 870 runs in his Test career at an average of 37,57, hitting nine centuries with a highest score of 207 against India in Madras in 1984/85.

Having been dropped by England, he made his decision to play in South Africa knowing that he would be banned from Test cricket for five years and aware that there might be political consequences. An honest and open man, he could not possibly have been prepared for the controversy that exploded around him.

board and on Tuesday, February 13, Geoff Dakin, president of the SACU, issued a statement saying the decision had been taken because dramatic political developments had overtaken the tour.

The English tour had been planned to be played over two seasons. Another bombshell came from Krish Naidoo. The second leg of the tour was cancelled. This caused an enormous row within the SACU. Dakin said the second leg had not been called off, but the board would meet in Durban on Sunday the 18th. Dr Bacher was unable to attend, and nothing further emerged from the meeting. But the executive met on the 22nd with Dr Bacher present, and finally it was confirmed that he had indeed agreed to call off the second leg. Dakin said: 'Dr Bacher concedes that he had no mandate from the board to cancel the tour.' According to Dakin the full board would decide on the second leg.

Dr Bacher immediately issued a statement of his own: 'I believe vitally important decisions about the future of South African cricket have to be made as a matter of urgency ... it is necessary for me to convey these views to the full board of the SACU.' These were not comfortable times for the SACU, and there can be little doubt that the rift that developed between the president and the managing director can be traced back to the Gatting tour.

The full board finally met in Durban on March 30 and agreed that tours were counter-productive in the political climate. The second leg of the Gatting tour was therefore cancelled. Dr Bacher was appointed as a one-man commission to investigate all aspects of cricket.

Not only was it a traumatic decision, it was also expensive. Because of the political sensitivity of the tour, the SACU had been unable to obtain sponsorship. Now, not only did they have to meet the costs of the first tour, but they also had to honour their financial obligations to the English players in full without the benefit of any income from the second leg.

South African cricket at the end of the 1989/90 season was in turmoil. The leading administrators were at loggerheads, the era of rebel tours had suffered a death blow, and the de-

Ali Bacher, team manager David Graveney and Mike Gatting at a press conference to announce the curtailment of the tour.

velopment programme among black youngsters, so carefully nurtured since 1986, had come to a complete halt because of the political controversy.

Had there been any betting on which major sports would first gain recognition in the international arena, cricket would have been a rank outsider. But the SACU had a trump card in Ali Bacher. The former Springbok captain must take the blame for pushing ahead with plans for the tour, but he also deserves enormous credit for seeing the political realities and acting quickly to get his sport back into the the mainstream. Perhaps, indeed, the tensions and drama of the tour served as a shock lesson in the power of mass mobilisation. Already of a liberal political persuasion, Dr Bacher was able to see the justice in the anti-tour group's arguments and he had the natural grace to deal with his opponents in an honest, trusting manner. What was really meant by his 'one-man commission' was that Ali Bacher would take a three-month plunge into the real political world. His first step, two days after the SACU board meeting, was to issue a statement signifying an end to rebel tours and calling for unity in South African cricket.

At the time, the statement seemed more than a little wordy and ambiguous, but the earnestness with which Dr Bacher insisted that it was important gave a clue to its significance. It was a public signal to the NSC that the SACU were ready to talk business. He also wrote to the SA Cricket Board suggesting talks between the two bodies.

On May 26 the SACB responded. At its annual meeting it was agreed that, as the SACB was a natural extension of the sport and political events of the period, it was inevitable that SACB and SACU would have to meet.

The executives of the two controlling bodies finally sat down in Durban on September 8. The chairman was a man who was to become a central figure in South African sports politics, Steve Tshwete, the ANC's spokesman on sport, education and culture.

Tshwete, a former Robben Island political detainee like so many of his colleagues among the top executive of the ANC, is a tall, pipe-smoking man who wears thick spectacles which give him an air of inscrutability.

He had impressed SACU board members at a symposium chaired by Frederick van Zyl Slabbert, a former leader of the liberal parliamentary opposition who had become an influential extra-parliamentary 'facilitator'.

It was Tshwete who kept the Durban meeting on track when old rivalries and bitterness threatened to prevent progress. Said one delegate: 'He was everything a chairman should be. The whole idea of the meeting was to find points of agreement rather than differences, and Steve stepped in the moment anyone started to stray off course.'

The meeting agreed that it was essential that one nonracial, democratic controlling body be formed. It was also agreed to respect and maintain the moratorium on international sports contact.

The moratorium issue was a thorn in the side of many white administrators who felt agreement tied them to a timetable set by the ANC. The rationale of the moratorium was that there should be no international contacts until unified sports structures were in place. There was some concern about what exactly unity meant and who would decide whether it had been achieved. Dr Bacher's view was that trust was an essential element, and his opinion prevailed.

Despite the cordiality of the September 8 accord, the moratorium remained a tricky issue. Overseas cricket professionals, mainly English, have plied their trade in South Africa for almost as long as the game has been played. Some SACB delegates wanted the moratorium to extend to them, but Tshwete managed to defuse a potentially explosive issue by classifying the moratorium issue as a possible impediment to unity which could be overcome. A joint committee was formed to draw up a declaration of intent.

One of Dr Bacher's trump cards was his commitment to grass roots development in townships. The Gatting tour had been a major setback to his well-established programme but he was determined to get it back on track. At the September 8 meeting he offered to share the SACU's resources in the development sphere, and it was a major spur to the unity process when the SACB decided at a meeting two weeks later to take part in a joint development programme. Now, at last, the two sides were working together on the ground.

A further meeting of the executives of the SACU and SACB was held in Port Elizabeth on December 16, 1990, the day following the SACU's Nissan Shield final. Again, Tshwete was the chairman.

Remarkably, barely nine months after the end of the Gatting tour which had reduced the relationship between the two rival bodies to an all-time low, virtually all impediments to unity were blown away.

A joint declaration of intent was agreed. The main points were:

✻ To form one nonracial, democratic controlling body in which nonracialism would be the guiding principle.
✻ To develop, administer and make available opportunities for all those who wished to play cricket at all levels.
✻ To acknowledge the existence of imbalances with regard to separate educational systems, sponsorships and facilities, and to form a committee to formulate strategies to overcome imbalances.
✻ To contribute through cricket to the creation of a just society in South Africa.

KRISH MACKERDHUJ, born on August 15, 1939, used to walk 5 km from Overport to the Kingsmead ground in Durban to watch Test matches, but because of his colour had to sit in the area reserved for non-whites. He played under the SA Cricket Board of Control (Sacboc) as a legspin bowler and middle-order batsman for the Crimson club. He entered cricket administration in 1977 at the time of the formation of the SA Cricket Union. He became president of the Natal Cricket Board and vice-president of the SA Cricket Board which emerged in opposition to the SACU, succeeding Hassan Howa as president of the SACB in 1983.

Mackerdhuj, together with leaders of rugby and soccer, took his sport out of the fold of the SA Council on Sport (Sacos) and its doctrine of 'no normal sport in an abnormal society' and became a vice-president of the National Sports Congress when it was formed in 1989.

A chemical engineer with a BSc Honours degree from Fort Hare University, Krish Mackerdhuj is a process advisor with a major oil company.

* To respect the sports moratorium but to respect existing individual contracts of overseas professionals. (This neatly avoided a conflict on the overseas professionals issue.)
* To establish a working relationship with the SA Nonracial Olympic Committee (Sanroc) and the Supreme Council of Sport in Africa.
* To administer and share resources within the development field.
* To inform the respective constituencies of the SACU and SACB of the spirit and letter of the declaration.

Joint committees were formed to set up a structure for a unified body. Geoff Dakin, president of SACU, and Krish Mackerdhuj, president of SACB, wrote a joint letter to international cricket bodies informing them of the progress made.

After a further meeting of the two executives in Johannesburg on January 20, 1991, a final crucial meeting was held in Johannesburg on April 20. It was agreed:

* To form a united, nonracial body to control all cricket in South Africa on June 29.
* That the name of the new body would be the United Cricket Board of South Africa.
* That the executive committee of the board would consist of 10 members from the SACB and 10 from SACU.
* For the first year Geoff Dakin, president of the SACU, would be president and Krish Mackerdhuj, his counterpart from SACB, would be vice-president. For the second year the roles would be reversed.
* Dr Bacher would be managing director.
* At the end of the first two years the constitution would provide for an executive committee of 10 members to be elected annually by the affiliated provinces.

Events proceeded at a breakneck pace, with Dr Bacher and Steve Tshwete embarking on a mission to inform cricket administrators and their governments throughout the world of the unity decision and to enlist support for a South African application for membership of the International Cricket Council.

A significant factor was a letter signed by the ANC's spokesman on foreign affairs, Thabo Mbeki, endorsing the ef-

Sir Garfield Sobers meets schoolboy fast bowler Walter Masemola in Soweto, watched by Ali Bacher.

forts of the cricket administrators and calling for South Africa to be admitted to the world cricket community.

The United Cricket Board duly came into being on June 29. The meeting at the Wanderers Club was no more than a formality but it was nevertheless a significant and emotional occasion. It was witnessed by two of the world's greatest cricketers from countries that the old South Africa had never played against, Sir Garfield Sobers from West Indies and Sunil Gavaskar from India.

Barely a week later, the UCB was at Lord's to put its case for membership of the International Cricket Council. A delegation consisting of Dakin, Mackerdhuj, Dr Bacher and Tshwete lobbied member countries and on July 10 South Africa was formally admitted to the ICC.

Symbolically, it was India, the first country to impose sanctions against apartheid South Africa in 1948, who proposed South Africa's membership. There was no opposition to South Africa's application, but the West Indies abstained on the grounds that their delegates had no mandate from their board.

Behind the scenes there had been discussions between Dr Bacher and his Australian counterpart, David Richards, about the possibility of South Africa playing in the World Cup. Although it would mean considerable reorganisation, with tickets already on sale, the World Cup organisers recognised the marketing potential of a South African return to international matches. However, Colin Cowdrey, president of the ICC, announced after the meeting that although South Africa was a member of the ICC it would not be possible for the country to play in the World Cup. According to South African officials, Cowdrey's decision was taken from the chair to avoid a possible conflict with the West Indies and Pakistan, both opposed to South Africa being re-admitted to international matches so early.

This decision came as a blow. Although quite rightly the UCB had put the emphasis on unity and readmission to the ICC, rather than appearing eager to rush into international matches, there was no doubt that there was a strong desire among the former SACU administrators and, of course, the players, for a tangible sign of acceptability.

Sensibly the World Cup organisers merely issued a statement, several weeks later, that it would be feasible to accommodate South Africa if the UCB wished to apply to take part. A deadline of September 22 was set.

The ICC responded by announcing that the matter would be reconsidered. Because of the potential sensitivity, a special meeting of the ICC was arranged for Sharjah, in the United Arab Emirates, on October 23 to coincide with the staging of the Sharjah Cup tournament.

Cricket's unity was now so firmly established that the UCB executive decided with little debate to apply to play in the World Cup. A key factor was an announcement by the National Sports Congress that it supported the lifting of the international moratorium on cricket.

Once again, the UCB lobbyists got to work, with a letter from Nelson Mandela added to the strong support for South Africa's case. Dakin, Mackerdhuj, Bacher and executive member Percy Sonn headed for Sharjah, confident but not certain that South Africa would be playing in the World Cup.

Immediately after the meeting they would head for India, Pakistan, Sri Lanka and Kenya on a bridge-building exercise to introduce themselves to their new ICC colleagues.

Into the unknown. Jimmy Cook and Andrew Hudson go out to bat in Calcutta.

CHAPTER FOUR

THE MAGICAL MYSTERY TOUR

The news out of India was startling. The Board of Control for Cricket in India had issued an invitation for South Africa to send a team for a short tour. The first match would be on Sunday, November 10, less than two weeks away. Pakistan had been due to tour but had cancelled almost at the last minute after a threat of violence by anti-Muslim extremists. For India the situation was desperate. For one reason or another they had not had a major tour into their country in more than two years. The Pakistan trip had been planned as a much-needed revenue earner. With a UCB delegation arriving in India on Sunday, October 27, it suddenly seemed logical to ask South Africa to fill the gap.

What had been planned as a goodwill, 'getting to know you' tour by the UCB team after the ICC's World Cup meeting in Sharjah had assumed far greater significance and urgency. As Dr Bacher explained later: 'When we arrived in India we were greeted with the news of Pakistan's cancellation. It was a bitter blow to the Indians because the cancellation came just a few days before the tour was due to start.'

The UCB party had been invited to attend some of the India–Pakistan matches. Instead, they were asked to bring their own team for a historic series.

The idea of inviting South Africa appears to have originated with Jagmohan Dalmiya, president of the Cricket Association of Bengal and until recently the secretary of the Indian board. He had struck up a close friendship with Ali Bacher when the UCB delegation had been in London in July and it had been because of the rapport between the two men that India had proposed South Africa's membership. Since then there had been an internal coup which ousted Dalmiya from the national post, but he remained a powerful figure in Indian cricket, not least because his Bengali association controlled the huge 95 000-seater Eden Gardens Stadium in Calcutta, the scene of the 1987 World Cup final.

The sudden invitation provided the UCB with an opportunity they could not afford to pass up, although the timing was far from ideal. It was the start of the South African season and the players would have virtually no time to adjust to Indian conditions. But it was literally a case of now or never, because the Indian team was due to leave for Australia on November 15 and would not return until after the World Cup. An urgent meeting of the UCB was set up for Sunday, November 3, the day after the return of the UCB delegation, and the selectors were put on standby. Ali Bacher summed up the debate ahead: 'We have to ask whether we are rushing into international cricket so soon after achieving unity. We don't want to rock the boat when unification is going so well. But we also have to acknowledge the debt we owe India. Without them we would not be in the ICC or the World Cup. Now we have a situation of a friend in need, and we have to make a decision.'

Dr Bacher painted a vivid picture of the welcome that the South African delegation had received in India and of the potential impact of a South African team playing at Eden Gardens. 'If the board decides the team should go, we may well see one of the most dramatic moments in world cricket.' He also pointed out that India had been the first country to impose sanctions against South Africa after the election of an apartheid government in 1948 and had been the first to host an ANC office abroad. It would be highly symbolic if it were the first country to welcome a new South Africa back into the world.

In view of Dr Bacher's comments it was hardly surprising that the decision was made to accept the Indian invitation. The team would leave just four days later and play three one-day internationals, starting in Calcutta the following Sunday.

Peter van der Merwe, the convenor of the selectors, said the team had to be picked on the previous season's form, which

CLIVE RICE, born in Johannesburg on July 23, 1949, played first-class cricket throughout South Africa's period of international isolation. He was selected as a promising youngster for the cancelled tour of Australia in 1971/72 and 20 years later led the national team to India.

In between he built up a formidable record as an allrounder, scoring more than 25 000 runs and taking more than 900 wickets in first-class cricket. Educated at St John's College and Damelin College, he made his debut for Transvaal B against Northern Transvaal B in 1969/70, scoring 81 and taking 4 for 56.

He played for Nottinghamshire from 1975 to 1988, being appointed captain in 1978 and leading them to the county championship in 1981 for the first time in 52 years.

Rice was appointed Transvaal captain in 1981 and held the post until resigning in February 1992, leading Transvaal during one of the most successful periods in their history. He captained South Africa in nine unofficial Tests.

perhaps should have given an early warning of the shock waves that would accompany the selection of the World Cup squad two months later. A 14-man team for India was announced on Sunday night. It was:

Clive Rice *(Transvaal, age 42, allrounder, captain)*
Jimmy Cook *(Transvaal, 38, opening batsman)*
Allan Donald *(Free State, 25, fast bowler)*
Clive Eksteen *(Transvaal, 24, slow left-arm bowler)*
Andrew Hudson *(Natal, 25, opening batsman)*
Peter Kirsten *(Border, 36, batsman)*
Adrian Kuiper *(Western Province, 32, allrounder)*
Craig Matthews *(Western Province, 26, fast-medium bowler)*
Brian McMillan *(Western Province, 27, allrounder)*
Dave Richardson *(Eastern Province, 32, wicketkeeper)*
Tim Shaw *(Eastern Province, 33, slow left-arm bowler)*
Richard Snell *(Transvaal, 23, fast bowler)*
Kepler Wessels *(Eastern Province, 34, batsman)*
Mandy Yachad *(Northern Transvaal, 31, opening batsman)*

Only three of the players, Eksteen, Hudson and Matthews, had not appeared in rebel internationals, but for all 14 it was a first chance to play in matches recognised by the rest of the world. It was the completion of a full circle for Rice, who had been picked for the cancelled official tour of Australia in 1971/72 but had waited 20 years to make his debut.

There were some surprises, with the emphasis on opening batsmen particularly puzzling, while talented batsmen such as Mark Rushmere, Roy Pienaar and Daryll Cullinan were overlooked. And there had to be concern that the average age of the squad was a venerable 31, although the inclusion of the promising Transvaal spinner Clive Eksteen was a bold move.

For the players selected, there was joy and excitement. Although Rice and Cook had been wearing Springbok colours for 10 years in rebel tours the prospect of playing in an official series was what they had been waiting for throughout their careers.

Perhaps prophetically, Rice tempered his pleasure with words of caution. 'I'm excited but we are going into the unknown. When we play at home we have the security of knowing what to expect. While I want the team to do extremely well the important thing is that we will be getting the experience of going on a tour.'

Cook said: 'I had been playing club cricket. I arrived home and my sons Stephen and Ryan came running out to the car to tell me I was going to India. It has always been great to play for South Africa but going on an official overseas tour is something I have always wanted to do.'

Clive Eksteen had been playing in the same club game and like Cook had missed the television news broadcast of the team announcement. He was told by his girlfriend. 'I couldn't believe it,' he said. But his clubmates did. They arrived at his home with beers. 'When I left for work the next morning some of them were still sleeping in the lounge.'

Although one of the youngest players in the team, Eksteen made one of the most perceptive comments. 'One of the nicest things is how happy other people are that we are back and going on a tour.'

After the team announcement, and evidently under some pressure from administrators who felt the new unity in cricket should be reflected in the make-up of the playing members of the touring party, it was decided to add four young players to the squad in order to gain experience. Faiek Davids of Western Province and Hoosain Manack of Transvaal were selected from the former SACB together with Hansie Cronje and Derek Crookes from the old SACU.

The next few days were hectic as uniforms were hastily put together and the team assembled in Johannesburg for a Thursday afternoon take-off from Jan Smuts airport in a chartered Boeing 707.

As Eksteen intimated, the atmosphere was quite different from anything generated during a rebel series. Having been involved in all the rebel tours, I personally had never experienced the level of excitement from people both inside and out of cricket. There was a quite remarkable awareness of the tour and its significance. 'Don't you need someone to carry your bag?' became a common question after the *Sunday Times* decided to send me on the tour. It was an emotional whirl which

Indian spectators welcome the South African team.

culminated as the team practised at the Wanderers on the morning of departure watched by a horde of media representatives and well-wishers.

The Panasonic company, who had agreed to sponsor the team, provided a lunch at the Wanderers. Then it was off to the airport at the start of an adventure that none of the 170 passengers could have contemplated even a week earlier. In addition to the team, most of the UCB executive, journalists, commentators, technicians and sponsors, almost half the seats had been sold to the general public. With his usual attention to detail, Dr Bacher had approached a Transvaal cricket official and prominent businessman, Liq Nosarka, who assembled a party of South African Asians to give the group an appropriate racial mix in addition to the multi-hued UCB executive.

As the ancient, fully-laden aircraft laboured down the runway and into the air the chatter inside the narrow fuselage was animated and excited. Many hours later, after a refuelling stop in the Seychelles, the pilot advised that we were at the south-eastern tip of India. 'Madras is on your left hand side.' And there we had our first glimpse of India. Even the captain, a veteran pilot who had often flown State President F W de Klerk on international missions in the same aircraft, could not keep the excitement out of his voice as he announced the descent into Calcutta's Dum Dum airport. 'It is the first time any South African aircraft has landed in India,' he said.

We flew over swampy marshland and landed at 8 am Calcutta time. We were told to remain seated as a delegation of Indian cricket officials and immigration officers boarded. Our passports were collected and finally we stepped onto Indian soil.

The airport bus went to a side gate and girls in traditional costume daubed us with a tika of welcome on the forehead, placed garlands around our necks and threw flower petals over us. We were offered soft drinks and fruit juices while waiting for formalities to be completed. Then we were loaded onto buses lined up on the tarmac, each allocated to a specific group – team, officials, media, supporters.

At the airport exit, more than 100 motorcyclists in red tee-shirts of the Cricket Association of Bengal linked up with the convoy. There were banners of greeting. That's nice, we thought, they've laid on a little welcome. It was the start of an hour and a half of extraordinary emotion. Almost from the moment the buses left the airport precincts people lined the road to Calcutta. For 22 kilometres we passed through crowds of waving, cheering people. Twice the cavalcade stopped at pre-arranged places where loudspeakers had been set up and the crowds were addressed by Dalmiya, UCB president Geoff Dakin, Ali Bacher, Mike Procter and Clive Rice.

Vehicles on the outgoing lane simply stopped in the middle of the road, as drivers and passengers gaped and waved at the buses. Spectators stretched out their hands to try to touch a South African, even a journalist.

We were told that the street, the main road to the city centre, had been closed to all traffic until our convoy had passed. It was an incredible experience, even allowing for the fact that many people had nowhere to go until we passed and therefore had little else to do. The buses moved slowly past tenement blocks and shanties. We had our first sight of the ubiquitous holy cows, wandering along and across busy streets.

Finally we reached the city centre and pulled up at the Oberoi Grand hotel on the bustling Maidan, a wide boulevard

MIKE PROCTER, born in Durban on September 15, 1946, took 26 wickets at an average of 15,02 in just seven Tests before international isolation took effect. His first tour with an official South African team was as coach of the 1991 team to India.

In a first-class career spanning 23 years he took 1 417 wickets in 401 matches at an average of 19,53 with a best performance of 9 for 71 for Rhodesia against Transvaal. No South African has taken more wickets. He also scored 21 936 runs at 36,01 with a highest score of 254. The latter came at the end of a world record-equalling sequence of six successive centuries and was scored for Rhodesia against Western Province in 1970/71.

At his best a feared fast bowler and a swashbuckling batsman, Procter played in South African first-class cricket for Natal, Western Province and Rhodesia as well as Gloucestershire in England.

He was cricket director of Natal until resigning in 1992.

flanked by a park which would be attractive if it were not for the teeming people, ancient vehicles and pervading air of dust, grime and smoke. In the near distance, across the Maidan, were the towering grandstands of Eden Gardens.

In a city of 11 million, most of whom live in squalor and poverty, the Oberoi Grand is an opulent oasis. Outside the front entrance are makeshift stalls, cluttered tiny shops, beggars and endless crowds. Inside, past uniformed guards who keep the residents isolated from the masses, is a world-class hotel of marble pillars and colonial grandeur. For the duration of the cricketers' stay, dozens of guards formed a tunnel from the entrance to the team bus as crowds surged forward for a glimpse of the players.

The players had a first look at Eden Gardens on Friday afternoon when they had a light workout after being paraded at a media conference attended by more than 100 journalists. They had a full-scale practice on Saturday. In between, on a tour in which the actual games were seldom likely to be the first priority, was a visit to Mother Teresa, the 81-year-old Yugoslav-born founder of the Missionaries of Charity who has worked among the poor and down-trodden of Calcutta since 1938.

In the kaleidoscope of emotions, experiences, sights and sounds that made up the tour of India, the visit to Mother Teresa was among the most bizarre yet rewarding. It was a natural news event and the media bus was crowded with cameramen, photographers and journalists. Chris Day, the tour media liaison officer, suggested to the driver that it would be a good idea to try to pass the team bus so the photographers could set up their equipment before the team's arrival. The driver took this as a challenge and embarked on a terrifying bus chase through the streets of Calcutta until assured that arriving first was not a matter of life and death. Driving in Calcutta requires determination and a fatalistic courage. Pedestrians wander across the streets and drivers simply keep their hand on the hooter and their foot on the accelerator. Most traffic lights do not appear to be in working order, with the result that intersections are a maelstrom of converging vehicles.

Once assured that our driver had switched from being suicidal to merely reckless, we could wonder anew at the extent of the poverty of India's largest city. There are apparently some wealthy areas but on this day we ventured into the Gothic reaches of the poorest. We reached a narrow street and parked next to a huge banner of Lenin. In this city of little hope, Communism has one of its last bastions. Beyond the banner, a few metres down an alleyway, was a tiny plaque. It read, simply, Mother Teresa. Inside, in a crowded courtyard the players looked perplexed as they were jostled by newsmen. A tiny, bent figure moved among the throng, shaking hands and murmuring blessings. She distributed a small yellow card, 'my business card' she told some of the recipients. I have kept mine in my briefcase. It reads: 'The fruit of Silence is Prayer, the fruit of Prayer is Faith, the fruit of Faith is Love, the fruit of love is Service, the fruit of Service is Peace – MOTHER TERESA.'

A church-going lady who said afterwards how moved she was by the experience, determinedly shoved aside all rivals to be side-by-side with the living saint and urged her husband to take a picture. 'Quick, take another,' she implored and smiled for the camera.

Clive Rice was wearing a hideous pair of purple anti-glare sunglasses. Would he take them off before he met Mother Teresa and the photographers took their pictures? Did Mother Teresa have the faintest idea who Clive Rice was? He did and she shook hands with him momentarily before moving on. It is at times like these that one has to admire the alertness and skill of press photographers. The pictures that went around the world froze a fleeting moment and gave it an air of sanctity.

The brief audience over, it was back to the buses and a visit to one of Mother Teresa's homes. There are 200-odd in Calcutta alone and some 600 in total, most in India but some in other impoverished areas of the world. This particular sanctuary was in, if anything, an even poorer area of the city. On the pavement sat derelict men in rags, hair long and eyes blank. People live and die in the streets and, we were told, the bodies were simply covered up and collected by mortuary vans

ALLAN DONALD, born in Bloemfontein on October 20, 1966, first attracted attention when he bowled extremely fast for Free State against Kim Hughes' Australian team in 1985/86. He was still raw and unskilled in the subtleties of the game but his promise was unquestioned. Within a year, the former Technical High School boy was playing for South Africa, having forced his way into the team by taking 8 for 37 in an astonishing performance against Transvaal at the Wanderers.

Donald was quickly snapped up by Warwickshire in 1987. He took 86 wickets in the 1989 English season and 83 in 1991 when he spearheaded a sustained challenge by Warwickshire for the country title and rewarded a county committee who had chosen him as their overseas player ahead of the high-scoring Australian batsman Tom Moody. His 1991 performance earned him nomination as one of Wisden's Five Cricketers of the Year.

in the morning. At the entrance to a drab, three-storey building, children queued for cups of soup. We were taken upstairs and saw crippled children in cots. Others played on the floor with a few meagre toys.

Clive Rice said he was humbled by the experience, as did Geoff Dakin, who also declared himself 'spiritually uplifted' and pledged 100 000 rupees (about R11 000) from the UCB to the Missionaries of Charity. He and vice-president Krish Mackerdhuj went back to Mother Teresa the same afternoon with the money.

At Eden Gardens, the South African and Indian teams practised side by side. It was a chance to explore one of the world's most imposing sporting edifices. All the public seating is made of concrete and is designed for small people. Gerald de Kock of SABC and I, neither of us particularly tall, sat down and didn't have enough legroom between the narrow, shallow seat and the backrest of the seat in front.

The pitch was bleached, bare earth, rolled hard and flat with not a blade of grass. The practice pitches, also on the main arena, had some grass and, according to the players after the game the next day, were quite unlike that in the middle.

Watching the Indians practice was educational. Not all the batsmen had a net but those who did, in particular the captain Mohammad Azharuddin and opening batsman Navjot Sidhu, worked hard on their attacking strokes and were especially strong on the legside. Azharuddin was seemingly able to place searing drives with pinpoint accuracy with no more than a late flick of the wrist.

Afterwards Azharuddin chatted easily to De Kock and me, expressing his pleasure that it would be a historic match which he hoped would be played in the best spirit of the game.

Clive Rice acknowledged that the South African team was under-prepared but said he felt they were '80 per cent ready'.

Because cricket is played in the winter months in India to avoid the worst of the summer heat, the match started at 9 am so that it could be finished before 5 pm when the light fades rapidly. Kepler Wessels, with the benefit of previous experience in India, warned that the danger time in Calcutta was

Allan Donald builds up pace in Calcutta.

at the beginning of the match when the ball was liable to swing sharply under early-morning cloud. South Africa's case would be helped immeasurably if Rice could win the toss and put India in to bat.

The morning was hazy, with mist hanging over the Hooghly River, which runs close to Eden Gardens. Half an hour before the start it seemed impossible that predictions of a capacity crowd could possibly come true. Huge, yawning empty spaces dominated the vast expanses of concrete grandstands. Azharuddin won the toss and decided to field. Round one to India.

As this was no ordinary cricket match, it was felt necessary for the South Africans to make a ceremonial gesture. The players, including the padded-up opening batsmen Cook and Hudson, walked on to the field and waved to the crowd shortly before the start of play. The crowd had increased markedly and the ground was more than half full. The players were cheered generously. Months later, Hudson said that going on the field just before the match instead of the normal pre-innings procedure of several minutes of calm contemplation had been unsettling. Indeed it must have been.

The Indians took the field to the cheers of the crowd. Cook and Hudson left the sanctuary of the dressing room, a pleasant, private area fronted by the only grass in the stadium other than that on the playing surface.

Kapil Dev's first two balls from the Hooghly River end swung wildly away from Cook who did not need to offer a shot. The third ball was glanced neatly down to fine leg for a single. Hudson faced four away-swingers, two of which were so far from him that they were called wide. Dev bowled a better delivery closer to the stumps, Hudson nudged forward, the ball swung enough to nick the edge of the bat and wicketkeeper Kiran More was presented with a simple catch. Hudson's international career had started in ignominy.

The slightly-built Manoj Prabhakar bowled a tidy over from the pavilion end which yielded a single to Cook, who then survived a loud appeal for lbw by Dev, although Dev smiled broadly when the appeal was turned down. The ball was swinging disconcertingly. International cricket seemed an awfully difficult game to play.

Wessels was off the mark in the fourth over with a typical nudge to third man off Prabhakar but the total was only seven when Cook broke the tension momentarily in the sixth over by pulling a short delivery from Prabhakar to the midwicket boundary. Nevertheless, the total was just 15 when Dev and Prabhakar were rested after nine overs.

Jawagal Srinath, a gangling youngster bowling swinging in-duckers, conceded six runs off his first over, but four were from Cook's inside edge, and Srinath struck in his next over when Cook played across an in-swinger and was leg before for 17 in a total of 28 for 2.

The crowd were eager for action and thousands rose to their feet when Wessels produced a rare aggressive stroke, a powerful coverdrive for four off Srinath in the 20th over. Firecrackers, a feature at Indian grounds, exploded when Kirsten was bowled by the diminutive left-arm spinner Venkatapathy Raju three overs later to leave South Africa precariously placed at 49 for 3 with 22,4 overs gone.

While Wessels calmly collected runs, Adrian Kuiper lifted the tempo and earned a huge roar from the crowd when he pulled a full toss from Srinath over the high security fence and into the spectators at square leg.

Just when Wessels seemed to have gained complete control, he dragged a ball from the innocently slow seamer Tendulkar onto his stumps.

Clive Rice looked calm and competent, but he and Kuiper were out in quick succession and despite some uninhibited strokes by Snell, the innings petered out at 177 for 8 with India bowling only 47 overs in the time allotted.

The total did not seem nearly enough, but Allan Donald came steaming in off his long run and his speed induced an involuntary jab at the ball by Ravi Shastri to provide wicket-keeper Richardson with a catch in the first over of the Indian innings. Poor Shastri. Unpopular in Calcutta, he had been whistled and jeered when he misfielded, had bowled poorly in conceding 17 runs off three overs, and now was out for nought. He was booed all the way to the pavilion.

Donald had more in store. In his next over the acclaimed young batsman Sanjay Manjrekar was yorked by another ball of blistering pace and Donald struck a third time when Sidhu was caught in the slips to reduce India to 20 for 3.

It could have been worse for the home team. The boy prodigy Sachin Tendulkar had been stranded metres out of his crease soon after arriving at the wicket when Sidhu played Snell to square leg, but Snell could not hold the throw from fielder Hudson and Tendulkar survived to play an innings of extraordinary charm and maturity. Tendulkar, just 18, went on the attack almost immediately and hit a scorching cover drive off Snell. It was the first of eight fours and he also flicked Snell effortlessly for six over midwicket to unleash another frenzied burst of firecrackers from a crowd which had swelled to an official count of 90 450.

Although Donald's first spell brought him 3 for 11 off five

Kepler Wessels forces the ball to leg in Gwalior.

overs, Snell conceded 21 in his first four and McMillan 23 in four as Tendulkar and Azharuddin went on the attack. Neither bowler was able to come to terms with the fuller length required for bowling on a pitch far slower than anything they had previously encountered.

Shaw dismissed Azharuddin when the Indian captain went down the wicket to drive and was stumped, but he also struggled against the nimble Indian batsmen. Anything too full was driven, anything even fractionally short was hit powerfully off the back foot as the ball bounced agonisingly slowly off the pitch. The ease with which the Indians played Shaw in what was his only bowling spell of the tour probably contributed to Shaw's later omission from the squad for the World Cup, although his figures of 1 for 46 from 10 overs were no worse than those of many of his teammates.

The match turned India's way in a quick-scoring partnership of 56 between Tendulkar and another young batsman, Praveen Amre, who followed Tendulkar's aggressive example. Although Donald came back to dismiss both Tendulkar and finally Amre when only one more run was required for victory, India reached their target with 10,2 overs and three wickets to spare.

Donald took 5 for 29 but the only other bowler who could feel satisfied with his performance was Rice, who bowled accurately at enough pace to slow down the Indian assault.

After a function at the ground that night, which provided a feast of eating but not a drop of alcohol under the strict liquor regulations in force, the team flew to Agra the next morning. They visited the Taj Mahal before reboarding the aircraft for the short flight to Gwalior, home of Madhavrao Scindia, president of the Indian cricket board and descendant of one of the great maharajah families of India.

It was on this Tuesday, when the lessons of Calcutta needed literally to be put into practice, that the tour lost its way in a cricket sense. While the Taj Mahal is every bit as impressive as the guide books and pictures suggest, it took up valuable cricket hours. To add to the team's problems, by the time they arrived in Gwalior in mid-afternoon, they were unable to practise because the kit had been sent to the wrong place. So, after a day of flying and sightseeing, they went to bed on the eve of match two.

Because the only hotel of suitable standard was small, only the players had travelled to Gwalior. The supporters, officials and media had stayed overnight in Agra and were transported to Gwalior, 118 km away, in a convoy of buses.

Unfortunately for those of us in the last bus, a crunching sound became apparent midway through the journey and a stop in the small village of Dholpur revealed that the driveshaft needed repair. It meant a two-hour delay and a remarkable demonstration of ingenuity as a local mechanic, working from a tiny shelter next to the main road, dismantled the offending part and repaired it while the stranded passengers were able to stroll around the village, including a visit to a local temple.

Agitation about the delay ended when we finally reached Gwalior, a moderate-sized city of relative prosperity, to find that the start of play had been delayed for nearly an hour by early morning mist, reducing the match to 45 overs a side.

India had made a flying start with the unorthodox Srikkanth scything away with his wristy shots square of the wicket and the turbanned Sidhu hitting the ball with relentless power. The openers put on 130 in 27 overs and with Manjrekar playing a delightful innings of 52 not out off 52 balls India posted a handsome total of 223 for 6.

FIRST ONE-DAY INTERNATIONAL

Eden Gardens, Calcutta, November 10, 1991
Toss won by Mohammad Azharuddin

SOUTH AFRICA
J Cook lbw b Srinath 17
A Hudson c More b Kapil Dev 0
K Wessels b Tendulkar 50
P Kirsten b Raju 7
A Kuiper
  c Amre b Prabhakar 43
C Rice b Prabhakar 14
R Snell c Amre b Kapil Dev 16
B McMillan run out 2
D Richardson not out 4
T Shaw not out 0
A Donald did not bat
Extras 24
Total (8 wickets, 47 overs) 177
Falls: 1/3, 2/28, 3/49, 4/109, 5/151, 6/156, 7/167, 8/176
Bowling: Kapil Dev 9-2-23-2, Prabhakar 10-1-26-2, Srinath 10-0-39-1, Raju 10-0-32-1, Shastri 3-0-17-0, Tendulkar 5-0-27-1.

INDIA
R Shastri c Richardson
 b Donald 0
N Sidhu c McMillan
 b Donald 6
S Manjrekar b Donald 1
S Tendulkar c Snell
 b Donald 62
M Azharuddin
 st Richardson b Shaw 16
P Amre lbw b Donald 55
K Dev b Kuiper 11
M Prabhakar not out 12
K More not out 0
V Raju, J Srinath did not bat
Extras 15
Total (7 wickets, 40,4 overs) 178
Falls: 1/1, 2/3, 3/20, 4/60, 5/116, 6/148, 7/177
Bowling: Donald 8,4-0-29-5, Snell 6-0-35-0, McMillan 6-0-30-0, Shaw 10-0-46-1, Rice 5-0-14-0, Kuiper 5-0-22-1.

India won by three wickets.
Man of the Match:
Sachin Tendulkar and
Allan Donald (shared).
Crowd: 90 450

Donald was again the best bowler, taking 3 for 36 from nine overs and ending the innings in spectacular style when a fast delivery to Amre broke a stump. Clive Eksteen, in his only two overs of the tour, had the mortifying experience of conceding 18 runs including a straight six by Sidhu.

The South African reply started disastrously with Kapil Dev repeating his feat of taking a wicket in the first over. This time it was Cook who played forward and edged an away-swinger to wicketkeeper More without a run on the board.

Mandy Yachad and Wessels set about repairing the damage but they did so painfully slowly, with only two scoring strokes in the first seven overs. They took the score to 94 before Yachad was lbw to Raju in the 25th over. Kirsten was trapped by Prabhakar and although Kuiper flared briefly in scoring 21 off 28 balls, with Wessels also picking up the pace, the South African effort fizzled when Kuiper and Wessels were out in successive overs to leave the total at 146 for 5 with 78 still needed for victory off 62 balls. Rice, Richardson and Snell all fell in a futile chase and the eventual margin was 38 runs.

While a packed and sometimes unruly crowd of 25 000 had been absorbed in the action on the field, another drama was going on in the pavilion.

The South African players noticed that the ball used by the Indians in Calcutta appeared to have been tampered with. It had several gouges on one side, while being kept shiny on the other. Clive Rice, for one, had been bowled by a ball which swung unnaturally for one in use for more than 40 overs on a grassless pitch.

In typical crusading fashion, Dr Bacher discussed the issue with Scindia and before the Gwalior game the two had told the Indian media that they had agreed that 'roughing-up' the ball was a practice which should be stamped out of international cricket. Not surprisingly, the Indian media deduced that Dr Bacher had only raised the issue because of events in Calcutta. The conclusion they drew was that the Indian team were being accused of cheating.

Scindia, apart from his involvement in cricket, is a full-time politician and India's Minister of Civil Aviation. He realised that his image could be adversely affected and immediately launched a counter-attack, going to UCB president Geoff Dakin to complain about the allegations against the Indian team. Dakin responded by discussing the matter with some of his board members in the presence of Scindia and agreed to apologise. He did not consult the man most directly involved in the controversy, which was especially surprising in view of Dr Bacher's dual role as team manager and UCB managing director. At the close of play Scindia and Dakin addressed the media. Scindia said he was 'surprised at the reference made by Dr Bacher to the alleged roughing up of the ball by the Indian team'. He categorically denied that his team had indulged in such a practice. In his statement Dakin said: 'It would appear that certain unfortunate remarks have been made. My executive were never approached in respect of this matter. To me there is no controversy – the matter is a storm in a teacup and we find the statement most embarrassing. I as president of the United Cricket Board and my executive totally dissociate ourselves from the statement allegedly made by Dr Bacher. I apologise on behalf of the executive, team management and the team to Mr Scindia and the Board of Control for Cricket in India.'

Having read this statement, Dakin turned to Scindia and apologised once again. As an observer, I felt the apology far exceeded the supposed insult, especially as there seemed little doubt, from having spoken to the players, that the Indians did in fact tamper with the ball. Dr Bacher, who sometimes naively believes everyone in cricket shares his consuming passion for the game and its ethics, may well have erred in making the issue public. It might have been far better to have discussed it quietly with Scindia, reached an agreement on future conduct, and then let it rest. Dakin, on the other hand, should surely have discussed the issue with the man accused to at the very least establish whether Scindia's outburst was justified.

The issue was, as Dakin said, a storm in a teacup, but it was meat and drink to the contingent of English reporters present, as well as many of the Indian journalists. Dakin took issue with me later for describing his apology as 'grovelling' when I wrote

SECOND ONE-DAY INTERNATIONAL

Gwalior, November 12
Toss won by
Mohammad Azharuddin

INDIA
K Srikkanth c Yachad b Snell	68
N Sidhu c Kirsten b Rice	61
S Manjrekar not out	52
S Tendulkar c Richardson b Matthews	4
M Azharuddin c Kirsten b Donald	19
K Dev b Donald	3
P Amre b Donald	4

M Prabhakar, K More, V Raju, J Srinath did not bat
Extras 12
Total (6 wickets, 45 overs) 223
Falls: 1/130, 2/144, 3/159, 4/202, 5/218, 6/223
Bowling: Donald 9-1-36-3, Snell 9-0-43-1, Matthews 9-0-41-1, Eksteen 2-0-18-0, Rice 9-0-46-1, Kuiper 7-0-38-0.

SOUTH AFRICA

J Cook c More b Kapil Dev	0
M Yachad lbw b Raju	31
K Wessels c More b Srinath	71
P Kirsten lbw b Prabhakar	2
A Kuiper c Azharuddin b Kapil Dev	21
C Rice c sub b Raju	12
D Richardson c Kapil Dev b Raju	5
R Snell c Tendulkar b Srinath	2
C Matthews not out	9
C Eksteen not out	7
A Donald did not bat	
Extras	25
Total (8 wickets, 45 overs)	185

Falls: 1/0, 2/94, 3/97, 4/144, 5/146, 6/162, 7/164, 8/166
Bowling: Kapil Dev 9-3-27-2, Prabhakar 9-1-19-1, Tendulkar 7-0-31-0, Srinath 9-0-24-2, Raju 9-0-43-3, Srikkanth 2-0-14-0.

India won by 38 runs
Man of the Match:
Kepler Wessels and
Sanjay Manjrekar (shared)
Crowd: 25 000

about the controversy in the *Sunday Times*. Although it was a strong word, I still feel with the benefit of hindsight that none of the participants emerged well from the affair. It undoubtedly widened the rift between Dakin and Bacher which had existed since the Gatting tour.

There was yet another gala function to attend that very night at Scindia's palace in Gwalior. He had laid on a dinner for the entire touring party, including supporters, at an ancestral home similar in design to Buckingham Palace, with 1 000 rooms and spacious formal gardens. Drinks were served in a reception area of baroque, gilded magnificence which according to a guide book boasts the largest chandeliers in the world. Guests were invited to step onto an enormous balcony to view a spectacular fireworks display before going down to the banqueting hall for a buffet meal. Down the centre of the room was a long table with a splendid model train attached to a silver carriage loaded with liqueurs. Although the train was not used on this occasion, it was tempting to create a mental picture of well-fed men enjoying the patronage of an all-powerful maharajah together with their post-prandial cognacs and cigars. It was from this same palace that an earlier Madhavrao Scindia had launched legendary tiger shoots to impress visiting British nobility and they undoubtedly celebrated their success from the same silver train.

As the clock pushed towards midnight, the convoy of buses headed out of the palace gates, past the homeless poor in the streets and on to Gwalior airport for a short flight to New Delhi. It was nearly 3 am by the time I went to bed. It had been an awfully long day, and I hadn't played in a tough game of cricket.

The final match of the tour was a day-night fixture at the 60 000 seater Jawaharlal Nehru Stadium, scene of the 1982 Asian Games. Another hard-baked pitch had been prepared in the centre of a field which also incorporated a tartan athletics track. Patches of green carpet covered throwing and jumping areas.

First, though, was yet another function hosted by Scindia, this time at the poolside of the Ashoka hotel. Once again there were welcoming Indian ladies, and a corridor of flowers led to a splendid occasion which included elephant rides, a display by a levitating man, and traditional dancers as well as unlimited food and drink.

The match the next evening continued with a depressingly familiar pattern of Indian domination. With Sidhu having been injured by an object thrown from the crowd in Gwalior, Shastri returned to the side. Although no more popular in New Delhi than in Calcutta, Shastri played superbly to register his third one-day international century and highest score of 109. Srikkanth hit 52 off 61 balls in an opening partnership of 86 before Manjrekar joined Shastri in a brilliant partnership of 175 off just 153 balls. Starting the last over on 94, Manjrekar reached 105 off only 82 balls.

India's total of 287 for 4 off 50 overs seemed out of reach, but Cook and Wessels gave South Africa an ideal start, scoring 71 for the first wicket in 16 overs. Kirsten then joined Wessels and the runs rattled along.

At last the South African batting order seemed to be right, with the right-handed Cook and left-handed Wessels providing an ideal blend to start the innings. Wessels, capable of being bogged down lower in the order, was at his best on a warm night, placing his cuts and pulls with deft timing. Kirsten, disappointed with his failure to score runs in the first two matches, realised he was playing for the continuation of his international career. He was superb, using his feet well and caressing the ball off his bat with all his old mastery. A confident two-step down the wicket and an effortlessly lofted straight six off Raju revealed his return to form.

Wessels and Kirsten achieved total domination over an attack which at last was reduced to mediocrity. Wessels seemed set for the third century of the match before he was given out lbw to Raju. From the press box square of the wicket it seemed Wessels was too far down the wicket for even the most gifted umpire to make a decision with certainty, but it was one of the few truly dubious decisions on the tour. Wessels had scored 90 off 105 balls, and he and Kirsten had put on 111 off 114 deliveries.

THIRD ONE-DAY INTERNATIONAL
(day-night),
Jawaharlal Nehru Stadium,
New Delhi, November 14
Toss won by Clive Rice

INDIA
R Shastri run out — 109
K Srikkanth st Richardson b Kirsten — 53
S Manjrekar c McMillan b Rice — 105
S Tendulkar c Cook b Donald — 1
K Dev not out — 3
P Amre, C Pandit, M Prabhakar, V Raju, J Srinath did not bat
Extras — 16
Total (4 wickets, 50 overs) — 287
Falls: 1/86, 2/261, 3/264, 4/287
Bowling: Donald 10-0-55-1, Snell 10-1-56-0, Matthews 10-1-50-0, McMillan 8-0-40-0, Rice 9-0-54-1, Kirsten 3-0-23-1.

SOUTH AFRICA

J Cook c Prabhakar b Srinath	35
K Wessels lbw b Raju	90
P Kirsten not out	86
A Kuiper not out	63
A Hudson, C Rice, B McMillan, D Richardson, R Snell, C Matthews, A Donald did not bat	
Extras	14
Total (2 wickets, 46,4 overs)	288

Falls: 1/72, 2/183
Bowling: Kapil Dev 8-0-37-0, Prabhakar 8,4-0-64-0, Srinath 10-0-69-1, Tendulkar 6-0-38-0, Raju 10-0-48-1, Srikkanth 4-0-25-0.

South Africa won by eight wickets.
Man of the Match: Peter Kirsten.
Man of the Series: Sanjay Manjrekar and Kepler Wessels (shared).
Crowd: 60 000

Andrew Hudson had been due to bat at number four, but with 105 still needed off 15,1 overs Rice wisely decided that Kuiper should be promoted. It was the ideal situation for the hard-hitting Western Province player and he immediately hammered Srinath through extra cover for four and lofted the same bowler over cover for six. There was simply no stopping the South Africans, and victory was achieved with no further loss of wickets and 3,2 overs to spare. Kirsten's unbeaten 86 was made off 92 balls, while Kuiper faced only 41 in scoring 63 not out.

After a tour of so many official functions, this was a night for South African celebrations and it was an elated group of players and officials who toasted victory into the small hours as an understanding management at the Oberoi hotel allowed the bar to remain open far later than usual.

It had been the week of a lifetime for virtually everyone who went to India, but it was also time for reflection. Sitting on the crowded flight home amid boisterous supporters I started my articles for that week's *Sunday Times*. 'South Africa', I wrote, 'can be a force in the World Cup – but only if the harsh lessons of India are absorbed.' The emotion and euphoria of victory in New Delhi could not be allowed to obscure glaring weaknesses – lack of agility in the field, an inability of the bowlers to keep the Indian batsmen in check, and a need to improve the urgency of the batting.

I suggested that Cook and Wessels were the logical pair to open the batting, with Peter Kirsten at number three to be followed by a classy specialist number four, and for Jonty Rhodes, with his sublime fielding ability, to follow Kuiper and Rice at the expense of a specialist fifth bowler. My suggestion for a number four was Daryll Cullinan, but the subsequent form of Free State's Hansie Cronje settled any discussion on this score. The basic structure thus suggested became the model for the eventual World Cup team, although the selectors had some shocks in store.

What is certain, though, is that without travelling to India, the South African team at the World Cup would indeed have been like babes in the wood.

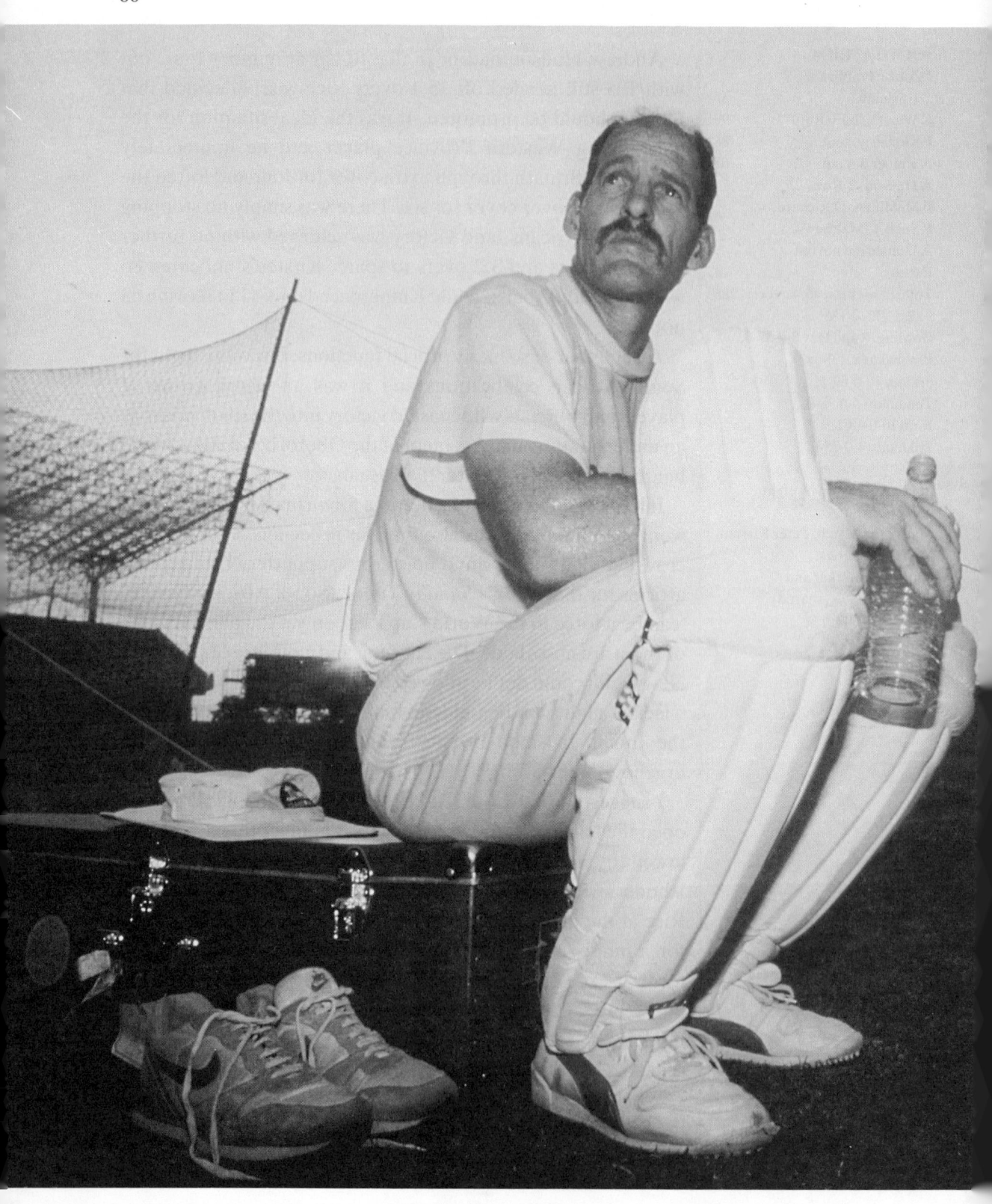

The captain in India. Clive Rice takes a break during a practice in Calcutta.

CHAPTER FIVE

THE SELECTION BOMBSHELL

The tour of India appeared to have secured Clive Rice's tenure as captain of South Africa. On the flight home, tour manager Ali Bacher made a speech across the aircraft speaker system and said India had been Rice's finest hour both on and off the field. His captaincy had been mature and his off-field conduct exemplary. He had handled both media and public with statesmanship and skill.

In playing terms, Rice was still the bowler best able to maintain an economical line and length, and his batting showed the experience and confidence of many years at top level. Despite being 42, he remained outstandingly fit and was certainly no liability in the field. It was therefore widely assumed that Rice would be the captain of the South African team for the World Cup.

But Rice had been dropped from the national captaincy once before – against Mike Gatting's rebel team in 1990, when his provincial teammate Jimmy Cook was appointed instead.

At the time it was widely alleged that there was a personal grudge between Rice and the convenor of the selectors, former Springbok captain Peter van der Merwe. The origins of the alleged feud are not entirely clear, but the pair are dissimilar in character. Van der Merwe, who led South Africa to series victories over England in 1965 and Australia in 1966/67, is of the 'old school', a conservative man in appearance and style. Rice, by contrast, had been involved in numerous brushes with authority since his days with Kerry Packer's World Series Cricket in the late 1970s, when he demanded an appearance fee before playing for Transvaal in a limited overs final.

If there was a direct clash of wills it might have been in 1983/84, when Rice was captain of the South African team in the series against Lawrence Rowe's West Indians and Van der Merwe was on the selection panel. Chris Burger, the convenor, handed Rice the team for the final 'Test' in Port Elizabeth. The incident happened in the dressing room after a match at Berea Park in Pretoria. The selectors had dropped Kenny McEwan. Rice refused to accept the team and insisted the selectors have a re-think. The next morning they announced a team which included McEwan, who repaid Rice's loyalty by scoring a century.

Van der Merwe was appointed convenor for the 1985/86 season when South Africa played against Kim Hughes' Australian team and Rice was appointed captain, retaining the job for the following season as well.

Rice was expected to retain the leadership against Gatting's team. The appointment of Cook came as a bombshell. The message from the selectors appeared to be that they no longer considered Rice to be a player capable of giving his best for the five days of a Test match. He was, however, recalled to the team for four one-day internationals although Cook retained the captaincy.

Before the India tour team was announced, Van der Merwe gave an assurance in the *Sunday Times* that he would not let personal feelings affect his choice. He said: 'It is not my job to confirm or deny anything about Clive Rice. But whether I like him or don't like him I will consider any player if he is good enough to be in the team.' He concluded: 'I have no axes to grind.' Later that day Rice was named captain for India and it seemed that any old grudges had been buried. But Van der Merwe had pointed out that the team would of necessity be picked on past form because it was too early in the current season to make a fair assessment.

The inquests after the India tour dwelt at some length on the age of the team and their lack of mobility in the field, but it also seemed that players like Rice and Jimmy Cook, together with Kepler Wessels and Peter Kirsten, could be considered certainties for the World Cup.

JIMMY COOK was born in Johannesburg on July 31, 1953. Educated at Hyde Park High, he is one of the few top-class cricketers not to have been selected at Nuffield interprovincial high schools level. He made his debut at the age of 19 for Transvaal against Natal at the Wanderers, scoring 54.

Although at the beginning of his career he was a middle-order batsman, he soon developed into a consistent opener. He made a century on his debut for South Africa in the unofficial Test against the 1982 English 'rebel' team and was the only player selected for every Springbok team throughout the rebel era. He captained the national side against Mike Gatting's Englishmen in 1990.

After three high-scoring seasons for Somerset in the English county championship, with more than 2 000 runs each season, he boasted a career first-class average above 50 with 55 centuries, including a highest score of 313 not out for Somerset against Glamorgan in 1991. University sports officer.

The first task of the selectors was to name a preliminary squad of 20 by the end of December. This was purely for administrative purposes, to enable the World Cup organisers to prepare brochures, publicity material and clothing. The squad did not bind the selectors to selecting from them alone in finalising their team.

The selectors, Van der Merwe, Lee Irvine, Tony Pithey, Peter Pollock, all former Springboks from the SACU, and Rushdie Majiet and Syd Reddy from the former SACB, gathered in Durban on Saturday, December 28. Mike Procter, the national team coach, was at Kingsmead where the selectors were meeting, in his capacity as the Natal coach. To his surprise he was not called in or consulted.

Cook, despite having scored a remarkable 2 755 first-class runs for Somerset in English county cricket in 1991, at an average of 81,03, was struggling to find his best form at home. This was a continuation of a three-year trend, with Cook scoring more than 2 000 runs in each of his three seasons with Somerset and then having moderate seasons in South Africa. As an opening batsman, Cook was vulnerable to the vagaries of a Wanderers pitch which was prepared to help seam bowlers, to the extent that he seemed to have lost much of his confidence in home matches. In first-class matches away from the Wanderers he continued to average about 50.

The Wanderers pitch, though, was not the villain in his current malaise. Rather it seemed that he simply had not had enough time to settle into a routine after taking some time off cricket immediately after the English season, and then going to India under-prepared. As he said in an interview shortly before Christmas, he had not planned to hit his peak until February. He had only batted five times since India, and had managed just 69 runs with a top score of 27. He had missed Transvaal's first four-day match of the season while in India, and Transvaal had then had a bye in the seven-team competition. As a result his first first-class innings of the season was on December 26 when he scored 23 against Eastern Province. This was far from an ideal situation for a batsman out of form.

Rice had suffered minor injuries and had not played a great

amount of cricket since India. His bowling, even when he was not restricted by one-day limitations, had generally consisted of short spells. His critics wondered if he had lost his pace and his stamina.

Kirsten, after starting the season with a torrent of runs, had suffered a minor slump in form but scored 107 and 54 in a Castle Cup four-day match for Border against Northern Transvaal in the days leading up to the announcement of the preliminary squad.

Although selection matters are supposed to be confidential, whispers about Rice and Cook had started to go the rounds. A week before the announcement, the Argus group writer Trevor Chesterfield, who spoke regularly to Van der Merwe, speculated that Kepler Wessels might be made captain. Other journalists speculated that Cook would be dropped and some said he should be dropped. The fatuous argument was promoted that the selectors had to pick on what they saw in South Africa and therefore Cook's English record should count for nothing. Amazingly, this is the argument the selectors seemed to accept.

Following the Wessels speculation, which seemed a deliberate leak, I spoke to Van der Merwe before writing for the *Sunday Times* of December 29, the day of the announcement. Van der Merwe denied that any decision had been made on the captaincy or the balance of the side. 'We have not previously got together to discuss specific issues,' he said. The Wessels report he dismissed as speculation. But he gave an indication that younger blood was being sought when he spoke of the need to pick a side specifically for the World Cup. 'We will be looking for a team which includes men who can field, run and throw well, and who can play a wide variety of strokes.'

Van der Merwe said he could give no indication as to whether a captain would be announced at the same time as the shortlist.

Despite Van der Merwe's disclaimers, Wessels was named captain on the Sunday evening and the shortlist did not contain Rice, Cook or Kirsten. The announcement was greeted with shock. Rice angrily said he had been dropped because of a per-

PETER VAN DER MERWE, born in Paarl on March 14, 1937, was educated at St Andrews College, Grahamstown, and Cape Town University. He captained SA Schools in 1955 and made his first-class debut for South African Universities against the MCC in 1956/57.

A solid middle-order batsman and useful left-arm spinner, he played for both Western Province and Eastern Province and made his Test debut as vice-captain on the 1963/64 Springbok tour of Australia and New Zealand. He captained victorious Springbok teams in England in 1965 and against Australia in South Africa in 1966/67.

He played in 15 Tests, scoring 533 runs at an average of 25,38 with a highest score of 76 against Australia in 1966/67. In first-class matches he averaged just under 30 and had a highest score of 128 for Eastern Province against Transvaal in 1966/67. Managing director of a group of companies in Port Elizabeth.

Right: Clive Rice meets Mother Teresa in Calcutta.

Below: All peace. Kepler Wessels, Clive Rice and Jimmy Cook during the opening ceremony before the match between South Africa and India at New Delhi.

Bottom: Clive Rice and the SA team greet the crowd before the start of the match marking South Africa's return to official international cricket at Eden Gardens, Calcutta.

Above: South Africa's touring party in India. Standing, from left, Mandy Yachad, Craig Smith (physiotherapist), Brian McMillan, Craig Matthews, Tim Shaw, Richard Snell, Clive Eksteen, Dave Richardson, Andrew Hudson. Sitting: Allan Donald, Kepler Wessels, Jimmy Cook, Clive Rice (captain), Dr Ali Bacher (manager), Mike Procter (coach), Rushdie Majiet (assistant manager), Peter Kirsten, Adrian Kuiper. On ground (non-playing members of squad): Hansie Cronje, Derek Crookes, Hoosain Manack, Faiek Davids.

Right top: The crowd of 90 450 for the match between India and South Africa at Eden Gardens in Calcutta.

Right: Allan Donald celebrates after taking a wicket against India in Calcutta.

Left: Mohammad Azharuddin and Clive Rice before the toss at Eden Gardens, Calcutta.

Below: South Africa take the field against India at Eden Gardens, Calcutta.

Right: A huge floodlight pylon towers over the crowd of 60 000 at the day-night match between India and South Africa at New Delhi.

SAIL SAIL
PALM BEACH
OPTONIKA
Rapport Elke Sondag
Tropicana
International Airports Authority of India

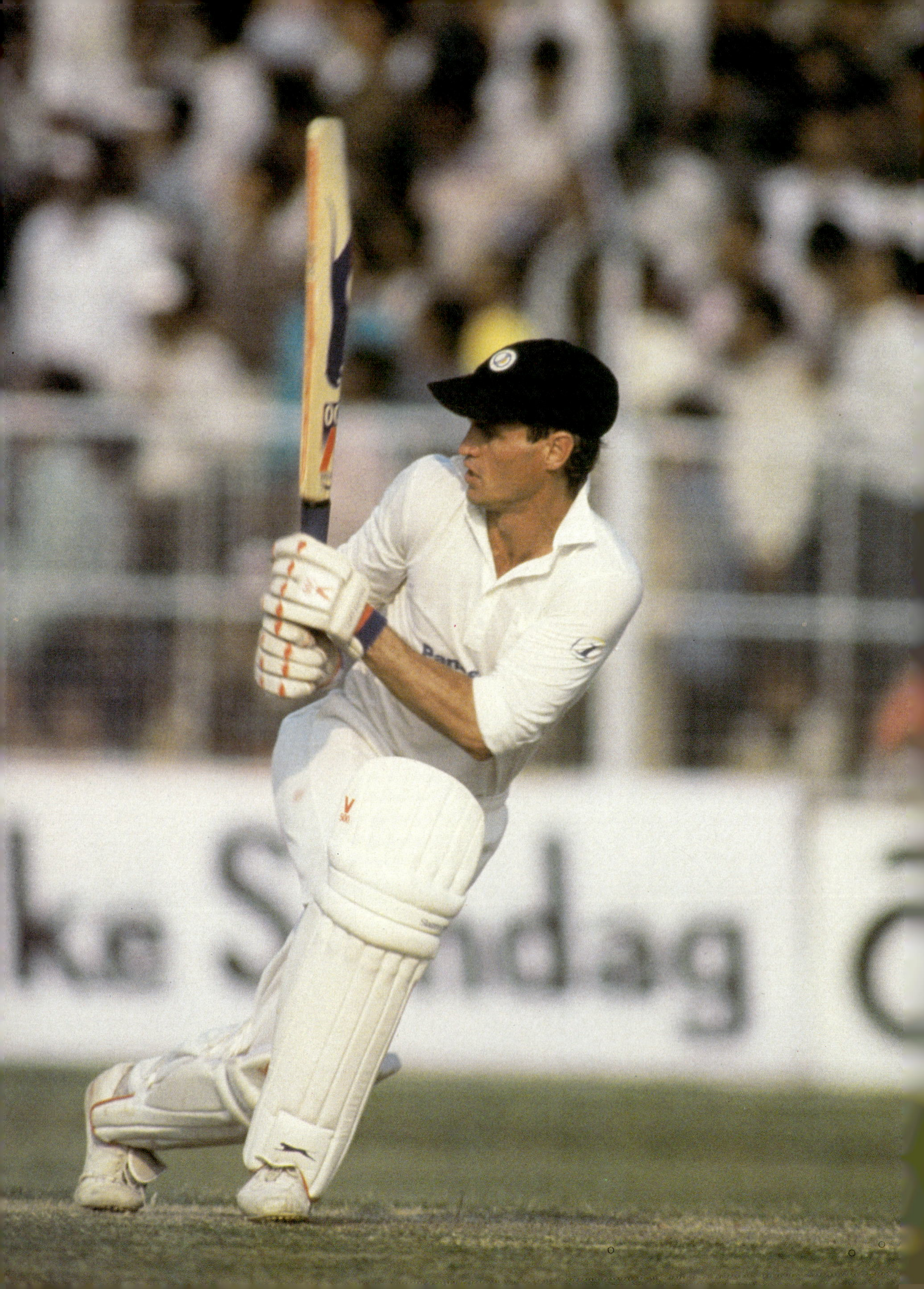

Left: Kepler Wessels during his top-scoring innings of 71 against India at Gwalior.

Right: The crowd at Gwalior welcome the South African touring team.

Below: Action during the second match between India and South Africa in Gwalior.

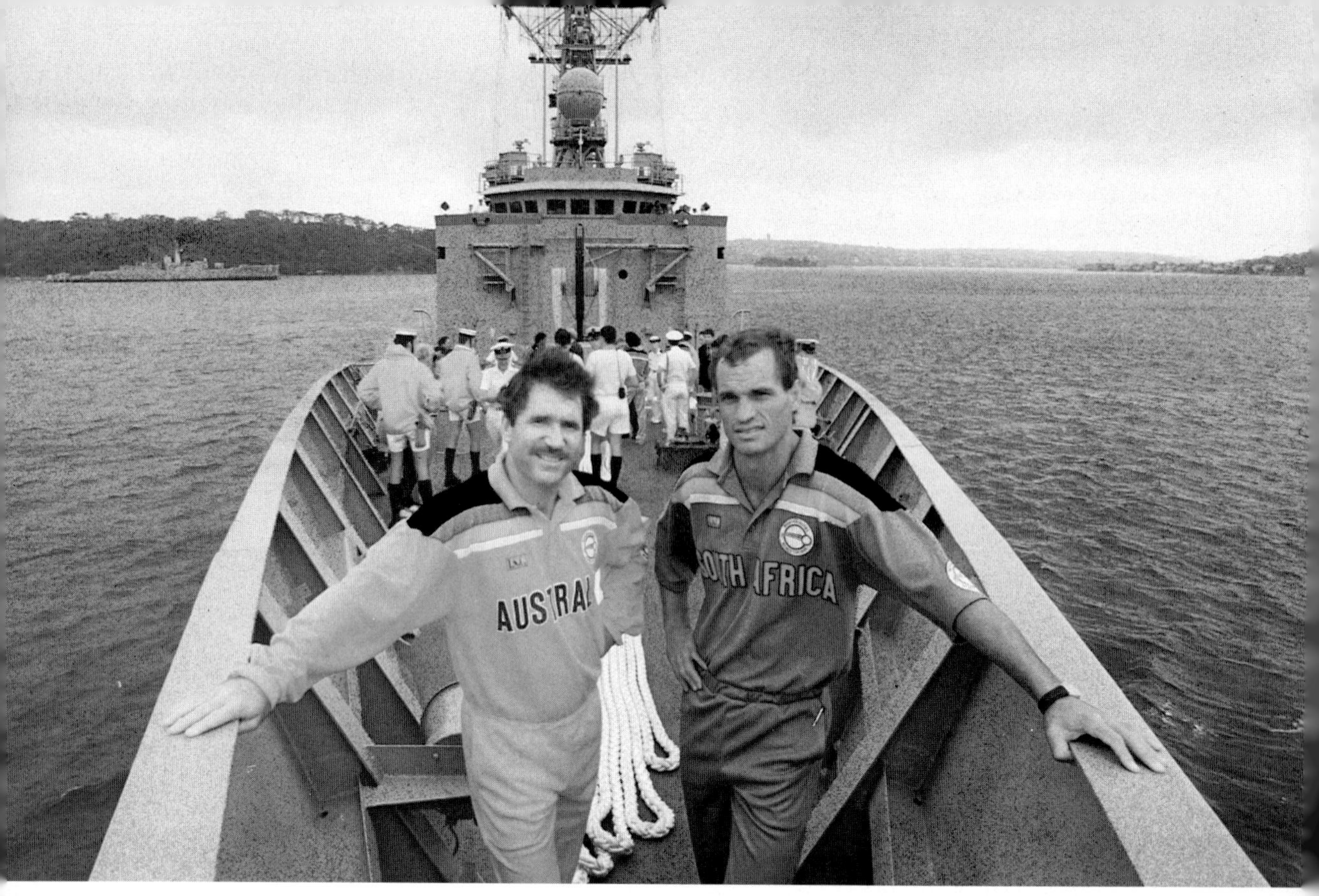

AUSTRAL
OUTH AFRICA

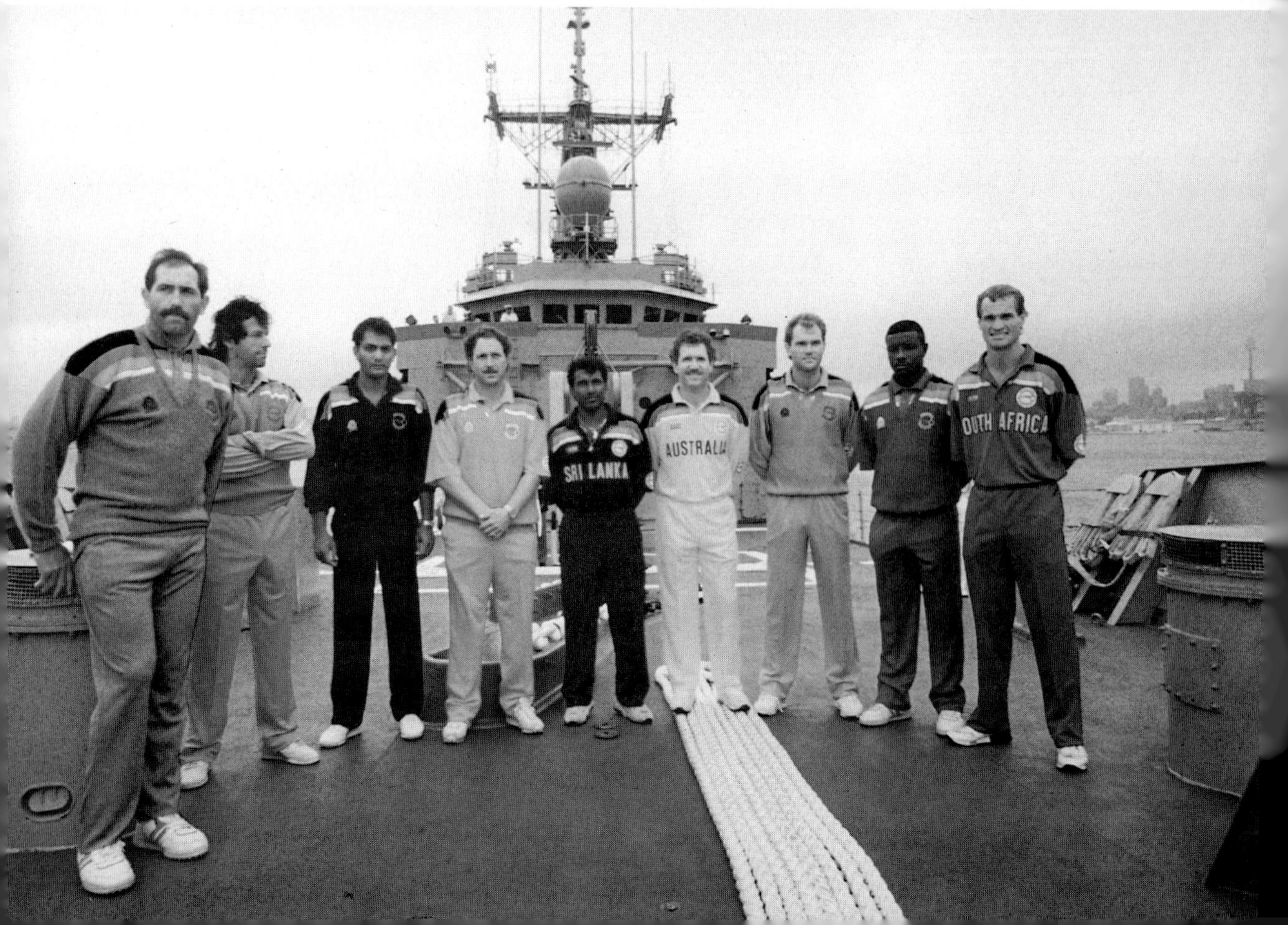

SRI LANKA
AUSTRALIA
OUTH AFRICA

Left: Ready for battle, Australian captain Allan Border and South African captain Kepler Wessels during the World Cup opening ceremony aboard the Canberra.

Left Bottom: Who'll rule the world? The captains line up aboard the Canberra. *From left: Graham Gooch (England), Imran Khan (Pakistan), Mohammad Azharuddin (India), Dave Houghton (Zimbabwe), Aravinda de Silva (Sri Lanka), Allan Border (Australia), Martin Crowe (New Zealand), Richie Richardson (West Indies) and Kepler Wessels (South Africa).*

Right: David Boon on the attack during his innings of 100 for Australia against New Zealand in the World Cup opening match in Auckland.

Below: The Sydney Cricket Ground during the match between Australia and South Africa.

Above: South Africa's World Cup squad. Standing (from left): Tertius Bosch, Richard Snell, Mark Rushmere, Craig Smith (physiotherapist), Faiek Davids (non-player), Jonty Rhodes, Omar Henry, Yasien Begg (non-player), Andrew Hudson, Hansie Cronje, Meyrick Pringle. Sitting: Brian McMillan, Allan Donald, Adrian Kuiper (vice-captain), Alan Jordaan (manager), Kepler Wessels (captain), Mike Procter (coach), Peter Kirsten, Dave Richardson.

Left: Captain triumphant. Kepler Wessels leaves the field after the victory over Australia in Sydney.

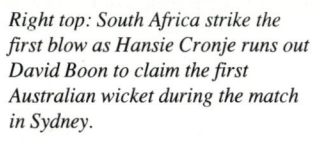

Right top: South Africa strike the first blow as Hansie Cronje runs out David Boon to claim the first Australian wicket during the match in Sydney.

Right: Still mates. Former Australian teammates Allan Border and Kepler Wessels after South Africa had beaten Australia in Sydney.

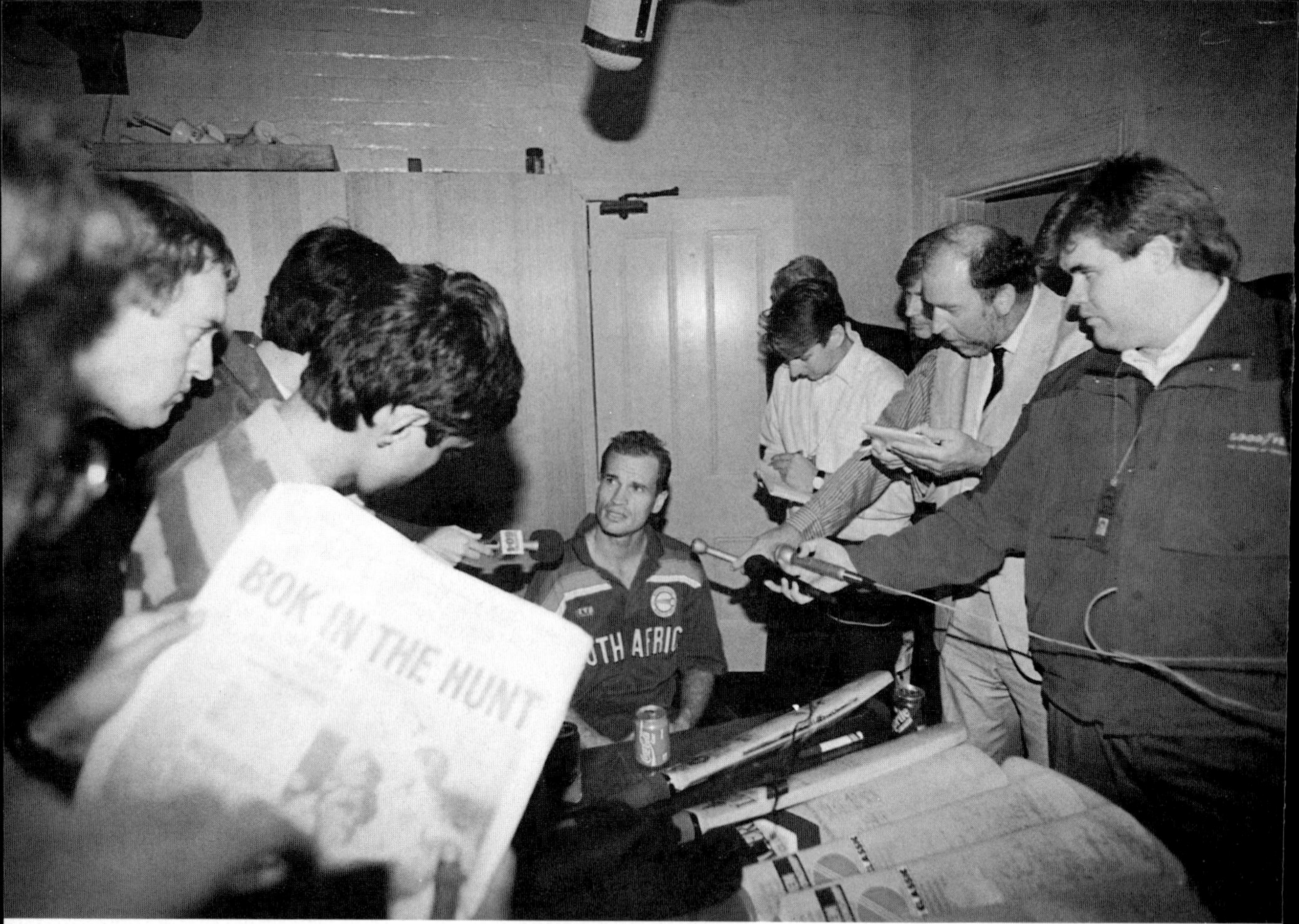
BOK IN THE HUNT

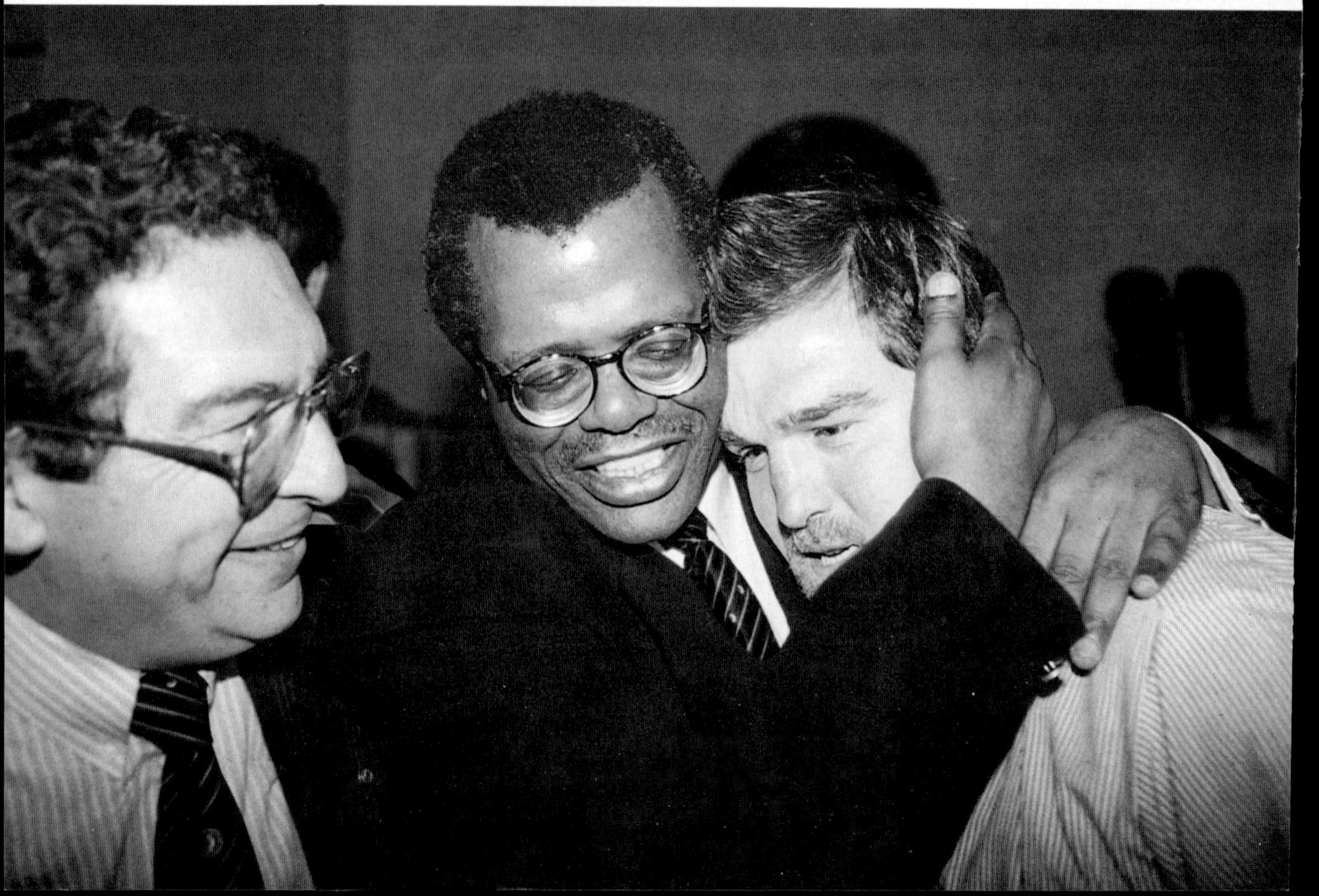

Left top: Kepler Wessels during the press conference after South Africa's win over Australia in Sydney.

Left bottom: Old wounds healed. Mike Gatting, captain of the last rebel team to South Africa, is embraced by the ANC's Steve Tshwete after South Africa's victory over Australia in Sydney, watched by Ali Bacher.

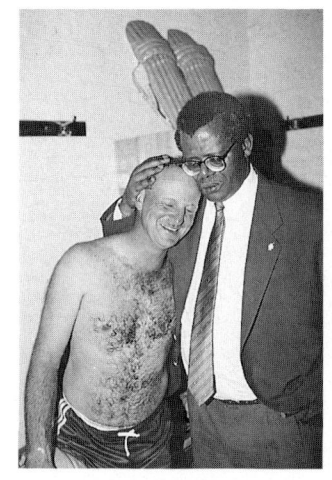

Above: Congratulations. Peter Kirsten and ANC spokesman on sport Steve Tshwete after South Africa's historic win over Australia in Sydney.

Right: The South African team celebrate on the players' balcony after beating Australia in Sydney.

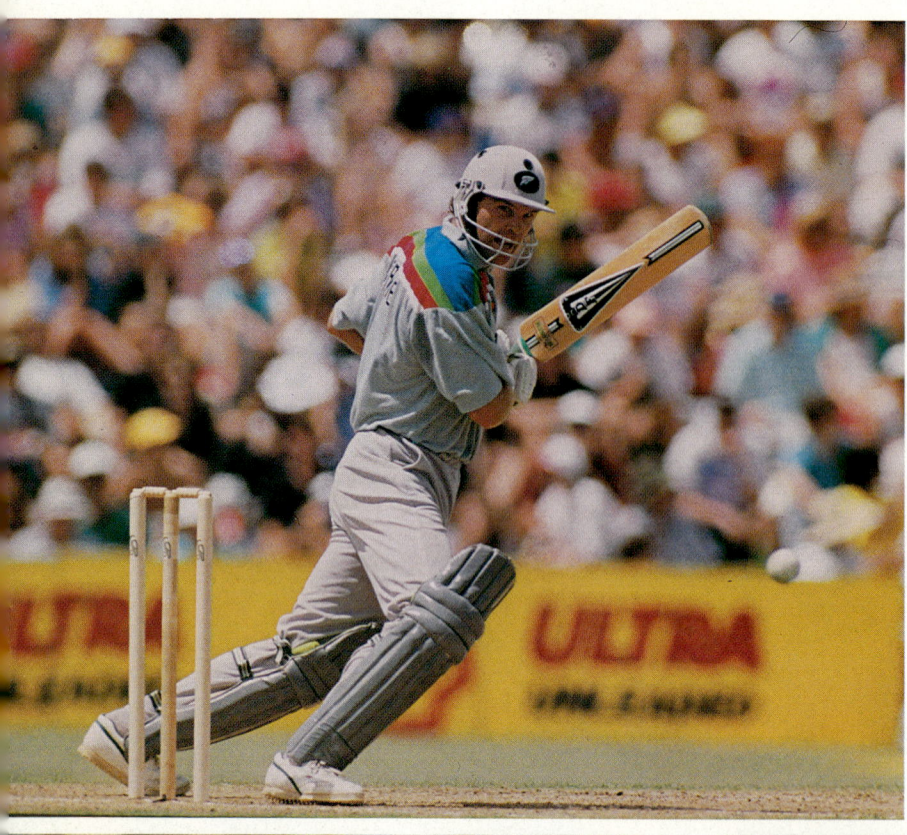

Left: New Zealand captain Martin Crowe, the most successful batsman at the World Cup, who scored 456 runs at an average of 114, during his century against Australia in the opening match in Auckland.

Below: Dave Richardson during his innings of 28 against New Zealand in Auckland.

Right top: Mark Greatbatch bowled after his bludgeoning innings of 68 for New Zealand against South Africa in Auckland.

Right bottom: Brian McMillan hits to leg during his innings of 33 not out against New Zealand in Auckland.

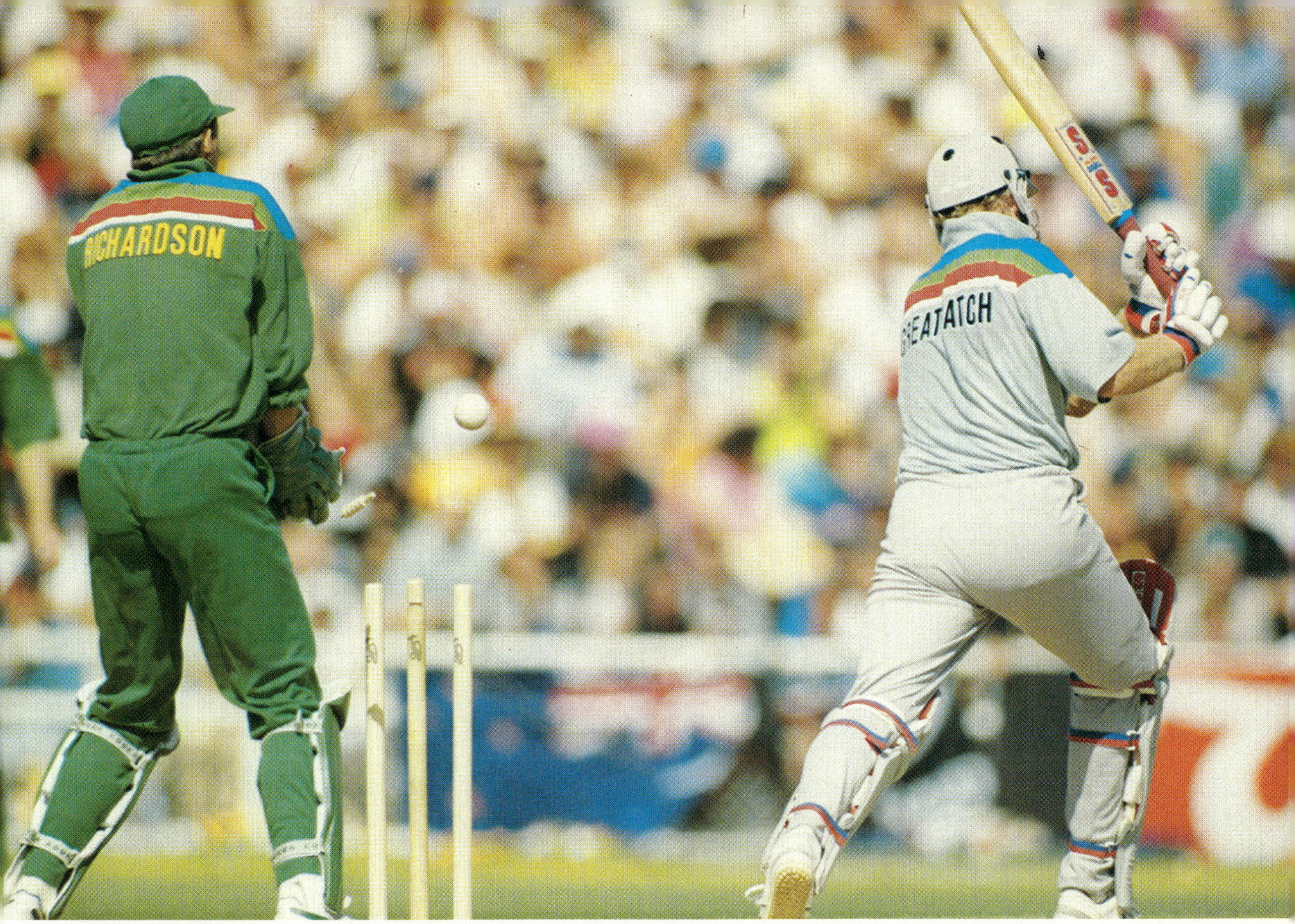
RICHARDSON

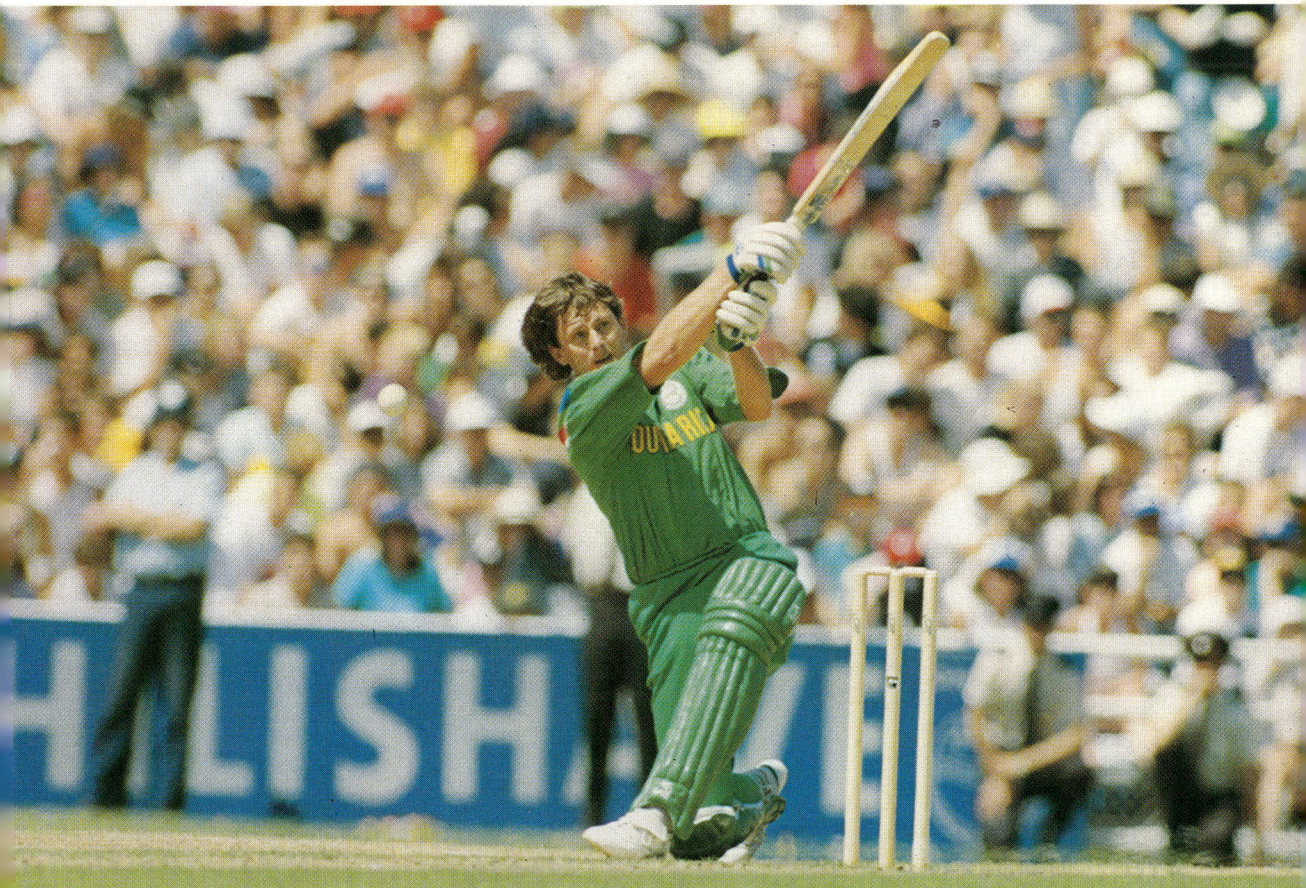

Left Arjuna Ranatunga plays a typical square cut on the way to a match-winning 64 not out against Sri Lanka against South Africa in Wellington.

Below: Arjuna Ranatunga and Champeke Ramanayake celebrate after scoring the winning runs for Sri Lanka against South Africa in Wellington.

sonality clash, and Cook was quoted as wondering whether the selectors were trying to pick 'a team of athletes' rather than a cricket side, although he later denied this remark. Kirsten merely expressed his bitter disappointment.

Surprisingly, older generation cricketers such as Johnny Waite and Roy McLean supported the selectors, but the almost unanimous opinion of current and recent players was that the selectors had made a dreadful mistake.

The squad named was: Kepler Wessels (Eastern Province, captain), Adrian Kuiper (Western Province, vice-captain), Tertius Bosch (Northern Transvaal), Rudi Bryson (Eastern Province), Hansie Cronje (Free State), Daryll Cullinan (Transvaal), Allan Donald (Free State), Omar Henry (Free State), Andrew Hudson (Natal), Ray Jennings (Northern Transvaal), Craig Matthews (Western Province), Brian McMillan (Western Province), Jonty Rhodes (Natal), Dave Richardson (Eastern Province), Mike Rindel (Northern Transvaal), Mark Rushmere (Eastern Province), Brett Schultz (Eastern Province), Tim Shaw (Eastern Province), Richard Snell (Transvaal) and Corrie van Zyl (Free State).

Axed from the squad that had returned from India only six weeks previously were Rice, Cook, Kirsten, Mandy Yachad and Clive Eksteen.

The reaction was so vociferous that Edward Griffiths, sports editor of the *Sunday Times*, decided to ask the people most directly involved, the players themselves, what they thought. An attempt was made to contact each regular provincial-level player in South Africa and ask them: Do you have confidence in the national selectors' ability to pick the strongest available side?

No fewer than 66 players from seven provinces were contacted and 46, a staggering 71 per cent, said No.

Attempts were made to discredit the poll. Free State coach Eddie Barlow felt it was harmful to cricket and a story was published in a Bloemfontein newspaper to the effect that journalists from the Transvaal were trying to influence cricketers to rebel against the selectors. This was presumably based on a conversation Griffiths had with one player after having noted his reply to the question. I still have my working list of players, which for obvious reasons must remain confidential, and I am confident that all the players, if asked to swear to the nature of the question posed by Griffiths and myself, would acknowledge that it was put in a fair manner without any attempt to insert a loaded preamble.

Van der Merwe responded to the poll result by saying that the selectors were elected by the United Cricket Board and were responsible only to the board.

UCB president Geoff Dakin refused to accept the result of the survey. 'I don't believe it,' he said. Later that week he harangued Johannesburg cricket writers about the campaign mounted by the 'Johannesburg press' and made some stinging comments about Clive Rice to the effect that Rice had cut his own throat with his statements after the announcement. On the same day it was announced that Rice had been reprimanded for breaching the players' code of conduct.

One has to accept Dakin's word that he did not play any role in the selection process, but there is no doubt that he took a hand in the appointment of Alan Jordaan as manager.

After Ali Bacher had managed the team in India, he made himself available, after some soul-searching, for the same task at the World Cup. He felt that with modern communications he could as easily run day-to-day UCB matters from Australia or New Zealand as he could from his office in Johannesburg. But Bacher's availability did not meet with universal acclaim. It would appear that Dakin was of the view that the managing director should not be away from his desk for seven weeks. It was Dakin, two nights before the UCB meeting to discuss the appointment of a manager, who telephoned Alan Jordaan, president of the Northern Transvaal Cricket Union, to establish whether he would be available as manager.

One view expressed about the mass sacking of Rice, Cook and Kirsten was that if Wessels was to be captain, the 'old guard' needed to be sacrificed to make sure there was no potential dissent within the team. But this argument has as much validity as the opinion that Jimmy Cook was an ordinary player simply because he had not made huge scores in South Africa.

Jimmy Cook ... thousands of runs in England.

There had been some bad feeling between Cook and Wessels at the time of the Gatting tour, which may have led to Wessels' resignation from the team after the first five-day international. Cook was one of the prime movers of a campaign to prevent Wessels from playing for South Africa only three years after representing an Australian side in South Africa. Rice was also involved in that particular controversy as a member of the players' committee that discussed the matter with the South African Cricket Union.

But such issues had become part of the past. In India, Rice, Cook, Wessels and Adrian Kuiper were a top management team who worked closely together. As for Kirsten, he and Wessels had always got on well.

Having been made captain, Wessels was given a voice but not a vote on the selection committee. Both he and Procter were consulted by the selectors in Port Elizabeth after a Nissan Shield semi-final on January 18, the day before the team was announced. It is understood that Wessels and Procter made a strong case for both Cook and Kirsten, although by this time the claims of Rice had virtually been disregarded. At least in the case of Rice it could be argued that his age was starting to slow him down and affect his performance. But it could not be said of Cook or Kirsten. Although neither was as spritely as he had been a decade earlier, they both remained highly competent fielders.

Finally, the team was announced from the pavilion balcony at St George's Park. Dakin congratulated the selectors and then read out the following names:

Kepler Wessels *(Eastern Province, 34, opening batsman, captain)*
Adrian Kuiper *(Western Province, 32, vice-captain, all-rounder)*
Tertius Bosch *(Northern Transvaal, 25, fast bowler)*
Hansie Cronje *(Free State, 22, batsman)*
Allan Donald *(Free State, 25, fast bowler)*
Omar Henry *(Free State, 40, left-arm spinner)*
Andrew Hudson *(Natal, 25, opening batsman)*
Peter Kirsten *(Border, 36, batsman)*
Brian McMillan *(Western Province, 28, allrounder)*
Meyrick Pringle *(Western Province, 25, fast bowler)*

Jonty Rhodes *(Natal, 22, batsman)*
Dave Richardson *(Eastern Province, 32, wicketkeeper)*
Mark Rushmere *(Eastern Province, 26, batsman)*
Richard Snell *(Transvaal, 23, fast bowler)*

It was announced that two former SACB players, Faiek Davids of Western Province and Yasien Begg of Transvaal, would travel with the team to gain experience and to play in some of the warm-up matches. Davids was a logical choice, but the selection of Begg was surprising. The fact that he was a wicketkeeper who could provide some relief for Dave Richardson was presumably a decisive factor.

The selectors had bowed to pressure by selecting Kirsten, who had done nothing more nor less than he had before being left out of the shortlist, while Pringle had been called in from outside the 20 after some good performances.

In view of the way the team played at the World Cup, there have been some self-congratulatory views expressed by the selectors, mainly aimed in the direction of the *Sunday Times*. It should be pointed out that a panel of *Sunday Times* cricket writers had picked a team which included 10 of the eventual squad. All of our 10 were in what became the established first team in Australia and New Zealand. We would have included Jimmy Cook, Tim Shaw, Corrie van Zyl and Rudi Bryson in place of Rushmere, Henry, Pringle and Bosch.

Although Pringle was an inspired choice by the selectors, I still believe that Shaw would have been a better bet than Henry, and that although Rushmere and Bosch are quality players well worthy of international honours they are both better suited to Test matches than limited overs games.

The debate had been acrimonious, but Wessels had remained dignified. The controversy had not been inspired by the players, who had all gone about their business of playing as well as they could. It was now time for the country to get behind the selected team as they assembled in Cape Town for a two-day training camp. Then it would be the Nissan Shield final, and finally the get-together in Johannesburg before departure to Harare and the first warm-up match.

Festival time in Harare as a record crowd watches South Africa play Zimbabwe.

CHAPTER SIX

THE WARM-UP MATCHES

A buoyant group of cricketers gathered in Johannesburg on Monday, February 3, 1992, to be kitted out for the great adventure. An eve-of-departure function hosted by team sponsors Benson and Hedges was a festive occasion, with a sense of excitement dominating the evening.

Early the next morning the team flew to Harare. Among the well-wishers who bade the team farewell in the ironically named Springbok VIP room at Jan Smuts airport were UCB vice-president Krish Mackerdhuj and National Olympic Committee chairman Sam Ramsamy. The price of support from the community as a whole was the sacrifice of the Springbok emblem for a bland and neutral United Cricket Board badge. Mackerdhuj emphasised, however, that the Springbok was not necessarily dead. 'The whole concept of flags, emblems and national anthems is sensitive. We are in the transition phase and these things have not yet been debated properly.'

Neither the South African flag nor a recording of 'Die Stem' were in team manager Alan Jordaan's luggage when the party took off for Harare and the first match involving any official team from South Africa since Zimbabwe had achieved independence in 1980.

Before independence, the old Rhodesia had played in the South African Currie Cup competition and Rhodesian players, although not South African citizens, had been eligible to play Test cricket for South Africa. Among those who achieved Springbok colours were Colin Bland, Joe Partridge, Jackie du Preez and, most recently, John Traicos, who played in three Tests against Bill Lawry's Australians in 1970.

The 44-year-old Egyptian-born Traicos, still wheeling down offspinners, was in the side for the match against South Africa, the first 'international' between the two countries, although not recognised as a full one-day international by the ICC because Zimbabwe do not have Test status.

As in pre-independence days, Zimbabwe's cricket hopes are inextricably linked with those of South Africa. The renewal of ties with their southern neighbours will make it easier to host tours, with teams visiting Zimbabwe on the way in or out of South Africa. If Zimbabwe are successful in their efforts to gain Test status they will join Sri Lanka as one of the lesser Test powers, and can expect to host one Test and two or three one-day internationals against sides touring South Africa, as well as staging regular matches against their neighbours.

The first match between the two countries was played at the Harare Sports Club. A gabled, colonial clubhouse stands in lush greenery a cricket ball's throw away from what used to be the home of the Governor General and which now houses President Robert Mugabe behind armed guards, who patrol menacingly with automatic weapons, and a high wall topped by razor wire.

The previous biggest cricket crowd since independence had been 3 500, but the lure of South Africa ensured that 9 000 packed the marquees and temporary stands around the ground on a hot day. The crowd had a pre-independence look to it, with scarcely a black face to be seen. Battling with a limited budget of only 600 000 Zimbabwe dollars a year, the ZCU have been unable to make the inroads into black areas that Ali Bacher and the UCB have managed 'down south'.

Wessels won the toss and decided to bowl in order to take advantage of early morning cloud cover. It was a mildly surprising decision because it would have seemed logical for the South African batsmen to get in some practice at setting biggish targets. Besides, there was always the possibility that Zimbabwe would fail to set a challenging target, thereby reducing the benefit of the match as a practice opportunity.

An early finish certainly seemed in prospect when Wayne James found himself hopelessly confused by the outswing of

KEPLER WESSELS ascended to the captaincy of the South African team by a remarkable route. Born in Bloemfontein on September 14, 1957, he was a schoolboy prodigy at Grey College and played in five Nuffield Weeks, gaining three caps for SA Schools. He made his first-class debut for Free State aged 16 while still at school. He played for Sussex from 1976 and subsequently moved to Australia, representing that country in Kerry Packer's World Series.

Wessels made his Test debut for Australia against England in Brisbane in 1982/83 and scored 162. He scored three other centuries in the course of 24 Tests for his adopted country. Wessels played in the 1986/87 rebel series for Kim Hughes' Australian team, having moved back to South Africa to captain Eastern Province. Three years later he was in the Springbok team against Mike Gatting's English side. Finally, in 1991, he was selected for South Africa's first official tour to India, becoming the only man to have played officially and in rebel series for two countries.

Meyrick Pringle... good bowling in Perth.

Meyrick Pringle, being dropped by Kuiper at second slip on nought, then opening his score with an edged four.

Allan Donald quickly built up formidable pace, but was no-balled four times in his second over before yorking the promising left-hander Andy Flower in the seventh over. Another left-hander, Alastair Campbell, seemed still to be halfway through his backlift when the next ball sent his offstump flying.

Without at any stage getting on top of the bowling, the Zimbabwe batsmen managed to take the score to 170 with the last wicket falling in the 50th over. James made a streaky 27 and Andy Waller the same score with somewhat more aplomb. The outfield was exceptionally slow, with only six boundaries being scored.

Donald, Pringle and Bosch all bowled at a good pace but no-balls and wides abounded. Donald's figures of 3 for 29 included 10 wides.

Henry sent down 10 accurate overs and a competent bowling performance was rounded off by Kuiper and Cronje sharing the fifth bowler's duties and taking 1 for 30 between them.

Eddo Brandes, a burly 28-year-old chicken farmer, opened the Zimbabwe bowling attack with surprising aggression while the left-arm seamer Malcolm Jarvis maintained an awkward line and length.

Hudson, having scored his first runs for South Africa with a push through cover for two, reached eight before being caught behind off a top edge against Brandes, who then had the crowd roaring in delight when he trapped Wessels leg before.

Kirsten and Cronje restored the equilibrium, but it was slow going with Kirsten clearly determined to have a good, long look at the bowling. Cronje displayed the greater aggression and at one stage had scored 35 to his more experienced partner's 16. But Kirsten increased in confidence, hitting his first boundary over midwicket after he had been at the crease for 27 overs.

The partnership was worth 99 before Cronje was caught at midwicket off the medium-paced Shah for 47, giving Kuiper a chance to contribute to the remaining 42 runs needed off nine overs.

There was mild alarm when Kirsten was caught in the deep off the last ball of the 49th over for 64. Five runs were still needed. With the batsmen having crossed, new man Rhodes had to face the first ball of the last over, which had to be bowled by the captain, David Houghton, who had somehow miscalculated the overs of his frontline bowlers. Rhodes scrambled a single and Kuiper crashed a boundary, but South Africa had won with only four balls to spare.

Coach Procter had come laden with dozens of new white Australian Kookaburra balls of the type to be used in the World Cup. With his men having sent down 19 wides and six no-balls, he had them in the nets the next morning in the first of what were to become the 'channel schools'. He placed a shirt on the spot reckoned to be ideal for limited overs cricket, just short of a length and in the region of offstump, and told the bowlers to bowl with new balls at full pace at the target.

So festive had been the crowd the previous day that the sports club had to send out for cold drinks to the adjacent Royal Harare golf club. Every beer and every soft drink had been consumed by the cricket spectators.

Practice completed, the players packed for Perth. Even Procter, a great cricketer who had at least been able to play in seven official Tests, had never been on overseas tour with a

ZIMBABWE v SOUTH AFRICA
Harare Sports Club, February 5
Toss won by Kepler Wessels

ZIMBABWE
W James run out	27
A Flower b Donald	5
A Campbell b Donald	0
A Pycroft c Richardson b Bosch	21
D Houghton c Cronje b Henry	14
A Waller c Richardson b Bosch	27
A Shah c Richardson b Donald	11
I Butchart lbw b Cronje	10
E Brandes not out	14
J Traicos c Richardson b Pringle	4
M Jarvis run out	7
Extras (5lb, 6nb, 19w)	30
Total (all out, 49,3 overs)	170

Falls: 1/20, 2/20, 3/54, 4/81, 5/83, 6/107, 7/134, 8/134, 9/158
Bowling: Donald 10-2-29-3 (10w),
Pringle 10-0-35-1 (3nb, 3w),
Bosch 9,3-0-44-2 (3nb, 4w),
Kuiper 6-1-12-0,
Henry 10-1-27-1,
Cronje 4-0-18-1 (2w).

SOUTH AFRICA
K Wessels lbw b Brandes 19
A Hudson c Flower
    b Brandes 8
P Kirsten c Shah b Traicos 64
H Cronje c Waller b Shah 47
A Kuiper not out 23
J Rhodes not out 1
D Richardson, O Henry,
M Pringle, A Donald and
T Bosch did not bat
Extras (4lb, 1nb, 4w) 9
Total (4 wickets, 49,2 overs) 171
Falls: 1/21, 2/30, 3/129, 4/166
Bowling: Brandes 10-3-26-2
(2w), Jarvis 10-1-29-0 (1nb, 1w),
Shah 10-1-32-1 (1w),
Butchart 10-0-32-0,
Traicos 9-0-43-1,
Houghton 0,2-0-5-0.

South Africa won by six wickets.

South African team. The nine-hour flight passed quickly.

A Press conference had been set up at the Perth airport and manager Jordaan steeled himself to handle what he feared might be tricky political questions. But he need not have worried. The dozens of journalists, including three camera crews, were interested almost solely in how strong a cricket challenge the prodigal sons of the cricket world would mount.

Wessels, too, might have anticipated some tougher questioning in view of his Australian Test career followed by a defection to join a rebel tour. But there was just one tester. 'Given the circumstances in which you left last time, are you relaxed about the reception you will receive?' 'Certainly,' smiled Wessels, 'I have a lot of friends in Australia. I enjoyed my time in this country and I look forward to playing here again.' He expressed his gratitude to the Australian Cricket Board, whose permission had been needed before he could play for another country in the World Cup.

The Press conference complete, the first South African team abroad in 27 years drove through flat countryside with vegetation reminiscent of the western Cape to an opulent hotel on the edge of the city. It was within walking distance of the Western Australian Cricket Association ground with its towering floodlights, known throughout the world as 'the WACA'.

A reception that night featured speeches by the West Australian Minister of Sport and Colin Egar, president of the Australian Cricket Board. Among the guests were Don Mackay-Coghill, once a feared left-arm fast bowler, later chairman of the Transvaal Cricket Council, and now heading a gold coin marketing operation in Perth. Also there was Kim Hughes, leader of the Australian rebel team. It was the first time he had been invited to the WACA in six years. Never the consummate diplomat, Hughes wore his cream rebel tour blazer.

A practice was scheduled the next day, but unseasonal rain had started falling on Friday night. In between showers, the team were able to have little more than a limb-loosener watched by a large media contingent. A gruelling test lay ahead on Sunday, and the team were under-prepared.

At least there were no great expectations from the media or local cricket experts. Western Australia were a formidable team on a pitch renowned as one of the fastest and bounciest in the world. Kim Hughes said: 'Your blokes will do well even to get close. They should not think about winning, just approach it like a Test match and try to play properly.'

Earlier in the same season India had been shot out for 64 and the West Indies had been beaten by nine wickets. In the previous season England and Pakistan had been the victims. If the raw South Africans suffered a similar fate no one would be astonished.

Sunday morning dawned grey and unpromising. In 24 hours 107 mm of rain had fallen, a record for a 24-hour period in Perth. And this was supposed to be the dry season.

Not surprisingly, South Africa placed their faith in an all-seam attack. With the exception of Mark Rushmere, who opened the batting in place of Hudson, the team for this match was the 'first XI' which was to carry the nation's hopes in the World Cup.

The weather started to clear before the 2.30 pm start but it was still overcast when Wessels won the toss. It had been surprising that he bowled in Harare, now it was surprising that he chose to bat in conditions likely to favour the bowlers. Missing, though, was the 'Fremantle doctor', a steady south-westerly prevailing wind off the ocean and the Swan River, which has been used to perfection by the contrasting Western Australian opening bowlers, the right-armed Terry Alderman and tall left-armer Bruce Reid.

Reid was making a comeback after injury and needed to prove to the Australian selectors that he was fit enough to be included in his country's World Cup squad. Approaching the wicket with surprising rhythm for a man standing more than two metres tall, he gave Wessels and Rushmere almost nothing to score from. His opening spell of 0 for 8 in seven overs included two wides.

Alderman, meanwhile, made the breakthrough, having old Test teammate Wessels caught behind, then Rushmere held by the towering Tom Moody at second slip.

JONATHAN 'Jonty' RHODES, born in Pietermaritzburg on July 26, 1969, was head boy of Maritzburg College and played for SA Schools in 1986 and 1987. He scored a century on his first-class debut for Natal against Western Province in Durban in 1988/89 but had to wait until shortly before the World Cup before notching his next century, a match-winning effort against Northern Transvaal in Pretoria.

Rhodes has made his reputation in one-day cricket and has become a huge crowd favourite, particularly in his home province, because of his electrifying fielding ability and his aggressive attitude as a middle-order batsman.

A student at Natal University in Pietermaritzburg, Rhodes is a talented hockey player whose speed and skill has taken him to the verge of national honours in a second sport.

Geoff Marsh ... impressed by the South Africans.

Peter Kirsten looked in good form, cutting a rare loose ball from Reid to the distant square boundary on the first of the big Australian fields that make both batting and fielding different for players used to smaller playing areas.

Survival seemed the game plan and although the scoring was slow the batsmen were looking reasonably sound before Cronje was beaten by the left-arm medium-pace of Brendon Julian. Kirsten responded with the stroke of the day, a searing cover drive off Martin McCague, but was caught in the same over. With Kuiper also falling to McCague, it was left to Rhodes and McMillan to rescue the innings from 66 for 5.

Rhodes, a perky newcomer with a schoolboy's enthusiasm, and the bulky McMillan, nicknamed 'The Incredible Hulk' by an Australian opponent in South Africa, were sharing a room and had immediately struck up a rapport. Their running between the wickets was a revelation. Rhodes is so quick to run that he provokes nightmares among teammates, but he and McMillan were positive and decisive as they doubled the total to 132 before Rhodes was quite brilliantly caught at short midwicket by Alderman for an encouraging 35.

The South African total of 157 for 8 off 47 overs was a long way short of being likely to win the match, but in testing conditions most of the batsmen had stayed in long enough to at least look competent.

Donald and Pringle were hostile from the start on a pitch which most fast bowlers would like to take around the world with them. Pringle whipped one through Moody's defences and the free-scoring Western Australian, fresh from a hugely successful season with Worcestershire in England, was caught behind.

Donald trapped veteran Australia opener and WA captain Geoff Marsh lbw for nine and the pressure was on the home team. Another Test player, Mike Veletta, and the promising Mark Lavender slowly pulled their team out of trouble before Pringle, in his second spell, dismissed both batsmen.

McMillan persuaded a ball to fly viciously off a good length to have the highly rated young Damian Martyn caught behind, and when Wayne Andrews skied Cronje to deep midwicket to provide Rushmere with a catch after an agonising wait – it would have been six on most South African grounds – Western Australia were in trouble at 112 for 6. The wicketkeeper, Tim Zoehrer, who had earlier held five catches, batted with a mixture of good sense and good fortune, and although Pringle struck one more blow by bowling Julian, South Africa simply did not have enough runs to play with.

Nevertheless, a three-wicket defeat, with only five balls remaining, was no disgrace. The large South African contingent in a crowd of 19 000 could feel satisfied. 'I feel proud to be South African,' said Mackay-Coghill.

Both WA captain Geoff Marsh and wicketkeeper Zoehrer said South Africa looked good enough to be a threat in the World Cup, as did former WA captain Kim Hughes. A major reason for satisfaction was the bowling of Pringle, who in his first important international match had taken 4 for 29 and given all the batsmen problems with his late movement away from the bat.

The tour was well and truly under way. After a flight across the Great Australian Bight, the next stop was Adelaide and a match against a team of young players from the Australian Cricket Academy, or to give them their full, imposing title, the South Australia Cricket Association/Australian Institute of Sport/Commonwealth Bank Australian Cricket Academy XI.

WESTERN AUSTRALIA v SOUTH AFRICA,
WACA ground, Perth,
February 9 (day-night)
Toss won by Kepler Wessels

SOUTH AFRICA
M Rushmere c Moody b Alderman	9
K Wessels c Zoehrer b Alderman	6
P Kirsten c Zoehrer b McCague	17
H Cronje c Zoehrer b Julian	7
A Kuiper c Zoehrer b McCague	3
J Rhodes c Alderman b Moody	35
B McMillan c Zoehrer b Reid	32
D Richardson not out	10
R Snell c Alderman b Moody	0
M Pringle not out	9
A Donald did not bat	
Extras (12lb, 7nb, 10w)	29
Total (8 wickets, 47 overs)	157

Falls: 1/9, 2/31, 3/46, 4/53, 5/66, 6/132, 7/134, 8/135
Bowling: Reid 10-3-12-1 (3w), Alderman 10-2-28-2 (5nb), Julian 10-2-35-1 (5w), McCague 10-0-36-2 (2nb, 1w), Moody 7-0-34-2 (1w).

WESTERN AUSTRALIA

T Moody c Richardson b Pringle	2
G Marsh lbw b Donald	9
M Lavender lbw b Pringle	28
M Veletta b Pringle	35
D Martyn c Richardson b McMillan	9
W Andrews c Rushmere b Cronje	10
T Zoehrer not out	28
B Julian b Pringle	9
M McCague not out	13
T Alderman, B Reid did not bat	
Extras (5lb, 3nb, 8w)	16
Total (7 wickets, 46,1 overs)	159

Falls: 1/5, 2/23, 3/83, 4/96, 5/98, 6/112, 7/133

Bowling: Donald 9,1-0-30-1 (1nb, 2w), Pringle 10-1-29-4 (3w), McMillan 10-1-41-1 (2nb, 1w), Snell 10-1-24-0, Kuiper 3-0-19-0, Cronje 4-0-11-1.

Western Australia won by three wickets.

The Academy is run by the former Australian wicketkeeper Rodney Marsh. Young players selected by their state associations spend about three months in Adelaide in a cricket environment in a scheme which Australian officials believe has lifted the overall standard of the first-class game.

The South Africans were due to play a one-day match at the Adelaide Oval on Wednesday but Procter and Wessels were concerned about the shortage of match practice of the batsmen and requested an additional, unofficial game on the Tuesday. South Africa batted first by agreement, which was just as well because an afternoon thunder shower ended the Academy innings after just 8,2 overs.

Once again the South African batsmen were far from dominating but there were useful innings from Hudson (33), Cronje (62) and Kuiper (54) in a total of 205 for 7 off 50 overs.

In the match the next day Hudson struck good form to score 81 off 123 balls while Kirsten made 63 and Rushmere 24 in a total of 224/7. The Academy XI replied with 179 for 9 and relied greatly on Darren Webber, a tall student from Adelaide University, who played a splendid attacking innings of 78 not out off 87 balls, including six fours and three soaring sixes into the old grandstand square of the wicket. All his boundaries, with the exception of one four, were struck off the hapless Omar Henry.

The Adelaide Oval is an unusual ground, almost cigar-shaped. The fences square of the wicket are relatively close to the pitch whereas the straight boundaries are almost 100 metres away. It can be argued that batsmen can go for lofted hits to the sides of the wicket confident that a reasonably vigorous miscue might clear the fence, but it was nevertheless a disappointing performance by Henry who conceded 60 runs off nine overs. It not only affected his own confidence but that of the tour selectors who thereafter relied exclusively on seam in most important matches.

The seamers had done well, with Cronje entrenching his claims as an extra bowler by taking 1 for 18 from six overs.

The pattern for the World Cup had already been set and the team which played Pakistan in a friendly match in Canberra was to be that which started in the World Cup. Left out were Rushmere, Bosch and Henry.

There was a great deal of anticipation about the Pakistan game, played at the Manuka Oval where Bob Hawke and Robert Menzies before him had hosted matches between Prime Minister's XIs and visiting teams. As far as the South Africans were concerned it was an official international game, but this belief was to be dashed by the Pakistanis afterwards. Both countries are required to back an application for official status and the Pakistanis were adamant that it was, in Imran Khan's words, 'just a warm-up game'.

The anticipated clash between Allan Donald and Waqar Younis, the two fastest bowlers in the world, did not take place because Younis was suffering from a persistent back injury which was to prevent him from playing in the World Cup. Also missing from the Pakistan team were left-arm fast bowler Wasim Akram with a thigh strain and star batsman Javed Miandad, who had only rejoined the team the previous day after being treated at home for a back injury.

Imran Khan won the toss and sent South Africa in on an overcast, blustery day. Wessels and Hudson made a cautious but confident start against Imran and Aaqib Javed and it was a disappointment when Hudson drove the innocuous-looking left-armer Ijaz Ahmed, bowling with a slingy action, straight to cover with the total on 35.

Wessels, already under some media pressure because he had not made runs on the tour, was rising to the occasion with typical determination and he found a good partner in Kirsten, who batted well to score 30 before being bowled by Iqbal Sikander, a young legspinner whose arrival with Miandad the day before had surprised the Pakistan media and brought to 18 the number of Pakistanis from whom a World Cup squad of 14 had to be nominated the following week. Wessels went on to make a solid 72 off 114 balls and South Africa's total of 205 for 5 was always likely to set a reasonable challenge on a slow pitch, especially as the outfield was both large and slow. The South African total included only 12 boundaries.

Donald made a dreadful start, bowling two no-balls and two

MARTIN CROWE, born in Auckland on September 22, 1962, is one of two brothers to have captained New Zealand, following in the footsteps of his elder brother Jeff. Martin made his debut for Auckland at the age of 17 and played in his first Test at the age of 19.

A classic stylist, Crowe is one of the finest middle-order batsmen in the world and a superb fielder. By the start of the World Cup he had played in 59 Tests, scoring 4 205 runs at an average of 47,78 with 13 centuries.

His highest Test score, 299 against Sri Lanka in Wellington in 1991, is a New Zealand record. During this innings he was involved in a third wicket partnership of 467 with Andrew Jones, a world Test record for any wicket.

Crowe was appointed New Zealand captain in 1990 and led an inexperienced team, dubbed the 'Young Guns' into the World Cup.

Imran Khan ... practice plans went awry in Canberra.

ACADEMY XI v
SOUTH AFRICA
Adelaide Oval, February 11
No toss.
SOUTH AFRICA 205 for 7 in
50 overs
(A Hudson 33, H Cronje 62,
A Kuiper 54, P Wilson 3 for 28).
ACADEMY XI 24 for 0 in
8,2 overs.
Match drawn – rain.

ACADEMY XI v
SOUTH AFRICA
Adelaide Oval, February 12
No toss.
SOUTH AFRICA 224 for 7 in
50 overs
(A Hudson 81, P Kirsten 63).
ACADEMY XI 179 for 9 in
50 overs
(D Webber 78 not out,
M Pringle 2 for 30,
B McMillan 3 for 32).
South Africa won by 45 runs.

wides in conceding 11 runs off two overs, prompting Wessels to bring McMillan on to bowl as early as the fifth over. The all-rounder had immediate success, with the experienced Rameez Raja touching an away-swinger to be caught behind.

Two young players who were to play big roles in the World Cup, the left-handed Aamir Sohail and the tall right-hander Inzamam-ul-Haq, took the total to 85 with Inzamam giving an early glimpse of his free-scoring ability before he was trapped leg before by Pringle.

Imran Khan, by his own admission later, came to the wicket looking for batting practice. All was going well for the aristocratic captain until Sohail was caught behind for 58 in the second over of McMillan's second spell. Zahid Fazal followed in the same over, chipping the ball gently to mid-on. Sixty runs were needed off 13 overs.

Ijaz Ahmed helped Imran take his side within 34 runs of victory but only five overs remained when Ijaz edged a ball from Snell into his stumps. Salim Malik, a leading batsman batting low down in the order after injuring an ankle while fielding, was yorked second ball, and Moin Khan was run out off Snell's next delivery, optimistically backing his ability to steal a second run against Pringle's rifling return from fine leg.

Imran had still not found his timing and with boundaries

needed could only manage ones and twos. McMillan struck twice more in the 49th over, and Imran was finally out in the last over as South Africa pulled off a surprising and morale-boosting victory by 17 runs.

With the exception of Donald, who conceded an alarming 57 runs from 10 overs, the seamers had performed exceptionally well, and McMillan rated his return of 5 for 32 as a career highlight. For Donald, though, it meant that plans to give him a short rest before the World Cup were shelved. 'He needs to keep bowling to get his rhythm right,' said Wessels.

But Wessels was delighted with the win, although he pointed out that Pakistan were missing good players and there was still much room for improvement by South Africa. He was satisfied with the way the bowlers had maintained pressure on the batsmen despite Donald's poor form. 'We are learning and improving all the time.'

The World Cup was only a week away, with South Africa's opening match four days after that.

The South African team travelled south to Hobart in Tasmania, where Donald had the locals gasping as he vented the frustrations of the previous day with a fast and furious spell of bowling in the nets.

Dave Richardson had aggravated an old ankle injury against Pakistan. As the team's only wicketkeeper his fitness was crucial. Although he would undoubtedly have enjoyed a break, he had to prove his durability with the deadline for squad nominations just two days away. Not only was he strapped up and thrown into the fray against Tasmania, he was asked to open the batting as well.

Tasmania are one of the weaker Sheffield Shield states, but even so South Africa could feel satisfied with a menacing all-round performance at the picturesque Bellerive Oval on the edge of the Derwent River estuary.

Donald signalled a return to form with a lightning-fast delivery which had Dene Hills caught behind off the second ball of the match, and despite an innings of 47 by the left-hander Michael Farrell, the Tasmanians were always struggling against tight, accurate bowling.

SOUTH AFRICA v PAKISTAN,
Manuka Oval, Canberra,
February 15
Toss won by Imran Khan

SOUTH AFRICA
K Wessels c Ijaz b Aaqib 72
A Hudson c sub
 (Mushtaq Ahmed) b Ijaz 18
P Kirsten b Sikander 30
A Kuiper c Sohail b Jaffer 10
H Cronje c Sikander
 b Imran 19
J Rhodes not out 21
B McMillan not out 7
D Richardson, R Snell,
M Pringle, A Donald did not bat
Extras (2b, 8lb, 4nb, 14w) 28
Total (5 wickets, 50 overs) 205
Falls: 1/35, 2/94, 3/116, 4/162, 5/182
Bowling: Imran Khan 9-3-33-1 (1w), Aaqib Javed 10-0-39-1 (3nb, 3w), Ijaz Ahmed 10-0-29-1 (3w), Saleem Jaffer 10-0-45-1 (1nb, 7w),
Iqbal Sikander 10-0-41-1,
Aamir Sohail 1-0-8-0.

PAKISTAN
Rameez Raja c Richardson b McMillan	11
Aamir Sohail c Richardson b McMillan	58
Inzamam-ul-Haq lbw b Pringle	30
Imran Khan b Pringle	43
Zahid Fazal c Snell b McMillan	0
Ijaz Ahmed b Snell	15
Salim Malik b Snell	0
Moin Khan run out	1
Iqbal Sikander b McMillan	4
Saleem Jaffer b McMillan	0
Aaqib Javed not out	0
Extras (4b, 2lb, 11nb, 9w)	26
Total (all out, 49,3 overs)	188

Falls: 1/23, 2/85, 3/146, 5/172, 6/172, 7/173, 8/186, 9/186
Bowling: Donald 10-0-57-0 (7nb, 4w), Pringle 9,3-1-34-2 (1nb, 2w), McMillan 10-0-32-5 (2nb, 2w), Snell 10-1-27-2, Kuiper 6-1-18-0 (1w), Cronje 4-0-14-0 (1nb).

South Africa won by 17 runs.

Donald took 2 for 26 and Bosch 2 for 22 while Henry picked up 3 for 36. Faiek Davids, given his only chance to play in a game at state level, bowled tidy medium-pacers to take 1 for 30 from nine overs including a spell of 4-3-1-1.

Richardson could feel delighted with his efforts, holding four catches, making a stumping and showing no ill-effects from his injury. South Africa cruised to victory by seven wickets with 10,3 overs to spare, with Kuiper hitting a flurry of boundaries to end the match before a threatened rain shower broke over the ground.

With two warm-up matches to go, South Africa were looking a competent team on schedule to go into the World Cup at a peak of preparation after the distraction of the official World Cup launch in Sydney on Wednesday, February 19. All the teams travelled on an Australian naval vessel and posed for a giant group picture with the harbour bridge in the background. Then it was a day of nets, interrupted by an official autograph-signing session. The contestants endured a day in which their every hour was prescribed, culminating in the official opening banquet (which at 175 Australian dollars a head was ignored by most of the world's media). It turned out, according to those who were there, to be an exceptionally featureless evening.

A match against Queensland at the Gabba ground in Brisbane was an opportunity to field the shadow World Cup team, but a cyclone was swirling off the Queensland coast. Rain started to fall while the team were practising on Thursday. It fell steadily through the night and early on Friday it was obvious there could be no play. Barry Richards, the former Springbok batsman who is executive director of the Queensland Cricket Association, re-scheduled the match for Saturday but the rain continued and not a ball was bowled.

It was a serious blow to the team and there was no let-up when they travelled to Bowral, where Australia's greatest cricketer grew up, for a match against the Sir Donald Bradman XI on the Sunday. Bradman is thought of as having lived in the outback, but his boyhood town is a prosperous, wooded enclave between Sydney and Canberra. The Bradman Oval, where a plaque proudly proclaims that the young Bradman played much of his early cricket, owes much to the famous name. A pavilion and terracing have clearly been added long since the young cricketer played there.

It would have been a pleasant occasion, with Barry Richards captaining a team consisting mainly of young New South Wales players, including the talented Michael Bevan, against the tourists. For the likes of Bosch, Rushmere and Henry, it would have been a last chance to persuade the selectors to change their thinking on the XI for Sydney.

All the tickets had been sold. Marquees surrounded the tiny Oval. Sadly, though, the rain fell virtually all day. Three overs were bowled by the South Africans before rain stopped play. An attempted re-start resulted in just one more ball being sent down, and the last chance to get in some match practice before the World Cup had gone. It was therefore a less than joyful group that I caught up with at the country lodge outside the town that afternoon. An attempt was to be made to play the game the next day, but it was always a forlorn hope with the outfield sodden, and the idea was quickly abandoned on Monday morning.

I, meanwhile, had flown from Brisbane to Auckland on Friday evening to see the opening World Cup match between the host nations, New Zealand and Australia, on Saturday. Having taken off in rain so heavy I could barely see the aircraft's wing tips, I arrived in Auckland after midnight, reached my hotel room at 1.30 am, and left again for Sydney on Sunday at 8 am. As a first visit to one of the world's more remote major countries it could hardly have been more fleeting.

The World Cup opening, though, was a memorable occasion. A float parade preceded the match, with each of the competing nations represented. It was an unexpectedly emotional moment. I was on the telephone to my home (it was still Friday evening in SA) and found myself choked up trying to describe the scene as the South African float was announced to a huge roar of approval from a big crowd. Ironically, it was Clive Rice who became the first man to represent South Africa in the World Cup. The deposed captain, at the match as part of the Channel Nine TV commentary team, had been asked to go on

---

TASMANIA v SOUTH AFRICA
Bellerive Oval, Hobart,
February 17
Toss won by Dave Gilbert

TASMANIA
D Hills c Richardson
  b Donald   0
G Hughes b Bosch   11
M Farrell c Richardson
  b Henry   47
J Cox b Kuiper   14
R Tucker st Richardson
  b Henry   20
A Dykes not out   25
S Young c Richardson
  b Davids   2
M Atkinson c Richardson
  b Henry   0
C Matthews c Henry
  b Donald   13
D Gilbert c Hudson b Bosch   5
T Bower run out   2
Extras (11lb, 4nb, 7w)   22
Total (all out, 48.2 overs)   161
Falls: 1/0, 2/36, 3/57, 4/101, 5/110, 6/113, 7/114, 8/146, 9/149
Bowling: Donald 9.2-3-26-2 (2nb), Pringle 4-0-15-0 (1nb, 4w), Bosch 10-1-22-2 (1nb, 1w), Kuiper 6-1-21-1, Henry 10-0-36-3, Davids 9-3-30-1 (2w).

SOUTH AFRICA
A Hudson lbw b Farrell 35
D Richardson c Atkinson
    b Matthews 18
M Rushmere lbw b Young 10
B McMillan not out 40
A Kuiper not out 38
J Rhodes, F Davids, O Henry,
M Pringle, A Donald and
T Bosch did not bat
Extras (2b, 10lb, 1nb, 9w) 22
Total (3 wickets, 39,3 overs) 163
Falls: 1/39, 2/61, 3/87
Bowling: Gilbert 5-1-13-0,
Bower 7-0-35-0 (2w),
Matthews 5-0-19-1 (1nb, 1w),
Young 8-1-33-1 (3w),
Farrell 7-2-17-1,
Tucker 5-0-17-0 (3w),
Dykes 2,3-0-17-0.

South Africa won by seven wickets.

the South African float to represent his country in the same way as former players such as Richie Benaud, Tony Greig and Richard Hadlee. It was a somewhat embarrassed Rice who said afterwards: 'I was only asked on the day. I thought they should find someone else after all the controversy about the captaincy, but there wasn't anyone, so I thought I had better do it rather than have no one representing South Africa.'

The pomp and ceremony over, there was a splendid game of cricket on the oddly shaped field. It is primarily a rugby stadium and the cricket pitch lies diagonally across it. As a result the backward square-leg boundaries, or backward point for left-handers, are extraordinarily short.

Martin Crowe, the New Zealand captain, peppered the short boundaries with a merciless display of hooking and pulling as New Zealand recovered from the loss of two early wickets. The Australian opening bowler Craig McDermott had started the match by bowling two wides. Then the New Zealand left-hander John Wright went too far across in trying to play the first legal ball of the World Cup to leg and had his leg stump knocked back. Andrew Jones was lbw to Bruce Reid with the total on 13 and it seemed that the World Cup favourites were well on the way to performing an efficient demolition of the outsiders. But Crowe found capable partners in Rod Latham (26) and Ken Rutherford (57) as he played an innings of immense power and grace, reaching a majestic century off the fourth ball of the final over as New Zealand reached 248 for 6 in 50 overs.

David Boon replied in similar vein for Australia but achieved no worthwhile support. All the batsmen struggled against New Zealand's slow-ball tactics, which included the use of offspinner Dipak Patel as an opening bowler. Chris Cairns, the only New Zealand bowler of any pace, conceded 30 runs off four overs with the new ball and did not bowl again.

Despite Boon scoring exactly 100 before being run out by a superb throw from Chris Harris at mid-on, Australia could score only 211 as New Zealand delighted 28 000 spectators by causing the first big shock of the World Cup. The tournament was under way, with South Africa about to take centre stage.

Kepler Wessels drives South Africa towards victory in Sydney. David Boon is the wicketkeeper.

CHAPTER SEVEN

THE IMPOSSIBLE DREAM COMES TRUE

The Sydney Cricket Ground is a mixture of old and new. The majestic green-painted wrought iron of the Members and Ladies Stands represents the ground on which legendary figures of the game – from Bradman to Benaud, Compton to Cowdrey, Lindwall, Sobers, Pollock and Gavaskar – performed heroic deeds. Elsewhere are the trappings of modernity – concrete stands with plastic seats, a giant electronic scoreboard and towering floodlight pylons.

What was once The Hill, and the historic old scoreboard which adorned its summit, is covered with plastic seating. The only reminder is a sign on the new scoreboard, Yarra's Hill, named after a famous barracker. In modern, crowded Sydney it is the new form of cricket, with its coloured clothing and close finishes, that packs the SCG. The new stars are the players who shine in limited overs cricket – Dean Jones, Steve Waugh and, of recent glory, Vivian Richards.

On February 26, 1992, a new chapter was written in the history of the famous ground. It was the night South Africa made its debut in the World Cup.

The days before the big night were anxious ones. Four successive days of rain had disrupted South Africa's preparation, and prevented a planned fielding practice under lights.

On Tuesday morning, the South Africans practised fielding side by side with the Australians on the playing arena. In this department Australia had set new standards. Even their practice is a highly polished form of entertainment, with players picking up, throwing, sprinting and shouting. Balls seem to fly everywhere but always there are players swooping to whip them in at the stumps. While the Aussie fielding show amused spectators in front of the Members Stand, the South Africans went through their not dissimilar drill on the far Hill side of the ground.

In between ground staff rolled the pitch that would be used on the morrow. Before its pre-match cut, there was a fair amount of grass to be seen, but like all World Cup groundsmen, the SCG staff were under orders to prepare a pitch resembling as far as possible a 'day three, first-class Test pitch'.

The South African players moved across to the nets for their first proper bat-and-ball practice since the previous Thursday. Had they had enough time to prepare to take on the acknowledged world champions of limited overs cricket? Kepler Wessels analysed the prospects in his usual down-to-earth way. 'If we win it will be a tremendous boost for our chances,' he said. 'If we lose it will not be the end of the world. Then we will need to beat New Zealand in our next match.'

Wessels said one of his primary tasks was to motivate his players to play sound, good cricket without being overcome by the occasion. 'It is possible to get too psyched up for a game,' he said. 'That can be counter-productive because the players get too tense. Our preparation has gone well and we are ready for the World Cup. I want the guys to relax and play their normal game, concentrating on what is happening on the pitch and not the crowd.' He identified several key areas. 'Their first 10 overs with the ball will be vital. Bowlers like Bruce Reid and Craig McDermott will be able to swing the white ball around and are capable of taking early wickets. It is important for us to make a sound start. We have to be careful about their fielding. They are a very good, experienced fielding side and often hit the stumps if the batsmen try to take runs that are too risky. They also have a strong top six batting line-up. If the Sydney pitch plays as it normally does for a one-day game we will need to score around 220 to be competitive.'

The selection of the team for the opening match was a fairly easy task. Although the SCG had been known to give help to

PETER KIRSTEN was born in Pietermaritzburg on May 14, 1955. His father, Noel, played wicketkeeper for Border between 1946 and 1960. Educated at the SA College School (SACS) in Cape Town, Peter Kirsten made 101 not out for the SA Schools team against Northern Transvaal in 1974. In the same season he made his debut for Western Province before having played club cricket and scored 68 and 74 in his first two matches.

A fluent batsman who has batted at number three for most of his career, he made six centuries in seven innings in the 1976/77 season and was also a prolific scorer for Derbyshire, setting a county record of eight centuries in the 1982 season.

Although younger than many of his teammates, he was made Springbok captain against Sri Lanka in 1982/83 and led his country in seven unofficial Tests before being replaced as captain by Clive Rice. He subsequently resigned the Western Province captaincy as well. He became a captain again when he led Border during the 1991/92 season.

spin bowlers, even in one-day games, it was clear that South Africa's strength lay with the seamers. Omar Henry was therefore eliminated. Of the quicker bowlers, Bosch had played the least cricket and was the least athletic of the fielders. And Andrew Hudson's good form ensured that he would be in the side ahead of Mark Rushmere, who was named twelfth man.

Australia, meanwhile, had had their aura of invincibility dented by their defeat in New Zealand. Allan Border acknowledged that his team had not played to their full potential. 'We learnt a good lesson in Auckland,' he said. 'At this level, you can't afford to relax. We have to make sure we come out a lot better against South Africa. If we play at 100 per cent we'll be hard to beat.' The Australians made one change to the side that had been beaten in Auckland, bringing in specialist left-arm bowler and Sydney favourite Mike Whitney at the expense of Mark Waugh, who had been out of form in recent weeks.

Anxiety about the weather persisted on a squally Wednesday morning, but the weather forecasters who predicted clearer conditions were right. It remained overcast but the threat of rain had gone by the time Border and Wessels walked to the middle to toss. Border called correctly and decided to bat, a decision which would not have caused undue alarm in the South African dressing room. It is likely that Wessels would have chosen to field on this most nerve-wracking day for South African cricketers, to allow his bowlers to extract what life there might be from the pitch, to settle the nerves of inexperienced players and to enable the batsmen to know what target to chase.

The ground was filling rapidly as the starting time approached. Because no South African anthem was being played at any matches, the added tension of standing to attention before the start of play was avoided. But when the powerful sound system started beating out the drum roll that introduces the World Cup theme song, 'Who'll Rule the World', it is unlikely any South African in the ground escaped a sharp increase in pulse rate. In South Africa it was approaching 5.30 am. It was to be a day of low productivity in workplaces around a nation at last united in support of a sporting team.

On the field, Ali Bacher was being interviewed by Australian television. The interview over, he stayed on the field to experience the moment when Kepler Wessels led his men, running, into history. The crowd roared out a welcome. This, at last, was really it. India had indeed been a prelude. In the modern jargon this was a mega-event.

The green-shirted South Africans ran to take up their positions, going through last-minute loosening exercises as the Australian openers, Marsh and Boon, walked out.

Around the ground, the crowd settled as Allan Donald came racing in off his long run-up. A shortish delivery, lifting sharply, had Marsh jabbing involuntarily at the ball, a deviation, and exultation among the South African players as Richardson held the ball and threw it high in the air.

Television replays, and the Australian players afterwards, left no doubt that Marsh had indeed touched the ball. But these battle-hardened Australians do not walk unless the umpire puts his finger in the air. The New Zealand umpire, Brian Aldridge, stood immobile. It was the sort of moment that can undo the best of mental preparation. Donald bowled a wide down the legside, which Richardson scrambled to gather as the batsmen crossed for a run.

Boon edged the ball high and wide of the slips. Cronje raced around at third man and fumbled as he dived for the ball, enabling the batsmen to run three. The stocky Boon, in such prolific form all summer, calmly drove an over-pitched ball from Pringle to the cover boundary. Another edgy shot brought two runs.

Another Donald wide, a single from Marsh and an edged four by Boon took the total to 16 after just three overs. What might have been a triumphant start was disintegrating rapidly.

A handsome off-drive off Donald brought four more runs to Boon as the total reached 35 after seven overs. A tight first over from Richard Snell yielded just two singles.

Boon crashed Pringle through extra cover for four, but then disaster struck for Australia. Marsh squeezed Snell to the legside and started on a run but changed his mind. Boon was racing down the wicket. Snell reacted instantly and sprinted to pick up the ball. Cronje hurried from mid-on to guard the stumps at the bowler's end. Snell threw in, Cronje broke the wicket and Boon was out for 27.

The innings settled in to a more normal pace as Snell bowled accurately in a seven-over spell which cost only 10 runs. But Marsh and Dean Jones kept the score moving with sharp running between wickets including an all-run four to Marsh.

Adrian Kuiper, now regarded as no more than a sharer of the fifth bowling role, came into the attack in the 19th over. In his second over he bowled from slightly wider of the crease than usual, Marsh drove at an away-swinger and this time umpire Aldridge had no hesitation in confirming the catch to Richardson.

Allan Border, veteran of more than 200 one-day internationals, came out for his first tilt at a South African team. Kuiper bowled a splendid delivery which swung late into the left-hander and crashed into the stumps off an inside edge. Australia were 76 for 3 after 21 overs and South Africa had won back the initiative. Jones, a legend of one-day cricket, was unable to break loose against tight bowling by Kuiper and McMillan, who completed a second spell of 1 for 11 in four overs by having Jones caught behind.

Donald came back and trapped the tall Moody lbw to reduce Australia to 108 for 5 in the 33rd over. Since their early flurry Australia's leading batsmen had been held to three runs an over, losing wickets all the while. The South African players, their adrenalin under control, were sharp and efficient in the field while the bowlers were as steady as they would be in the nets bowling at Mike Procter's shirt in the 'channel school'.

Ian Healy pulled a hamstring while running a sharp single with Steve Waugh and resorted to desperate measures, lofting Pringle for two legside fours in an over which cost 12 runs, but then skied Donald to McMillan at wide mid-on. Waugh remained as Australia's last recognised batsman but in the next over he drove the tenacious McMillan straight to Cronje at extra cover and Australia's case was hopeless at 146 for 7 in the 42nd over. Donald claimed his third wicket when he bowled the left-handed Taylor and Jonty Rhodes swooped for his first run-out of the tournament, diving at cover to cut off a drive from Whitney to have McDermott stranded in mid-pitch backing up.

A target of 171 for victory was far fewer than South Africa might have dared to imagine. It was a situation tailor-made for Wessels, who needed only to bat calmly and methodically. But, as I joined some supporters in the Brewongle stand during the supper break, the excitement at South Africa's fightback was tinged with concern about the team's ability to chase a target. Did Australia's collapse indicate devils in the pitch? Could Reid and McDermott make an early breakthrough? Would the nerves and techniques of the young SA batsmen stand up to the pressure of the occasion?

McDermott, with his nose and surrounding areas daubed with zinc cream like warpaint, in the manner of Allan Donald, came charging in. A leg bye put South Africa's first run on the board and Hudson survived several fast, testing deliveries before, in the fifth over, he scored his first runs in official international cricket with a neat on-drive for three. Seventeen came off the first seven overs before Border swopped one left-armer for another, with Whitney replacing Reid. The change suited Hudson who greeted Whitney with one of the strokes of the night, a sweetly timed square cut which raced all along the turf to the boundary.

Wessels hit legside boundaries off Whitney and the 50 was raised in the 16th over. With his score 23 and the total 51 Wessels edged Whitney to the left of Boon, who was keeping wicket in place of the injured Healy. Although Boon reached the ball he was unable to hold a sharp chance.

Hudson, looking more and more confident, drove Reid through the covers and the batsmen ran four as the ball held up short of the distant boundary. He played the coverdrive again in the same over and this time the ball sped to the fence.

Wessels and Hudson had put on 74 in 19 overs when Taylor came on to bowl offspinners. Hudson, perhaps too confident, went down the wicket to drive a well-flighted ball which spun back, beat the bat and hit the stumps. Fewer than 100 runs

ALLAN BORDER, born on July 27, 1955, has played in more international cricket matches than any man in history, having set a world record of 130 Tests during the series against India before the World Cup. His appearances in the World Cup lifted his record number of matches in one-day internationals to 241.

The left-handed Border had scored 9 532 runs in Tests at an average of 52,37 by the end of the series against India. His tally included 23 centuries and a highest score of 205. As a middle-order batsman, his average in limited overs matches is understandably more modest in the lower 30s.

Border had enjoyed a good record of success as a captain, leading Australia to victory in the 1987 World Cup which they had started as outsiders. Australia subsequently re-emerged as a force at Test and one-day level, but their performances in the World Cup were disappointing. Border, however, remained unfailingly courteous and sportsmanlike in defeat.

were needed for a South African victory as the 36-year-old Kirsten joined his captain.

Kirsten had always dreamed of playing for his country at the SCG. As the years of isolation had passed it had seemed to become an impossible dream. Now, at last, in front of 39 789 packed spectators, it was coming true. With his balance and nimble footwork he was the ideal man to counteract Australia's only spinner. He had a good look at Taylor, taking just two runs of the first 10 balls. Then he struck a two, square cut a four and drove for three in an over which cost nine runs.

Wessels, looking in supreme form after his earlier let-off, square cut Waugh to the boundary. Border brought himself on to bowl slow left-armers. There was no need for South Africa's two most experienced batsmen to take any chances and they quietly accumulated runs to stay within easy striking range of victory. The Australian cause was not helped by uncharacteristic fielding errors, notably when Whitney fumbled a drive at mid-off to allow Kirsten two gift runs off Taylor.

McDermott, the Australian bowler most likely to break through, came back and was splendidly struck to the cover-point boundary by Wessels.

South African flags were flying all around the stadium. One banner proclaimed arrogantly: 'South Africa, unbeaten world champions 1970–1992' in a reference to the 4–0 thrashing of Australia 22 years earlier.

Wessels and Kirsten paced the run chase to perfection. Eleven were needed off the last three overs, and Wessels achieved them off five balls from Reid with a cut backward of square for four, a leg glance for two, a coverdrive for four and a nudge to third man for the winning run.

The victory had been achieved so calmly, convincingly and professionally that it almost defied belief. In the dressing room there were ecstatic scenes with no one more overjoyed than the ANC's spokesman on sport, Steve Tshwete, who hugged members of the winning team emotionally. Mike Gatting, two years earlier the ogre of Tshwete and his colleagues, came into the room and he too was embraced. South African cricket had never been more triumphant or more united.

Peter Kirsten was bubbling with joy. 'You thought I was good?' he asked when I congratulated him. Brilliant, I replied. 'I thought I was better than that,' he laughed.

The initial euphoria over, Wessels went to the treatment room for attention to a sore knee. Smiling, but calm, he praised his bowlers and fielders who had performed so well under pressure. This, though, was only the first game. A long road lay ahead. A disappointed Border acknowledged that his team would have difficulty in qualifying for the semi-finals. He gave full credit to the South Africans. 'They pegged us back and their fielding was fantastic. They were always a worry because they were an unknown quantity. A lot of teams will sit up and take notice after their performance tonight.'

In South Africa a joyful nation took pride in their sportsmen. I had been feeding regular reports to Radio 702, who were so swamped with calls about the game that they abandoned their scheduled phone-in discussion programme and talked about cricket instead.

In Sydney, it was a time for celebration. If nothing else was achieved by this team, they had made this one of the great nights of South African sport.

World Cup, AUSTRALIA v SOUTH AFRICA
Sydney Cricket Ground, February 26
Allan Border won the toss

AUSTRALIA	Runs	4	6	Min	Balls
G Marsh c Richardson b Kuiper	25	1	–	89	72
(driving at away-swinger)					
D Boon run out	27	4	–	31	32
(Snell/Cronje)					
(backing up, stranded)					
D Jones c Richardson b McMillan	24	1	–	97	51
(edged lifting ball)					
A Border b Kuiper	0	–	–	1	1
(ball swung in late)					
T Moody lbw b Donald	10	–	–	47	33
(trapped by off-cutter)					

S Waugh c Cronje b McMillan	27	1	–	58	51
(drove to extra cover)					
I Healy c McMillan b Donald	16	2	–	34	24
(skied to wide mid-on)					
P Taylor b Donald	4	–	–	18	9
(missed drive)					
C McDermott run out	6	–	–	20	12
(Rhodes/Snell)					
(diving stop at cover)					
M Whitney not out	9	1	–	19	15
B Reid not out	5	–	–	13	10
Extras (2lb, 4nb, 11w)	17				
Total (9 wickets, 49 overs)	170				

Falls: 1/42 (Boon), 2/76 (Marsh), 3/76 (Border), 4/97 (Jones), 5/108 (Moody), 6/143 (Healy), 7/146 (Waugh), 8/156 (Taylor), 9/161 (McDermott).
Bowling: Donald 10-0-34-3 (5w), Pringle 10-0-52-0 (2nb, 1w), Snell 9-1-15-0, McMillan 10-0-35-2 (2nb, 3w), Kuiper 5-0-15-2 (1w), Cronje 5-1-17-0 (1w).

SOUTH AFRICA	Runs	4	6	Min	Balls
K Wessels not out	81	9	–	173	148
A Hudson b Taylor	28	3	–	81	51
(down wicket, missed drive)					
P Kirsten not out	49	1	–	91	90
H Cronje, A Kuiper, J Rhodes,					
B McMillan, D Richardson,					
R Snell, M Pringle and A Donald					
did not bat					
Extras (5lb, 2nb, 6w)	13				
Total (1 wicket, 46,5 overs)	171				

Fall: 1/74 (Hudson).
Bowling: McDermott 10-1-23-0 (2nb), Reid 8,5-0-41-0 (4w), Whitney 6-0-26-0, Taylor 10-1-32-1 (1w), Waugh 4-1-16-0 (1w), Border 4-0-13-0, Moody 4-0-15-0.

South Africa won by nine wickets.
Man of the Match: Kepler Wessels. Crowd: 39 789.

Jonty Rhodes during a breezy innings of 22 against the West Indies in Christchurch.

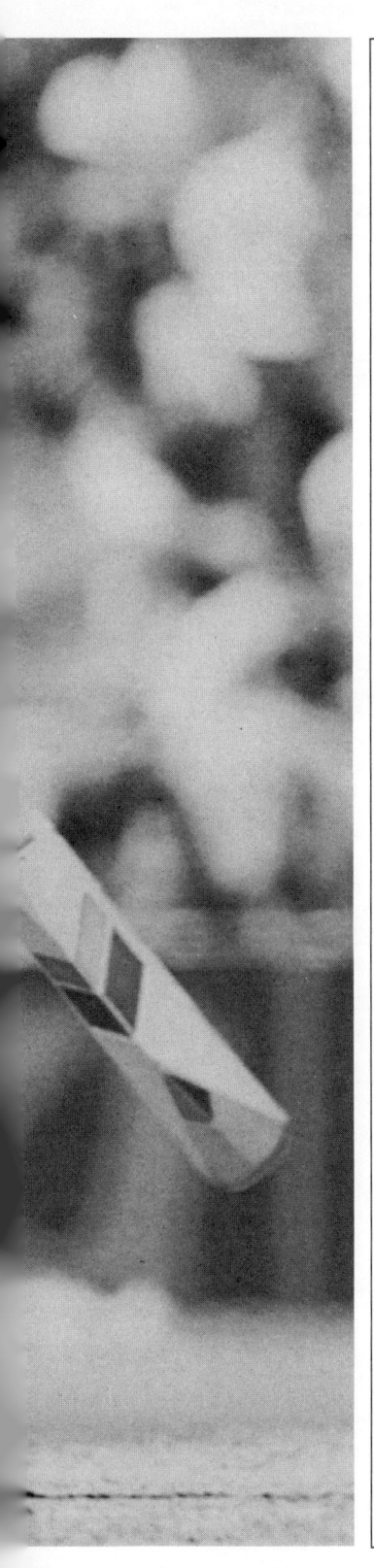

CHAPTER EIGHT

DISASTER AND TRIUMPH IN NEW ZEALAND

The euphoria of Sydney wore off quickly. The flight to Auckland was delayed by an hour, and, with a three-hour time difference on top of a three-hour flight, it was late afternoon when the team reached New Zealand's largest city for their match against the second host nation of the World Cup.

The Halt All Racist Tours organisation, HART, wanted the players to sign a declaration condemning, amongst other matters, the whites-only referendum to be held shortly to establish whether the white electorate supported President de Klerk's reform programme. It was a matter for Steve Tshwete and the ANC spokesman told HART members during a private meeting that their views were outdated. The ANC's support for the cricketers was unequivocal. The issue did not surface in public again.

On Friday morning the team practised at Eden Park. There was an edge of irritation about the preparations because the New Zealand players had been allocated the practice time requested by the South Africans. The nets were in poor condition, and the workout was disrupted by several rain showers.

The match against New Zealand was expected to be greatly different from the victory over Australia. The South African management had watched television coverage of the Kiwis' win over Australia at the same ground the week before and were well aware that the pitch would be slow, and that New Zealand would bowl slowly but accurately and force the South African batsmen to impart their own pace to the ball.

With hindsight, it would have been logical to play Omar Henry and his left-arm spin, but it was decided to stay with an all-seam attack with the option of using Peter Kirsten as an offspinner. Tertius Bosch replaced Meyrick Pringle, who had bowled so well in warm-up games, but had been the most expensive South African bowler in Sydney.

The weather cleared in time for the match and Wessels decided to bat after winning the toss. From the start the South African batsmen were ensnared in the web of New Zealand's bowling trickery. Offspinner Dipak Patel again used the new ball after Watson had bowled a maiden to Wessels. Patel followed with a maiden to Hudson. Only four runs had come from the bat, in addition to four leg byes, when Hudson, in a virtual repeat of his Sydney dismissal, went down the wicket to drive Patel in the sixth over and was bowled.

Kirsten was off the mark with a confident late cut for two off Patel, but Wessels was out in the next over from Watson, attempting to cut too close to his body and offering an easy catch to wicketkeeper Ian Smith.

Cronje cut his first ball in an official international for two but then found himself struggling for runs before being caught behind off the medium-pace of Harris trying to cut. It was 29 for 3 in the 16th over. Richardson was promoted to try to stabilise the innings rather than sending Kuiper in early, but although he played soundly runs came slowly.

Kirsten, though, was in excellent form. In order to break the stranglehold he had to loft the ball occasionally and he did so with assurance as he dominated a partnership of 79 off 115 balls with Richardson.

When Richardson was caught at mid-on in the 35th over trying to force the pace, Kuiper came and went in extraordinary circumstances. He clipped the first ball he faced, from Cairns, confidently to leg for two, then swung at the next, short-pitched ball, top-edging a simple catch to wicketkeeper Smith. In the way that batsmen do, he went down the wicket as though hoping the chance would be spilled. When it was held he continued towards the dressing room, which was beyond the far end of the pitch. He did not realise that umpire Khizar Hayat had called no-ball from square leg under the special condition outlawing balls above shoulder height. Neither Kuiper

Martin Crowe, New Zealand's innovative captain.

nor Kirsten heard the call amid the general hubbub of a noisy and enthusiastic crowd.

Bowler Cairns was the first to realise what had happened. Robbed of a wicket, he saw Kuiper was out of his ground and could be run out. He ran to the stumps, called for the ball from Smith, and although he fumbled and it was Harris, backing up, who broke the wicket, Kuiper was run out despite realising belatedly what was happening and making a futile attempt to get back. The laws of cricket state that umpires 'shall intervene if satisfied that a batsman, not having been given not out, has left his wicket under a misapprehension that he has been dismissed.' It might have been argued that if the dressing room had been at the other end of the pitch Kuiper would have been going in that direction and therefore not out of his ground. But there was also an argument that he had started in search of a run. It might well have changed the match if Kuiper had been able to strike his best buccanneering form over the final 15 overs, although it would have had to have been an exceptional innings in view of the batting form that the New Zealanders showed later in the day. In any event, there were no complaints from the South African camp.

The South African innings never gained full momentum despite Kirsten going on to make an excellent 90 off 129 balls, and McMillan scoring a valuable 33 not out.

Any ambitions South Africa might have entertained about defending a mediocre total of 190/7 were quickly dispelled by the left-handed Mark Greatbatch. Only in the side because John Wright had been injured in a midweek victory over Sri Lanka, the 28-year-old Greatbatch played an innings of stunning power. He clipped Donald to midwicket for four, cracked a straight six off McMillan who had opened the bowling, and square cut four more off Donald.

Greatbatch's tempo increased when Richard Snell came on and a slashed shot flew over the short boundary behind point for six. The chunkily built Rod Latham provided ideal support in an opening partnership of 114 off only 107 balls. Greatbatch grew ever more aggressive and 18 runs came from Kuiper's only over as he slammed three fours and a six over square leg in a scoring burst that would have done credit to Kuiper himself. Finally Kirsten, the seventh bowler in only 18 overs, bowled the left-hander when he tried to hit out once too often.

New Zealand raced to victory with 15,3 overs to spare, with Martin Crowe sending in his hitter Smith to accelerate the pace and increase New Zealand's net run rate, a factor in deciding log positions in the event of a tie on points. Smith hit 19 off eight balls against a demoralised attack.

World Cup, NEW ZEALAND v SOUTH AFRICA
Eden Park, Auckland, February 29
Toss won by Kepler Wessels

SOUTH AFRICA	Runs	4	6	Min	Balls
K Wessels c Smith b Watson	3	–	–	22	18
(caught behind, cutting)					
A Hudson b Patel	1	–	–	18	16
(down wicket, driving)					
P Kirsten c Cairns b Watson	90	10	–	156	129
(high hit to long-on)					
H Cronje c Smith b Harris	7	–	–	30	22
(caught behind, cutting)					
D Richardson c Larsen b Cairns	28	1	–	69	53
(drove to mid-on)					

A Kuiper run out (Smith/Harris)	2	–	–	1	2
(mix-up after caught off no-ball)					
J Rhodes c Crowe b Cairns	6	–	–	18	15
(diving catch, midwicket)					
B McMillan not out	33	1	–	45	40
R Snell not out	11	1	–	14	8

A Donald and T Bosch did not bat

Extras (8lb, 1nb)   9
Total (7 wickets, 50 overs)   190

Falls: 1/8 (Hudson), 2/10 (Wessels), 3/29 (Cronje), 4/108 (Richardson), 5/111 (Kuiper), 6/121 (Rhodes), 7/162 (Kirsten).

Bowling: 10-2-30-2, Patel 10-1-28-1, Larsen 10-1-29-0, Harris 10-2-33-1, Latham 2-0-19-0, Cairns 8-0-43-2 (1nb).

NEW ZEALAND	Runs	4	6	Min	Balls
M Greatbatch b Kirsten	68	9	3	80	60
(going for big hit)					
R Latham c Wessels b Snell	60	7	–	117	69
(caught at first slip)					
A Jones not out	34	4	–	64	63
I Smith c Kirsten b Donald	19	4	–	9	8
(caught deep extra-cover)					
M Crowe not out	3	–	–	17	9

K Rutherford, C Harris, C Cairns, D Patel, G Larsen and W Watson did not bat

Extras (1b, 1nb, 5w)   7
Total (3 wickets, 34,2 overs)   191

Falls: 1/114 (Greatbatch), 2/155 (Latham), 3/179 (Harris)

Bowling: Donald 10-0-38-1 (1nb, 1w), McMillan 5-1-23-0 (3w), Snell 7-0-56-1, Bosch 2,3-0-19-0, Cronje 2-0-14-0 (1w), Kuiper 1-0-18-0, Kirsten 7-1-22-1.

New Zealand won by seven wickets.
Man of the Match: Mark Greatbatch. Crowd: 30 000.

The turnaround from a victorious side to one vanquished in humiliating fashion had been swift and sudden, and there was precious little time for planning before the next match, against Sri Lanka in Wellington two days later. Such was the hectic pace of the World Cup that the players went from Eden Park to the airport to arrive in Wellington on the same night.

In purely logical terms, South Africa were where they might have expected to have been after two matches, with a win and a loss. But the extent of the defeat against New Zealand, with both batsmen and bowlers showing an inability to adapt to pudding-like slow pitches, prompted the tour selectors to try drastic action for the match against Sri Lanka on Wellington's similar surface.

Omar Henry was brought in and Bosch left out in an exchange of spin for speed. In the most drastic move, Adrian Kuiper was asked to open the batting in an attempt to lift the scoring tempo over the crucial first 15 overs when fielding sides were restricted to two fielders outside the 30 metre circle. Even in the warm-up matches South Africa's early rate had been painfully slow. With Kuiper opening, Hudson made way for Mark Rushmere.

Sri Lanka were known to be a capable batting side but their bowlers had taken a hammering. Zimbabwe had scored 312 for 4 on a small ground in New Plymouth only for Sri Lanka to blaze to victory with four balls to spare, and New Zealand had cruised home after being set to make 207 in Hamilton.

Because of the unpredictability of the Sri Lankan batting it would have been ideal for South Africa to have chased rather than set a target, but Aravinda de Silva won the toss and sent South Africa in on a chilly day of gusting wind.

The Kuiper experiment simply didn't work. Only six runs came off the first five overs against the lively Ramanayake and the medium-paced Wickremasinghe. Kuiper then hit the latter for two fours in the sixth over, a powerful offdrive followed by a characteristic flick to midwicket.

But after only one more boundary, a lofted drive over extra cover off Wickremasinghe, Kuiper was beaten and bowled by a well-flighted ball from the left-arm slow bowler Don

Arjuna Ratanunga plays a match-winning innings for Sri Lanka.

Anurasiri. It was the 14th over, and with Wessels virtually strokeless at the other end South Africa had scored 27 runs.

Kirsten joined his captain. He lofted Anurasiri with sweet timing for a straight six, but the runs came painfully slowly to the growing impatience of a large contingent of South African supporters. The crowd started to heckle Wessels to the obvious annoyance of the captain who glared at the grandstand where the most vocal spectators were sitting.

Wessels only reached double figures in the 18th over when the total was 47. After 25 overs the total had limped to 70, with Wessels on 19. Although not scoring at a much greater rate than Wessels, Kirsten was going for his shots when he was caught in the deep for 47. The total was 114 in the 36th over.

Wessels was caught and bowled for 40 off 94 balls in the next over, driving the slow medium-pace of Ranatunga, and the South African innings was in disarray. A succession of batsmen came and went in an effort to take the total beyond 200, but only Rhodes, whose 28 runs came off 21 balls, and the reliable McMillan made any worthwhile impression.

The Basin Reserve ground in Wellington.

The Sri Lankan bowlers stuck to their task with commendable accuracy and there was some superb fielding. The agile 22-year-old Sanath Jayasuriya held two quite brilliant catches at short cover to dismiss Rhodes and Rushmere, who both played what seemed good, decisive strokes.

All the South African wickets fell in the futile chase for runs and a score of 195 was a depressing return against a side that any World Cup contender would expect to beat without raising too much of a sweat.

Allan Donald gave South Africa hope of pulling the match out of the fire with a hostile opening spell in which he had Hathurusinghe caught at slip and left-handed Asanka Gurusinha lbw before he yorked the captain Aravinda de Silva, a player of genuine class.

Roshan Mahanama, taller than most of his teammates and of calm temperament, survived the carnage and kept the scoreboard moving with modest but effective strokes. The wicketkeeper Hashan Tillekeratne helped Mahanama add 52 for the fourth wicket before the chunky and aggressive left-hander Arjuna Ranatunga came in to play an innings which settled the destiny of the match.

While Mahanama held the innings together, Ranatunga, with the lightness of foot of a ballet dancer, played audacious strokes square of the wicket and took his runs quickly.

Mahanama's innings ended in the 43rd over when he was caught behind off McMillan with Sri Lanka 42 short of victory.

Jayasuriya was stumped off Kirsten, and Sri Lanka needed seven off the last over from Donald. Kalpage was run out giving the strike to Ranatunga, who made the sacrifice worth while by cracking Donald for four to midwicket. A scampered single meant the new man, Champeke Ramanayake, had to face with two needed off three balls. With the field brought in to save the singles, Ramanayake drove the second ball he faced through the cordon and it ran for four to point. The two batsmen sprinted off the field waving their bats in the air. De Silva said it was one of Sri Lanka's finest cricket moments.

Wessels blamed himself for getting out immediately after Kirsten, although his batting would have needed to find an extra gear to have made a substantial difference. He was also disappointed with a bowling performance that lacked discipline, as epitomised by the conceding of 13 wides and four no-balls.

For South African supporters it was a dismal day. For the first time, advertising boards were on display urging them to vote yes in the forthcoming referendum. Clearly a substantial no vote would have a negative effect on international sporting relations, prompting a gloomy spectator to say: 'If international sport is going to be like this, maybe I should vote no.'

Wellington, New Zealand's capital, is on the southern tip of the North Island. It is a city of spectacular mountains and seascapes reminiscent of Cape Town, but all the scenery in the world, even with a splendid seafood meal in a harbourfront restaurant, could not obliterate a dreadful defeat.

Within the space of five days, the success of Sydney had been superseded by serious setbacks. The next match, against the West Indies in Christchurch, assumed huge significance.

World Cup, SOUTH AFRICA v SRI LANKA
Basin Reserve, Wellington, March 2
Aravinda de Silva won the toss

SOUTH AFRICA	Runs	4	6	Min	Balls
K Wessels c and b Ranatunga	40	–	–	130	94
(mistimed drive)					
A Kuiper b Anurasiri	18	3	–	53	44
(beaten by flight)					
P Kirsten c Hathurasinghe b Kalpage	47	5	–	74	81
(lofted to long-off)					
J Rhodes c Jayasuriya b Wickremasinghe	28	2	–	27	21
(leaping left-handed catch, cover)					
M Rushmere c Jayasuriya b Ranatunga	4	–	–	7	9
(diving catch, cover)					
H Cronje st Tillekeratne b Anurasiri	3	–	–	10	6
(going for big hit)					
R Snell b Anurasiri	9	2	–	10	4
(going for big hit)					
B McMillan not out	18	–	–	35	22
D Richardson run out (Mahanama)	0	–	–	1	0
(direct hit from point)					
O Henry c Kalpage b Ramanayake	11	–	–	17	13
(lofted to long-off)					
A Donald run out	3	–	–	9	6
(trying to steal run, last ball)					
Extras (9lb, 1nb, 4w)	14				
Total (all out, 50 overs)	195				

Falls: 1/27 (Kuiper), 2/114 (Kirsten), 3/114 (Wessels), 4/128 (Rushmere), 5/149 (Cronje), 6/153 (Rhodes), 7/165 (Snell), 8/165 (Richardson), 9/186 (Henry).
Bowling: Ramanayake 9-2-19-1 (1nb),

Wickremasinghe 7-0-32-1 (1w), Anurasiri 10-1-41-3,
Gurusinha 8-0-30-0 (2w), Kalpage 10-0-38-1,
Ranatunga 6-0-26-2 (1w).

SRI LANKA	Runs	4	6	Min	Balls
R Mahanama c Richardson b McMillan	68	6	–	182	121
(attempted cut)					
C Hathurusinghe c Wessels b Donald	5	1	–	10	9
(caught first slip)					
A Gurusinha lbw b Donald	0	–	–	8	4
(beaten by pace)					
A de Silva b Donald	7	1	–	26	16
(beaten by yorker)					
H Tillekeratne c Rushmere b Henry	17	–	–	75	63
(skied attempted sweep)					
A Ranatunga not out	64	6	–	96	73
S Jayasuriya st Richardson b Kirsten	3	–	–	11	7
(trying to force)					
R Kalpage run out	5	–	–	20	11
(feeding strike to Ranatunga)					
C Ramanayake not out	4	1	–	3	2

P Wickremasinghe did not bat
Extras (1b, 7lb, 4nb, 13w)   25
Total (7 wickets, 49,5 overs)   198
Falls: 1/11 (Hathurusinghe), 2/12 (Gurusinha),
3/35 (De Silva), 4/87 (Tillekeratne), 5/154 (Mahanama),
6/168 (Jayasuriya), 7/186 (Kalpage)
Bowling: McMillan 10-2-34-1 (3nb), Donald 9,5-0-42-3 (8w),
Snell 10-1-33-0 (2w), Henry 10-0-31-1 (1nb, 2w),
Kuiper 5-0-25-0 (1w), Kirsten 5-0-25-1.

Sri Lanka won by three wickets.
Man of the Match: Arjuna Ranatunga. Crowd: 4 500.

There was a distinct air of tension as the South African players prepared for the match against the West Indies at Lancaster Park in Christchurch. Wessels felt aggrieved by severe criticism from back home, including some abusive messages that had arrived by fax. At an impromptu Press conference after a practice at the ground he raised eyebrows among a substantial international media corps by referring sarcastically to 'the South African media, those great experts who expect us to score eight runs an over against Curtly Ambrose.'

The West Indians were practising in an adjacent net, providing a cheerful contrast to the disciplined South Africans. Whereas the SA players were all dutifully attired in their sponsor's tee-shirts, the Caribbean cricketers appeared to have grabbed the first item of gear that came to hand, and their practice methods seemed equally haphazard. It has been alleged that there is disunity in the team, but if so it was well hidden by players who were clearly enjoying themselves.

I introduced myself to Richie Richardson, the West Indian captain, who was friendly and welcoming. He was greatly looking forward, he said, to the South African team playing in the West Indies soon after the World Cup.

The tour, though, was far from South African minds. The Christchurch match had become absolutely vital if South Africa's World Cup campaign were to remain viable.

The selectors went back to the successful seam formula of the Australia match by recalling Pringle. Hudson returned at the top of the order and Kuiper went back to number five. The only mild surprise was that Rushmere was preferred to Cronje at four, although Cronje had been struggling with a muscle injury that had prevented him bowling against Sri Lanka.

A big crowd was a tribute to the appeal of the first match between the two cricketing powers and to the general enthusiasm for the World Cup in New Zealand. Like Eden Park, Lancaster Park is etched deeper in South African sporting consciousness for rugby deeds than cricket, but the ground has more of a cricket atmosphere than its Auckland counterpart, and the pitch is conventionally situated in the middle of the field. Good news for both teams was that the pitch offered

MEYRICK PRINGLE, born in Adelaide, Eastern Cape, on June 22, 1966, was one of the surprise choices in the South Africa team. He was not in the original selectors' shortlist of 20, but forced his way into the final 14 with a string of consistent performances for Western Province.

Educated at Dale College and Kingswood College, Pringle played for the Eastern Province and South African Nuffield teams in 1983 and 1984. He made his first-class debut for Free State in 1985/86 and for Eastern Province two seasons later. He moved to Western Province in the 1989/90 season.

Pringle's main weapon is a late outswinger which brought him his best one-day international figures of 4 for 11 against the West Indies. His best figures in first-class cricket were 7 for 60 for Western Province against Natal in Cape Town in 1989/90. Professional cricketer.

some encouragement for seam bowling, being both harder and grassier than the surfaces in Auckland and Wellington.

With South Africa's difficulties in setting a target already well documented, Richardson had no hesitation in sending them in to bat when he won the toss. Hudson was off the mark with an unpromising inside edge for four off Ambrose and Wessels was out in the fourth over. The South African captain tried to work Malcolm Marshall to the leg side but succeeded only in getting a top edge which sent the ball spiralling to point where Desmond Haynes held the catch.

This brought Peter Kirsten to the crease for some of the best South African batting of the tour against a world-class pace attack. After his early edged shot, Hudson settled in to play with plenty of time against all the West Indian bowlers, while Kirsten was once again in confident form, square-cutting Marshall for four. Hudson hooked Ambrose to the fence. The second wicket pair saw off Ambrose and Marshall and were looking set to prosper against the replacement bowlers when Hudson was superbly caught by a diving Brian Lara at deep gully after a full-blooded back cut off Anderson Cummins.

Although it was not an imposing South African batting performance, a succession of batsmen reached 20, while Kirsten rated his 56 as one of his most satisfying innings despite hobbling with a calf muscle injury.

Adrian Kuiper hooked Benjamin for his first six of the tournament and was threatening to go on the rampage when he was bowled by a swinging full toss from Ambrose.

With Kuiper, Rhodes, McMillan and Richardson all batting at close to a run a ball, South Africa's total of 200 for 8 was reasonable in the conditions, although once again South African supporters lunched anxiously in the 45-minute break between innings.

Brian Lara, the exciting 22-year-old left-hander from Trinidad, launched the West Indian innings in style with a sizzling coverdrive off an over-pitched ball from Pringle, then hit a ferocious square cut to the boundary. He hammered another square cut only to see Rhodes, reacting instantly, scoop up a great catch centimetres off the turf at point from a searing hit which could so easily have been four more runs.

It was a turning point, not only in the match but for the World Cup campaign as a whole. An hour or so of Lara could well have settled the match in favour of the West Indies. Instead, Pringle was at the start of possibly the most significant spell of bowling of the entire tournament. Richardson was trapped lbw at the start of Pringle's next over and Hooper touched an away-swinger to Wessels at first slip four balls later.

The West Indies were in desperate trouble, but this did not prevent the left-handed Arthurton from chasing a ball wide of his offstump – and edging another catch to Wessels at slip. The West Indies were 19 for 4 and Pringle had taken all four wickets for no runs in the space of 11 balls.

In the meantime Haynes had taken a painful blow on his right index finger from a Donald lifter to aggravate an old injury. As the highest scoring batsman in the world in limited overs international cricket, he now carried his team's hopes together with the diminutive and enterprising Gus Logie.

Logie, in typical West Indian fashion, decided to fight fire with fire. A short ball from McMillan was slashed hard and high to the third man boundary and in McMillan's next over Logie made room for himself to square cut another four before scything another boundary behind point.

Haynes and Logie took the score to 50 with Haynes showing a rare discrimination and faultless technique in choosing which balls to play and which, often at the last micro-second, to allow past his bat. But Haynes was still suffering from his earlier injury and when a lifting ball from Snell crunched into the same finger he had to retire hurt with his score on 13.

Marshall helped Logie take the total to 70 before Snell struck a double blow, having Marshall smartly caught by Rhodes at point off a square cut, then Williams caught behind waving wildly at a lifting delivery.

Haynes, meanwhile, had been about to go to a nearby hospital for treatment, but news of the fall of Marshall's wicket caused him to put the pads on again, and he rejoined Logie at 70 for 6 with his team needing 131 to win off 28 overs.

To their credit, the last two recognised batsmen played posi-

DESMOND HAYNES, born in Barbados on February 15, 1956, is the only batsman in the world to have scored more than 7 000 runs in limited overs international cricket. His tally of 16 centuries is also a record. His highest score in a one-day international is 152 not out against India at Georgetown in 1989.

Haynes, a sound opening batsman, made his debut for Barbados in the 1976/77 season and his Test debut against Australia a year later. In 103 Tests until the end of the 1991/92 season, including the match against South Africa, he had scored 6 725 runs at an average of 42,30 with 16 centuries. His highest score of 184 was made against England at Lord's in 1980. He captained West Indies in one Test against England in 1990 and led the team on the tour of Pakistan in the same year which included three Tests.

Haynes was signed by Middlesex in 1989 and made his career highest first-class score of 255 for the county against Sussex in 1989.

tively and aggressively. Although a wicket would almost certainly seal the issue, West Indian hopes started to rise again when Logie hit four boundaries in an over from Kuiper. With Kuiper going for 36 in his first five-over spell, and Kirsten unable to bowl because of his calf injury, Wessels was running out of options.

But Kuiper's profligacy proved to be the undoing of the West Indies' last hopes when he returned to the attack in the 32nd over after two tight overs from Pringle had yielded only one run and set back the West Indian scoring rate. Logie and Haynes clearly decided that they had to hit the maximum number of runs from the least threatening of South Africa's seamers. Haynes went for a huge drive off the first ball of Kuiper's second spell and edged a catch to Richardson. After a leg-bye brought him to the striker's end Logie also went for a big hit and sent a high catch to Pringle at long-off. On this day of days in his cricket career, Pringle was hardly likely to spill the offering and he threw the ball high in delight after holding it safely. West Indies were 117 for 8 and as good as dead.

Ambrose was run out after a mix-up with Cummins, who in turn fell to a superb diving catch by McMillan at second slip off Donald as South Africa completed a 64-run win. In four matches they had beaten the two opponents they would least have expected to vanquish, and been beaten by those they would have expected to defeat.

After the match Richie Richardson said the South Africans had bowled well. 'They put the ball in the right spot, and that is half the job done.' He had felt, as indeed had numerous worried South Africans, that his side retained a chance of winning for as long as Logie and Haynes had been together.

Wessels, still prickling about earlier criticism, continued to be testy with the South African media. Whatever anyone else might think about the way he had approached batting, it had worked for him through a long career and he was not about to change now. The headline in *The Australian* the next morning was 'Prickly end to SA win'. The thought occurred that a touch more graciousness, whether in victory or defeat, might not be a bad thing. Such an issue was trivial, though, in the context of

South Africa's comeback in the World Cup. At the halfway stage, after four matches, they were in fourth place behind New Zealand, England and surprise package Sri Lanka.

There was a renewed spring in the steps of the South African players as they boarded the aircraft. A New Zealand campaign which started in disaster had ended in triumph.

World Cup, SOUTH AFRICA v WEST INDIES
Lancaster Park, Christchurch, March 5
Toss won by Richie Richardson

SOUTH AFRICA	Runs	4	6	Min	Balls
A Hudson c Lara b Cummins	22	3	–	68	60
(diving catch, deep gully)					
K Wessels c Haynes b Marshall	1	–	–	12	9
(intended leg shot top-edged to point)					
P Kirsten c Williams b Marshall	56	2	–	123	91
(edged lifter)					
M Rushmere st Williams b Hooper	10	–	–	24	24
(strayed momentarily out of crease)					
A Kuiper b Ambrose	23	–	1	32	29
(swinging full toss)					
J Rhodes c Williams b Cummins	22	–	–	32	27
(flashing outside off-stump)					
B McMillan c Lara b Benjamin	20	2	–	45	29
(hit to point in chase for runs)					
D Richardson not out	20	1	–	40	26
R Snell c Haynes b Ambrose	3	–	–	5	6
(skied to square leg)					
M Pringle not out	5	–	–	11	6
A Donald did not bat					
Extras (8lb, 7nb, 3w)	18				
Total (8 wickets, 50 overs)	200				

Falls: 1/8 (Wessels), 2/52 (Hudson), 3/73 (Rushmere), 4/119 (Kuiper), 5/127 (Kirsten), 6/159 (Rhodes), 7/181 (McMillan), 8/187 (Snell).

Bowling: Ambrose 10-1-34-2 (3nb), Marshall 10-1-26-2, Benjamin 10-0-47-1 (2w), Cummins 10-0-40-2 (4nb), Hooper 10-0-45-1 (1w).

WEST INDIES	Runs	4	6	Min	Balls
D Haynes c Richardson b Kuiper	30	3	–	110	83
(edged drive to wicketkeeper)					
B Lara c Rhodes b Pringle	9	2	–	13	13
(square cut, low catch at point)					
R Richardson lbw b Pringle	1	–	–	8	3
(played across line)					
C Hooper c Wessels b Pringle	0	–	–	2	4
(edged to first slip)					
K Arthurton c Wessels b Pringle	0	–	–	7	4
(chased wide ball, caught at slip)					
G Logie c Pringle b Kuiper	61	9	1	101	69
(lofted to long-off)					
M Marshall c Rhodes b Snell	6	1	–	14	10
(square cut to point)					
D Williams c Richardson b Snell	0	–	–	2	3
(flashed at lifting ball)					
C Ambrose run out (Kuiper)	12	2	–	24	15
(mix-up, direct hit from midwicket)					
A Cummins c McMillan b Donald	6	–	–	30	24
(diving catch, second slip)					
W Benjamin not out	1	–	–	9	4
Extras (9lb, 1w)	10				
Total (all out, 38,4 overs)	136				

Falls: 1/10 (Lara), 2/19 (Richardson), 3/19 (Hooper), 4/19 (Arthurton), 5/70 (Marshall), 6/70 (Williams), 7/116 (Haynes), 8/117 (Logie), 9/132 (Ambrose)
Bowling: Donald 6,4-2-13-1 (1w), Pringle 8-4-11-4, McMillan 8-2-36-0, Snell 7-2-16-2, Kuiper 9-0-51-2.

South Africa won by 64 runs.
Man of the Match: Meyrick Pringle. Crowd: 14 500.

Pakistani joy as Mushtaq Ahmed (right) takes a wicket, but there were no celebrations in Brisbane.

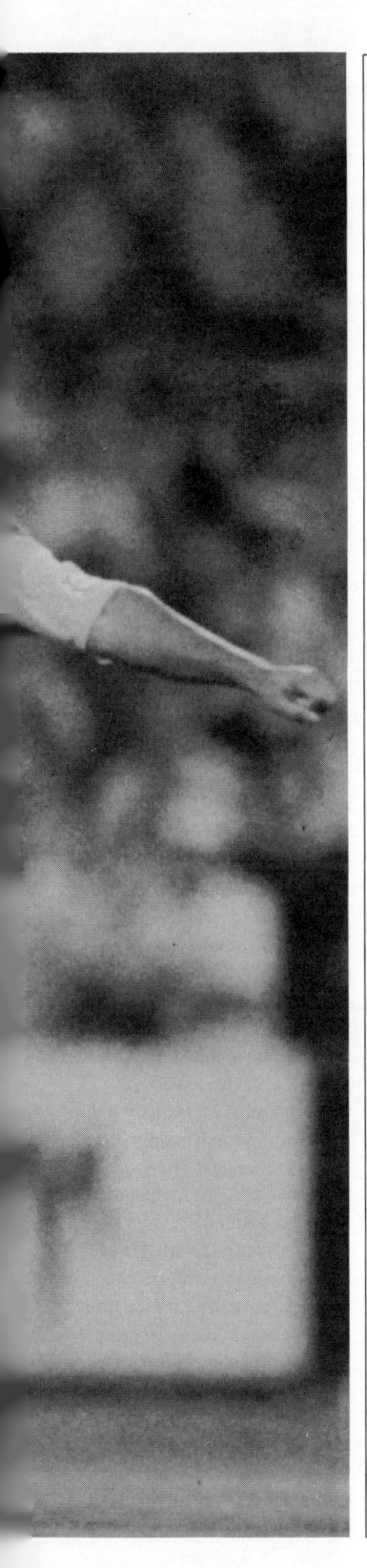

CHAPTER NINE

ON THE VERGE OF THE SEMI-FINALS

After their previous visit to Brisbane, when rain had prevented play on two successive days, the South African party were entitled to look with suspicion at the Queensland skies.

The match against Pakistan was pivotal for both teams, with South Africa on four points after four matches and Pakistan on three. Neither could afford more than one further defeat if they were to reach the semi-finals. Pakistan, listed as second favourites, had done virtually nothing to justify that rating. They had beaten Zimbabwe but had lost by 10 wickets to the West Indies and had suffered a 43-run defeat against arch-rivals India. Rain had saved them from a humiliating defeat by England in Adelaide after being bowled out for 74, England being 24/1 after just eight overs when a downpour ended play.

Imran Khan's team had also suffered further injury blows since fast bowler Waqar Younis had returned home. The team against South Africa literally picked itself with three of the 14-man squad being non-starters, including two key batsmen, Javed Miandad (stomach) and Rameez Raja (shoulder). All-rounder Wasim Haider had a thigh strain.

If the loss of Miandad was a huge blow to the Pakistanis, it was no more so in comparative terms than the withdrawal of Peter Kirsten from the South African team because of the calf muscle injury he had suffered in Christchurch.

It was a clear, sunny day but the forecast allowed for the possibility of showers. In the circumstances, Imran's decision to send South Africa in was not greeted with total dismay in the South African dressing room.

The match could not have started better for South Africa.

Wasim Akram's first ball was pitched short and Andrew Hudson, with perfect timing, square-cut it masterfully for four. Another short delivery suffered the same fate and for once South Africa had made a flying start.

With Aaqib Javed bowling two wides in his first over, followed by two from Akram, Hudson and Wessels needed only to pick up the ones and twos to be on target for a good total. Hudson was in his most confident form yet and although he played an edgy stroke for his third boundary, off Aaqib, he followed in the same over with another crisp back foot stroke, bisecting the cover field as the total raced to 27 off six overs.

After Wessels had skied a pull against Aaqib to be caught by wicketkeeper Moin Khan, Rushmere took advantage of a rare opportunity to play a meaningful innings as he helped Hudson put on 67 for the second wicket.

South Africa seemed comfortably placed, but when Hudson mistimed an on-drive off Imran to be caught at midwicket it signalled a collapse in which four wickets fell for 27 runs while 10 precious overs slipped by.

Hansie Cronje and Brian McMillan found themselves with a heavy responsibility, but with sensible and enterprising batting they put the innings back on course. Cronje's 47 not out was his highest score for South Africa, as had been Hudson's 54 and Rushmere's 35. It was a fine performance by the young Free State captain although he was lucky to survive a chance spilled by Inzamam at deep midwicket off the tricky legspinner Mushtaq Ahmed.

Wasim Akram showed in the closing overs just how dangerous a bowler he could be. The big left-armer ripped out both McMillan and Richardson with fast, swinging deliveries.

South Africa's total of 211 for 7 represented a continued improvement by the younger batsmen although the mid-innings stutter meant that they would have to bowl and field with rather more discipline than the Pakistanis, who showed a tendency to disintegrate when things were going wrong. Late in the innings Richardson was caught at long-off by Ijaz Ahmed off a no-ball, prompting an exaggerated display of dismay by the youthful Aaqib who was still performing when the ball was

ANDREW HUDSON, born in Eshowe, Zululand on March 17, 1966, made a nightmare start to his international career when he was out for nought in the first over of South Africa's return to international cricket against India in Calcutta. The level-headed and modest opening batsman did not allow this experience to unnerve him, however, and played well enough on his return to South Africa to justify a place in the World Cup squad. Hudson, educated at Kearsney College and Natal University, made his first-class debut in 1984/85 and after a string of solid performances forced his way into contention for the national team with a superb innings of 184 not out against Transvaal in Durban in 1990/91, his highest first-class score.

One of the few South African batsmen who is as competent off the back foot as he is off the front foot, Hudson became a mature international player during the World Cup, which set him up to become the first South African to score a century on Test debut when he toured the West Indies later in the year.

returned to him by wicketkeeper Moin. Aaqib was struck on the temple by the lobbed ball and had to leave the field after bowling one more delivery to complete his over.

Donald, whose ability to control the new white ball was anything but predictable, opened with an over in which he conceded six wides, although four were from a particularly wild delivery which flew beyond Richardson's reach to the boundary. With Pringle bowling two wides in his first over, the Pakistani batsmen scarcely had to put bat to ball in order to keep up their scoring rate. The 50, posted in the 14th over, included 16 extras but no sooner had the mark been reached than the left-handed Aamir Sohail swung wildly across the line and was bowled by Snell. McMillan, the match-winner in the warm-up game against the same opponents, had the other opening batsman Zahid Fazal caught behind in the next over.

Clouds were building up and Imran, usually a slow starter, square cut Snell for four and hit a powerful off-drive for another boundary as the first heavy drops of rain started to fall. The umpires kept the players on the field as long as possible but two overs later, after Imran had edged another four off Snell, play was suspended at 74 for 2 after 21,3 overs.

A torrential shower hit the ground. Rain hammered down on the roof and against the windows of the press box and it seemed that the chances of play were minimal, but in a way that was reminiscent of the Wanderers in Johannesburg, the storm passed and the players were on the field again with no more than an hour lost.

Under the rules 14 overs were deducted and the adjusted target was 194 from 36 overs. Pakistan had only another 14,3 overs in which to score 120. Although they claimed with some justification that this amounted to an almost impossible task, this was an example of the rules conspiring to create an exciting contest. Once again, however, it was a case which cried out for flexibility in order to extend the finishing time as a first resort before deducting overs.

In Pakistan's favour was that they could afford to be cavalier in their approach, as losing wickets was not as important as it would have been in a normal situation. Missing both Miandad

Inzamam-ul-Haq, Pakistan's exciting young batsman.

and Raja, Pakistan's approach would of necessity have needed to have been more cautious in a full 50-over contest because of their lack of batting depth.

The rules also reduced the maximum number of overs that could be sent down by each bowler. One could bowl eight, the others seven. Adrian Kuiper had only bowled one over, so six of the remaining 14 overs had to be entrusted to the problematical fifth bowler.

Pakistan approached the task methodically with 15 coming off 3,3 overs before Imran greeted the entry of Cronje to the attack with a hook and an off-drive for fours. Inzamam slammed two successive over-pitched balls from Kuiper to the leg boundary and swept Pringle for a four which he followed with a three. The tall 22-year-old from Multan, apparently a minor cricket centre, was threatening to take command.

A coverdrive by Imran off McMillan reduced the target to 59 off 35 balls with eight wickets in hand before Jonty Rhodes turned the course of the match with a sensational piece of fielding. Imran cut McMillan backward of square and Inzamam started for a run. Rhodes swooped at backward point, the batsmen hesitated, then ran again. Rhodes, disappointed with his low rate of direct hits on the stumps, backed his own speed across the ground and raced the charging Inzamam to the wicket, finally diving at full stretch, like a rugby player going for a try in the corner, and knocking over all three stumps.

It was a stunning piece of inventiveness and daring that confirmed the young Natalian's growing reputation as one of the personalities of the World Cup. Television replays showed that he beat Inzamam by mere centimetres. It was one of those moments when a split second made all the difference, but it is characteristic of great deeds that they are achieved with no margin for error. Rhodes had made the commitment and it had paid off.

Two balls later Imran was caught behind and Pakistan were effectively out of the game. The chase continued, however, in a flurry of boundaries, interspersed with catches in the deep.

Rhodes provided a second demonstration of his extraordinary fielding skill when he caught Ijaz Ahmed, who skied a ball well beyond Rhodes at point. Rhodes set off in pursuit of a ball which would land 30 metres away, watching the ball all the way and waving away other fielders. It was a signal that Andrew Hudson, who had started equidistant from the estimated point of descent at third man, was only too happy to follow having moments earlier dropped a difficult chance off the same batsman. Rhodes, having again backed his own speed, had to plunge backwards in order to take the catch.

South Africa's eventual victory by 20 runs established them among the leading contenders in the World Cup. Pakistan, with three points from five matches, were in desperate straits. They were, as Imran Khan said later, like wounded tigers. They were about to come bristling and snarling through the cricket jungle.

World Cup, SOUTH AFRICA v PAKISTAN
The Gabba, Brisbane, March 8
Toss won by Imran Khan

SOUTH AFRICA	Runs	4	6	Min	Balls
A Hudson c Ijaz Ahmed b Imran Khan *(mistimed on-drive to midwicket)*	54	8	–	97	81
K Wessels c Moin Khan b Aaqib Javed *(skied pull to wicketkeeper)*	7	–	–	32	26
M Rushmere c Aamir Sohail b Mushtaq Ahmed *(pulled short ball to midwicket)*	35	2	–	86	70
A Kuiper c Moin Khan b Imran Khan *(wicketkeeper ran 30 m to catch skied hook)*	5	–	–	13	12
J Rhodes lbw b Iqbal Sikander *(missed pull shot)*	5	–	–	25	17
H Cronje not out	47	4	–	78	53
B McMillan b Wasim Akram *(beaten by pace and swing)*	33	1	–	47	44
D Richardson b Wasim Akram *(beaten by pace and swing)*	5	–	–	9	10
R Snell not out	1	–	–	2	1

M Pringle and A Donald did not bat
Extras (8lb, 2nb, 9w) 19
Total (7 wickets, 50 overs) 211
Falls: 1/31 (Wessels), 2/98 (Hudson), 3/110 (Kuiper), 4/111 (Rushmere), 5/127 (Rhodes), 6/198 (McMillan), 7/207 (Richardson)
Bowling: Wasim Akram 10-0-42-2 (2nb, 7w), Aaqib Javed 7-1-36-1 (2w), Imran Khan 10-0-34-2, Iqbal Sikander 8-0-30-1, Ijaz Ahmed 7-0-26-0, Mushtaq Ahmed 8-1-35-1.

PAKISTAN	Runs	4	6	Min	Balls
Aamir Sohail b Snell	23	2	–	61	53
(swung across line)					
Zahid Fazal c Richardson b McMillan	11	1	–	63	46
(played forward, edged ball)					
Inzamam-ul-Haq run out (Rhodes)	48	5	–	70	45
(backing up, beaten by diving fielder)					
Imran Khan c Richardson b McMillan	34	5	–	70	53
(flashing outside off-stump)					
Salim Malik c Donald b Kuiper	12	–	–	15	11
(hit full toss to deep midwicket)					
Wasim Akram c Snell b Kuiper	9	1	–	15	8
(lofted to long-on)					
Ijaz Ahmed c Rhodes b Kuiper	6	1	–	4	3
(running backwards to deep point)					
Moin Khan not out	5	–	–	11	5
Mushtaq Ahmed run out (McMillan/Richardson)	4	–	–	5	4
beaten by throw from cover)					
Iqbal Sikander not out	1	–	–	2	3
Aaqib Javed did not bat					
Extras (2lb, 1nb, 17w)	20				
Total (8 wickets, 36 overs)	173				

Falls: 1/50 (Sohail), 2/50 (Zahid), 3/135 (Inzamam), 4/136 (Imran), 5/156 (Malik), 6/157 (Akram), 7/163 (Ijaz), 8/171 (Moin).
Bowling: Donald 7-1-31-0 (7w), Pringle 7-0-31-0 (1nb, 3w), Snell 8-2-26-1 (1w), McMillan 7-0-34-2 (4w), Kuiper 6-0-40-3 (2w), Cronje 1-0-9-0.

South Africa won by 20 runs
(target reduced to 194 in 36 overs, rain).
Man of the Match: Andrew Hudson. Crowd: 8 108.

While South Africa had been playing matches at Test grounds, their northern neighbours Zimbabwe had been relegated to the lesser venues of the World Cup – New Plymouth, Hobart, Napier and Hamilton. Their World Cup had adopted a depressing pattern of minimal interest, poor practice facilities and defeats on match days.

By the time the Zimbabweans arrived in Canberra for their match against South Africa, their captain, Dave Houghton, was unsurprised but nonetheless unhappy to find that the nets were damp and his team were therefore unable to prepare properly.

South Africa, in the middle of a hectic schedule with just one day between matches, only needed a light workout. Because Zimbabwe scarcely posed a major threat it was surprising that Peter Kirsten declared himself fit enough to play after missing the Pakistan match. He explained later: 'I had been in good form before the injury and didn't want to lose the momentum by missing games.'

Wessels won the toss and Zimbabwe were always struggling, with James out early and the promising left-hander Andy Flower forced to retire hurt after being hit on the finger by a lifting ball from Donald.

Houghton and Andrew Pycroft, the two most experienced batsmen in the team, took the score to 51 before Pycroft was caught off McMillan and then it was the turn of Kirsten to make a decisive contribution with the ball, albeit with considerable help from the batsmen.

The Manuka Oval, according to proud locals, has a bigger playing area than the massive Melbourne Cricket Ground, but Andy Waller decided to test his strength and try to clear the distant midwicket fence. He succeeded only in causing Cronje to hold a good catch.

In Kirsten's next over, Houghton, who should have known better, repeated Waller's experiment by offering Cronje another lofty test of character. The left-handed Ali Shah prodded forward to the next ball and hit a simple catch to Wessels at cover. Kirsten had taken three wickets within nine balls and although the wounded Flower returned to the crease

BRIAN MCMILLAN, born in Welkom on December 22, 1963, was educated at Carleton Jones high school in the mining town of Carletonville and did not make the usual progress through schoolboy weeks that is standard for most South African first-class cricketers. He attracted attention as a highly competitive allrounder while training as a schoolteacher in Johannesburg and made his first-class debut for Transvaal B in 1984/85.

He played county cricket for Warwickshire for one season in 1986 and scored 999 runs at an average of 58,76 including his highest first-class score of 136 against Nottinghamshire at Trent Bridge. He was selected for South Africa against Kim Hughes' Australian team the following season. He moved from Transvaal to Western Province in 1989/90.

Tall and powerfully built, McMillan is a solid middle-order batsman, bowls at a lively fast-medium pace and is a safe slip catcher. He was a key player during the World Cup.

Zimbabwe were in ruins at 80 for 5 after 27 overs.

Zimbabwean cricketers are extraordinarily persistent and the powerfully built Eddo Brandes succeeded where two teammates had perished when he cleared midwicket for a six off Kirsten in an over which cost 15 runs. Brandes made 20, a total exceeded only by 28 extras.

An eventual target of 164 was never likely to trouble the South Africans, despite their earlier defeat by Sri Lanka.

With net run rate, whereby the scoring rate of teams compared to their immediate opponents is taken into account, being the deciding factor in the event of a tie on points, it seemed sensible for South Africa to knock off the runs as quickly as possible, and with 19 scored off the first four overs this appeared to be the policy. But Hudson was yorked by the left-armed Jarvis with the total on 27 in the eighth over and Jarvis was treated thereafter as though he were tossing hand grenades at the batsmen.

Wessels and Kirsten made the match safe for South Africa with a partnership of 112 which took the team within 25 runs of victory, although with only nine overs remaining.

The eventual win by three wickets was achieved in 45,1 overs and seemed to represent an unnecessarily cautious approach. It was hard to quibble, though, with a third successive win.

The South African referendum was approaching fast, and there was a minor off-field drama. A consortium of South African businessmen had booked signs at the grounds where South African matches were being played, urging their countrymen to vote yes. But the sign in Canberra was taken down on the eve of the match, because of a telephone call demanding equal space for a 'no' sign. Rather than become involved in a political controversy, the Australian Capital Territories cricket authorities decided to accept neither sign.

The South African embassy in Canberra had made arrangements for special votes to be cast by the touring party. But because only three of the playing group had brought their identity books in addition to their passports, they were the only ones able to vote. It seemed an unnecessarily bureaucratic ruling, especially as the players were already out of the country when the decision to call a referendum was taken. Several supporters and journalists were able to vote, however.

World Cup, SOUTH AFRICA v ZIMBABWE
Manuka Oval, Canberra, March 10
Toss won by Kepler Wessels

ZIMBABWE	Runs	4	6	Min	Balls
W James lbw b Pringle	5	1	–	12	12
(played across line)					
A Flower c Richardson b Cronje	19	–	–	72	45
(playing forward defensively)					
A Pycroft c Wessels b McMillan	19	–	–	65	45
(driving, edged to slip)					
D Houghton c Cronje b Kirsten	15	–	–	75	53
(lofted to deep midwicket)					
A Waller c Cronje b Kirsten	15	1	–	28	28
(lofted to deep midwicket)					
A Shah c Wessels b Kirsten	3	–	–	9	4
(pushed to cover)					
E Brandes c Richardson b McMillan	20	1	1	49	29
(driving, caught behind)					
M Burmester c Kuiper b Cronje	1	–	–	8	9
(diving catch at midwicket)					
J Traicos not out	16	1	–	50	38
M Jarvis c and b McMillan	17	1	1	28	22
(mistimed drive)					
K Duers b Donald	5	–	–	9	12
(beaten by pace)					
Extras (11lb, 4nb, 13w)	28				
Total (all out, 48,3 overs)	163				

Falls: 1/7 (James), 2/51 (Pycroft), 3/72 (Waller), 4/80 (Houghton), 5/80 (Shah), 6/115 (Flower), 7/117 (Burmester), 8/123 (Brandes), 9/151 (Jarvis)
Bowling: Donald 9,3-1-25-1 (1nb, 1w), Pringle 9-0-25-1 (3nb, 6w), Snell 10-3-24-0, McMillan 10-1-30-3 (6w), Cronje 5-0-17-2, Kirsten 5-0-31-3.

SOUTH AFRICA	Runs	4	6	Min	Balls
K Wessels b Shah	70	6	–	148	127
(beaten by slower ball)					
A Hudson b Jarvis	13	1	–	25	22
(yorked, driving)					
P Kirsten not out	62	3	–	137	105
A Kuiper c Burmester b Brandes	7	–	–	9	8
(drove to mid-off)					
J Rhodes not out	3	–	–	4	3

H Cronje, B McMillan, D Richardson, R Snell, M Pringle and A Donald did not bat
Extras (4lb, 3nb, 2w)   9
Total (3 wickets, 45,1 overs)   164
Falls: 1/27 (Hudson), 2/139 (Wessels), 3/152 (Kuiper)
Bowling: Brandes 9,1-0-39-1 (1nb, 1w), Jarvis 9-2-23-1 (2nb), Burmester 5-0-20-0, Shah 8-2-33-1 (1w), Duers 8-1-19-0, Traicos 6-0-26-0.

South Africa won by seven wickets.
Man of the Match: Peter Kirsten. Crowd: 2 500.

In their travels around Australia and New Zealand, the South Africans had yet to visit Melbourne, home of the cavernous Melbourne Cricket Ground, with its new Great Southern Stand, seating 42 000 in a ground with a capacity of 100 000.

There was only one day between the win over Zimbabwe and an encounter with England at the MCG, but there was an air of confidence about Wessels and his men after three successive wins. One more victory would assure South Africa of a place in the semi-finals and there was a feeling that it could be achieved against England, despite the invincibility of the English team in 10 successive limited overs internationals.

England had suffered a severe blow when their captain, Graham Gooch, was ruled out with a hamstring injury, while former South African Allan Lamb, still recovering from a muscle injury, remained on the injury list. Allrounder Chris Lewis, with a side strain, was able to play but could not bowl.

Kepler Wessels on the way to 85 against England.

The MCG sets problems for batsmen not only because of the intimidating size of the towering grandstands but because of the vast playing area. Depending on the situation of the pitch, a square boundary can be more than 100 metres from the wicket. For this day-night encounter, however, the hazards were entirely peripheral. The pitch was probably the best surface for batting in South Africa's entire World Cup campaign, hard and true with a consistent bounce.

Despite a possibility of showers, Stewart decided to field after winning the toss. The feast of runs was not enjoyed immediately. After just four runs had been scored in the first three overs, Wessels' opening boundary was off the edge of the bat against DeFreitas, flying between Botham and Reeve in the slips.

In the fifth over Hudson set the pattern for a splendid innings, opening his score with a sweetly timed offdrive against Pringle which raced to the distant boundary.

The scoring rate increased steadily, with Wessels welcoming the introduction of Gladstone Small by hitting three fours in two overs from the new bowler and causing Small to be banished to the outfield for the rest of the innings.

Botham, the object of the undying affection of red-and-white painted England supporters, who waved banners and chanted throughout the match, had been one of the most economical bowlers in the World Cup. Although a somewhat portly figure compared to the young tearaway who had taken so many Test wickets early in his career, Botham had learnt guile and accuracy. Hudson, though, showed scant respect for one of the legends of cricket and handled Botham with fluent ease.

The 50 was raised in the 15th over and 100 in the 28th. A huge total seemed possible when Reeve pulled up lame in the middle of his third over and Hick had to come on as a replacement, bowling off-spinners. Wessels raised the 150 with a pulled four and a three off Hick in the 36th over, but Hudson drove a well-flighted delivery back to the bowler and South Africa's best start of the tournament was ended at 151.

Hudson's 79 was made off 115 balls with seven boundaries. He had established himself as one of the most accomplished batsmen in the World Cup, although he confessed: 'Sometimes I have to pinch myself to believe that I am playing at a ground like the MCG, making runs in the World Cup.'

The stage was set, with 14 overs to go, for an all-out assault, but Kirsten seemed over-keen to take on the bowling, opening his score with a splendid straight hit for six off the left-arm spinner Illingworth, only to fall on 11 with a hook to deep square leg off DeFreitas which would have sailed into the stands on any South African ground, but which instead dropped into the safe hands of Robin Smith.

With Wessels becoming another victim of the surprisingly effective Hick, after a highly impressive innings of 85, no South African batsman could take complete control in the closing overs. Adrian Kuiper, looking in good form, faced only 12 balls after coming in at the 46th over. It might have benefited the team for him to have batted at number four, which would have brought him to the crease with 11 overs remaining. Although 236 for 4 from 50 overs was easily South Africa's highest total, there was a feeling that it could have been 250 or more with a slice of luck in the late onslaught.

Donald started the bowling with a rare maiden to Stewart, with neither a wide nor a no-ball, and Pringle conceded just a single to Botham in his first over, but it did not take long before

Stewart, deputising as opening batsman as well as captain, started to show his ability to work the ball into open spaces. A fine judge of length, Stewart played impressively while Botham was content to yield most of the strike to his partner.

The threatened rain was starting to fall and the batsmen went on the attack with 40 runs coming off just five overs before rain drove the players off the field. England were 62 for 0 off 12 overs. With 40 minutes being lost, the overs were reduced by nine and the runs target by 11, which meant 164 were needed off 29 overs, a stiff but attainable goal.

An accurate over from Snell was followed by a dramatic double strike by McMillan, with Botham driving over a well-pitched ball which shattered the middle stump containing television's stump camera and provided a spectacular shot of exploding white light in the replays, followed by a worm's eye view of jubilant and curious South Africans staring down.

Two balls later Robin Smith, in his first tilt against his native land, flashed at a lifting ball outside the offstump and Richardson held the catch. Graeme Hick nudged a single to third man and faced Snell at the south stand end. He was beaten by a ball which hurried off the pitch and he too was caught behind. England had lost three wickets in seven balls, and at 64 for 3 seemed to be hopelessly out of contention.

English cricketers, though, have a wealth of experience in limited overs cricket and this team was not about to lie down and die. The left-handed Fairbrother was lucky to edge Snell for four to open his score, took a single, and runs were flowing again.

Stewart carried on where he had left off when the rain came, punching the ball away for twos into the wide spaces of the MCG and hitting rasping cuts off anything short.

Fairbrother started to find the measure of the bowling as 100 was reached off 23 overs. Cronje, after an economical first over, was lashed for two fours and a two by Stewart, using his feet to change the length of Cronje's slow medium-pacers. The next over, from Kuiper, cost 11 runs including a full toss which was hooked for four by Fairbrother.

Kirsten replaced Cronje and his first over yielded 10 runs,

Alec Stewart plays a match-winning innings in Melbourne.

including a leg bye. Drinks came fortuitously for South Africa, who were able to regroup with 95 needed off 15 overs at 6,33 runs an over.

Donald came back and conceded one run in a good over, and Pringle was brought on from the other end. Stewart was run out by another superb piece of fielding by Rhodes and the tide seemed to have changed in South Africa's favour. Stewart had played magnificently for his 77 off 88 balls and he turned to wave to the rapturous England supporters as he returned to the dressing room.

Fairbrother had no alternative but to attack. If he had been dismissed at this stage, South Africa would surely have won, but the little left-hander from Lancashire slashed Pringle for four before hitting out against Donald in an over which cost seven runs.

Fairbrother raced to 50 off 60 balls before Reeve was caught hitting out against Snell. With Fairbrother scoring two more in the over, 58 were needed off eight overs – 48 balls.

The tall, lithe Lewis could score only a single off an over from Cronje, but literally swung the match in England's favour when he hammered Kuiper for a two aided by a rare Rhodes misfield at point and a crunching lofted drive over mid-off for four in an over which cost 11 runs. The match was all but settled in the next over when Lewis hit McMillan for 2, 4, 2, and 4, hitting the ball with quite stunning power. It was down to virtually a run a ball, with 32 needed off 30 deliveries.

Although Lewis was run out by yet another Rhodes swoop and Pringle superbly held by Kuiper close in with one needed off three balls, De Freitas pushed the first ball he received through the covers. England had won by three wickets with one ball to spare. Fairbrother had played an excellent innings of 75 not out off 83 balls. He might have had some good fortune, but in a helter-skelter run chase in a reduced game, a batsman has to make his own luck. England deserved to win because Stewart and Fairbrother never stopped believing that victory was possible.

It had been a dramatic, emotion-charged night. England remained unbeaten and South Africa faced one more match, against India, three days later. They were still one elusive step away from ensuring a place in the semi-finals.

World Cup, SOUTH AFRICA v ENGLAND
Melbourne Cricket Ground, March 12
Toss won by Alec Stewart

SOUTH AFRICA	Runs	4	6	Min	Balls
K Wessels c Smith b Hick	85	6	–	170	126
(pulled to deep midwicket)					
A Hudson c and b Hick	79	7	–	132	115
(deceived by flight)					
P Kirsten c Smith b DeFreitas	11	–	1	14	12
(high hit to deep square leg)					
J Rhodes run out	18	–	–	25	23
Illingworth/Hick/Stewart)					
(went for impossible second run)					
A Kuiper not out	15	1	–	17	12
H Cronje not out	13	–	–	14	15
B McMillan, D Richardson,					
R Snell, M Pringle and					
A Donald did not bat					
Extras (4b, 4lb, 3nb, 4w)	15				
Total (4 wickets, 50 overs)	236				

Falls: 1/151 (Hudson), 2/170 (Kirsten), 3/201 (Wessels), 4/205 (Rhodes)
Bowling: Pringle 9-2-34-0 (3nb, 2w), DeFreitas 10-1-41-1 (1w), Botham 8-0-37-0, Small 2-0-14-0 (1w), Illingworth 10-0-43-0, Reeve 2,4-0-15-0, Hick 8,2-0-44-2.

ENGLAND:	Runs	4	6	Min	Balls
A Stewart run out	77	7	–	122	88
Rhodes/Pringle)					
(quick pick-up at point)					
I Botham b McMillan	22	1	–	54	30
(driving at well-pitched ball)					
R Smith c Richardson	0	–	–	2	2
b McMillan					
(flashing outside offstump)					
G Hick c Richardson b Snell	1	–	–	4	4
(beaten outside offstump)					
N Fairbrother not out	75	6	–	133	83
D Reeve c McMillan b Snell	10	–	–	29	15
(skied behind mid-on)					
C Lewis run out	33	4	–	29	22
(Rhodes/Donald)					
(backing up, stranded)					
D Pringle c Kuiper b Snell	1	–	–	11	3
(drive to short midwicket)					
P DeFreitas not out	1	–	–	2	1
R Illingworth and					
G Small did not bat					
Extras (3lb, 2nb, 1w)	6				
Total (7 wickets, 40,5 overs)	226				

Falls: 1/63 (Botham), 2/63 (Smith), 3/64 (Hick), 4/132 (Stewart), 5/166 (Reeve), 6/216 (Lewis), 7/225 (Pringle)
Bowling: Donald 9-1-43-0 (1nb), Pringle 8-0-44-0 (1nb, 1w), Snell 7,5-0-42-3, McMillan 8-1-39-2, Kuiper 4-0-32-0, Cronje 3-0-14-0, Kirsten 1-0-9-0.

England won by three wickets (reduced target).
Man of the Match: Alec Stewart. Crowd: 25 248.

Jonty Rhodes plays a short but sweet innings against India in Adelaide.

CHAPTER TEN

INTO THE HOME STRAIGHT

Having been the last of the nine teams to play a World Cup match, South Africa's eight-match round robin programme was crammed into 19 days. The final qualifying game, against India at the Adelaide Oval, would be followed by important matches involving rival contenders for places in the semi-finals.

New Zealand and England were already assured of first and second places, but South Africa, Pakistan, Australia and the West Indies all had hopes of winning through. A win over India would assure South Africa of a place. It was mathematically possible to qualify on eight points, which South Africa had already attained, but a moderate net run rate was not encouraging in the event of a tie.

The Sunday morning of the match against India gave rise to a further possibility, that of having nine points. Although Adelaide, in the words of cricket academy director Rodney Marsh, was the driest city in the driest state in the driest continent, steady rain was falling when the South Africans opened their curtains in the magnificent Hyatt Regency Hotel which overlooks the Oval. As rain persisted well beyond the scheduled starting time, it seemed more and more likely that both teams would have to settle for one point, which would mean uncertainty for South Africa until the final round robin games were completed three days later. Nine points could be enough, but if Pakistan won both their games and West Indies beat Australia, Pakistan's run rate was better than South Africa's ... and so the discussions and the scribbled calculations carried on.

The clouds off the Bight lifted gradually. A start was

planned for 12.30 but no sooner had the covers been taken off than there was another shower. Eventually it was resolved that there would be 30 overs a side, starting at 1.30. Each bowler would be restricted to six overs. It was an important toss, and Wessels was happy to win it and send India in to bat.

It clearly would be a slogging match and India promoted Sanjay Manjrekar to open with the ebullient and unorthodox Srikkanth, whose scything strokeplay seemed to be ideally suited to the short square boundaries of the Adelaide Oval.

Donald opened with what had almost become his statutory wide but he and his teammates had cause to leap for joy five balls later when Srikkanth tried to whip Donald away to leg and the ball miscued off the leading edge of the bat. Kirsten, at cover, leapt with a high-jumper's timing and precision to hold the looping ball with his left hand at full stretch.

It was a match in which each unearned run was likely to be even more important than usual, but Donald and Pringle between them bowled five wides and a no-ball before Azharuddin hit a thumping back foot drive through the covers off Donald's second over for the first runs from the bat.

South Africa had not seen the best of the Indian captain on the short tour of India in November; nor, for the most part, had Australian crowds in the months between. Win or lose, India were already out of the World Cup, but the tall right-hander was in commanding form in his team's last match of a four-month tour.

Although Manjrekar was not timing the ball well, 30 runs came off eight overs. Snell had started with a maiden to Manjrekar but 11 runs came off his second over, including two savagely struck square cuts for four by Azharuddin, who reached the distant boundary behind the wickets with his trademark shot, an imperious on-drive off Snell, as the scoring rate accelerated. Despite helping his captain put on 78 for the second wicket, Manjrekar at no stage played with the assurance he had displayed in India and it was no surprise when he was bowled, hitting out against Kuiper. The gifted Tendulkar was just getting into his stride when Kuiper struck again, with Wessels picking up a scooped chance at mid-on. At 102 for 3

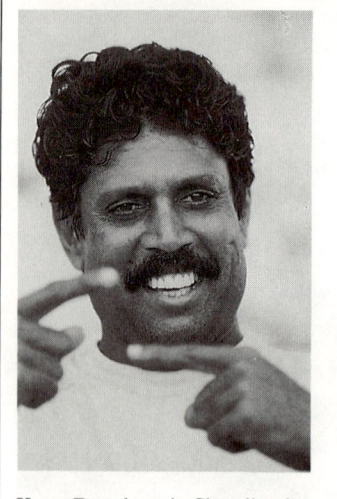

KAPIL DEV, born in Chandigarh on January 6, 1959, made a sensational debut in first-class cricket when at the age of 16 he took 6 for 39 for Haryana against Punjab in a Ranji Trophy match.

He was only 25 days past his 21st birthday when he became the youngest man to take 100 Test wickets and two days later he completed the double by scoring his 1 000th Test run. By the end of the 1991/92 season he had lifted this tally to 401 wickets and 4 690 runs in 105 Tests, with best bowling figures of 9 for 83 and a highest score of 163.

Dev, who over the years has reduced his pace while remaining a skilful fast-medium bowler with a deadly away-swinger, is the only man to have scored 3 000 runs and taken 200 wickets in limited overs internationals. His 226 wickets are a world record. He scored 175 not out, a world record since beaten by Viv Richards, in turning likely defeat into victory against Zimbabwe during the 1983 World Cup and went on to lead India to triumph in the final against the West Indies at Lord's.

The Adelaide Oval, with the Sir Donald Bradman Stand in the background.

from 20,3 overs, India needed an inspirational partner for the splendid Azharuddin. They found the right man in Kapil Dev, who almost immediately went on the attack. He and Azharuddin put on 71 off only 48 balls. Dev was racing along in a frenzy of scoring and had hit Donald for 6, 2, and 4 off successive balls before being bowled in the penultimate over.

In the circumstances, India were probably less than happy with scoring only six runs off the last nine balls, during which they lost three wickets – including Azharuddin, caught a huge distance from the bat at long-on from the fifth ball of the final over. His innings of 79 off 77 balls had been one of the most impressive of the World Cup.

South Africa's World Cup depended on the two hours of batting that lay ahead, with 181 required at a fraction over six an over. Kirsten came out to open with Hudson, with a quick tempo needed from the start, but the first two overs were not encouraging. Hudson took a single off Dev before playing out a maiden from Prabhakar.

Kirsten set the ball rolling for South Africa in the third over as, with massive assurance, he placed Dev through the covers for four off the back foot. After eight overs South Africa had scored 30, exactly the same as their opponents, and like India they had a prosperous ninth over with the gangling Srinath having nine runs taken off his first over including another back-foot cover boundary by Kirsten. A leg bye brought the haul from the over to 10. Srinath conceded 10 more in his next over, with Hudson joining the boundary act with a lofted pull for four.

Hudson, so correct and controlled in earlier innings, had been instructed to try to clear the inner ring of fielders in the

Sachin Tendulkar, India's talented teenager.

early overs and was succeeding admirably although one or two shots gave his supporters anxious moments as they looped tantalisingly close to grasping hands.

Kirsten displayed once again his superb footwork against slow bowling as he made the left-arm bowler Raju look ordinary with 29 coming off the first three overs from the spinner.

Surprisingly, the only bowler who slowed down the flow of runs was Tendulkar, who from the stands looks irritatingly on the slow side of medium pace and infinitely hittable. But he is full of oriental subtlety and changes of pace. Neither batsman could launch the sort of assault on him that they so clearly would have enjoyed. The frustration almost accounted for Hudson, who mistimed a drive and started for a run only to be sent back by Kirsten. Tendulkar, with instantaneous reactions, had scrambled across to pick up the ball and he threw down the stumps at the batsmen's end. If the umpire had had the benefit of a television replay, the partnership would have ended on 77 instead of the eventual 128.

It was a splendid partnership for South Africa, and 53 were needed, although with only 40 balls left, when Hudson went on the back foot to try to force Srinath and was bowled.

Kuiper was sent in to smash the remaining runs but was run out for seven after an lbw appeal against Kirsten was turned down. Kirsten went for the leg bye, Kuiper was forced to respond, and bowler Srinath rolled the ball into the stumps.

In the next over Kirsten went down the wicket and lofted Kapil Dev gloriously over extra cover for four. It was a stroke of such splendour that Kirsten was tempted to attempt a repeat and was bowled. He had played one of the innings of a lifetime, with 84 scored off 86 balls. Twenty-four were still needed off 19 balls.

Rhodes, having scored a single off the first ball he faced, whipped Prabhakar for a stunning six over square leg, then lashed a square cut which was caught at point. He had faced only three balls and scored seven. Of such miniatures are one-day cricket masterpieces made. Now it was only 18 needed off 16 balls.

Wessels had come in to steer the ship through the final overs. He was joined by the youthful Cronje. Only four runs came off the next four balls. Fourteen needed, 12 balls left.

Wessels took a single off Dev, Cronje ran a leg bye, Wessels pulled powerfully but only a single could be scored. Cronje stole a two, then a single. Victory was close, but it remained agonising for the spectators. Dev, with all his experience, overpitched his last ball of the match and Wessels calmly drove it to the cover boundary. Suddenly a place in the semi-finals was all but assured.

Four were needed off the last over and Cronje hammered the first ball from Prabhakar to the midwicket fence. He shook his fist in triumph and waved his bat above his head. This was a great moment for South African cricket.

At the press conference afterwards, Wessels was in a state approaching jubilation. 'There was a lot of pressure but the guys have come through it,' he said. 'We are very happy to have reached the semi-final, and it really doesn't matter who we play against.'

World Cup, SOUTH AFRICA v INDIA
Adelaide Oval, March 15
Toss won by Kepler Wessels

INDIA	Runs	4	6	Min	Balls
K Srikkanth c Kirsten b Donald	0	–	–	5	5
(caught at cover off leading edge)					
S Manjrekar b Kuiper	28	–	–	72	53
(drove over full-pitched ball)					
M Azharuddin c Kuiper b Pringle	79	6	–	125	77
(high hit to long-on)					
S Tendulkar c Wessels b Kuiper	14	1	–	17	14
(scooped to mid-on)					
Kapil Dev b Donald	42	3	1	33	29
(swinging across line)					
V Kambli run out (Wessels/Pringle)	1	–	–	4	3
(Azharuddin dropped mid-on, return to bowler)					
P Amre not out	1	–	–	3	1
J Srinath not out	0	–	–	1	0

M Prabhakar, K More and V Raju did not bat
Extras (7lb, 2nb, 6w) 15
Total (6 wickets, 30 overs) 180
Falls: 1/1 (Srikkanth), 2/79 (Manjrekar), 3/103 (Tendulkar), 4/174 (Dev), 5/177 (Kambli), 6/179 (Azharuddin)
Bowling: Donald 6-0-34-2 (3w), Pringle 6-0-37-1 (2nb, 2w), Snell 6-1-46-0, McMillan 6-0-28-0, Kuiper 6-0-28-2 (1w).

SOUTH AFRICA	Runs	4	6	Min	Balls
A Hudson b Srinath	53	4	–	75	66
(stepping back, trying to force)					
P Kirsten b Kapil Dev	84	7	–	104	86
(going down wicket to drive)					
A Kuiper run out (Srinath)	7	–	–	13	6
(direct hit by bowler)					

J Rhodes c Raju b Prabhakar	7	–	1	8	3
(slashed to point)					
K Wessels not out	9	1	–	13	6
H Cronje not out	8	1	–	9	6

B McMillan, D Richardson,
R Snell, M Pringle and
A Donald did not bat.
Extras (10lb, 3nb) 13
Total (4 wickets, 29,1 overs) 181
Falls: 1/128 (Hudson), 2/149 (Kuiper), 3/157 (Kirsten), 4/163 (Rhodes).
Bowling: Kapil Dev 6-0-36-1, Prabhakar 5,1-1-33-1, Tendulkar 6-0-20-0, Srinath 6-0-39-1 (3nb), Raju 6-0-43-0.

South Africa won by six wickets.
Man of the Match: Peter Kirsten. Crowd: 6 272

With a place in the semi-finals assured, the South African players at last had a chance to bask in the glow of achievement, to take a day off cricket and allow niggling injuries to heal. Some played golf, others relaxed around the pool, others caught up on some shopping.

As coach Mike Procter said, the programme for South Africa had been tough, but having reached the knockout stage, the timing now worked well for the team. They had a full week in which to prepare for their next match, although they did not know whether they would face a semi-final in Auckland or Sydney.

With Pakistan defeating Sri Lanka while South Africa were beating India, the match between Pakistan and unbeaten New Zealand in Christchurch assumed great importance. Pakistan had to win to have a chance of playing on, and if they did Australia would be eliminated. Australia could achieve a maximum of eight points, and a Pakistan win would take Imran Khan's team to nine. The situation for the West Indies was less complicated. If they beat Australia in Melbourne they would join South Africa at 10 points, while Pakistan would be out.

There was some suspicion in Australia about New Zealand's

motivation, because if they lost they would avoid a possible repeat match against a resurgent Australian team in Sydney. The rules allowed both New Zealand and Australia to play semi-final matches in their own countries, with the exception of a match between the two countries which had to be in Sydney because the opening game had been in Auckland. Although the attraction of a home semi-final doubtless was greater than the prospect of an away game against Australia, it is unlikely that New Zealand would consciously have set out to lose a match. They were unbeaten and keen to maintain their momentum. It would probably be true, nevertheless, that their will to win was something less than absolute because they were already assured of finishing top of the round robin table.

The New Zealand game would be virtually over by the time Australia's day-night match against the West Indies began, and with New Zealand slipping to 166 all out, Pakistan were well set for their eventual victory by the time Australia started their innings against the West Indies.

England, meanwhile, were slipping to an embarrassing defeat against Zimbabwe, having been set only 135 to win on an uneven pitch in Albury.

Despite having every reason to produce a good performance, West Indies were unable to beat Australia, who, having started as favourites, were at least able to finish the tournament on a high note.

The final log positions therefore were:

	Played	Won	Lost	No Result	Points
New Zealand	8	7	1	–	14
England	8	5	2	1	11
South Africa	8	5	3	–	10
Pakistan	8	4	3	1	9
Australia	8	4	4	–	8
West Indies	8	4	4	–	8
India	8	2	5	1	5
Sri Lanka	8	2	5	1	5
Zimbabwe	8	1	7	–	2

(Australia finished ahead of West Indies, and India ahead of Sri Lanka, on net run rate.)

Aamir Sohail of Pakistan sweeps Dipak Patel during the semi-final in Auckland.

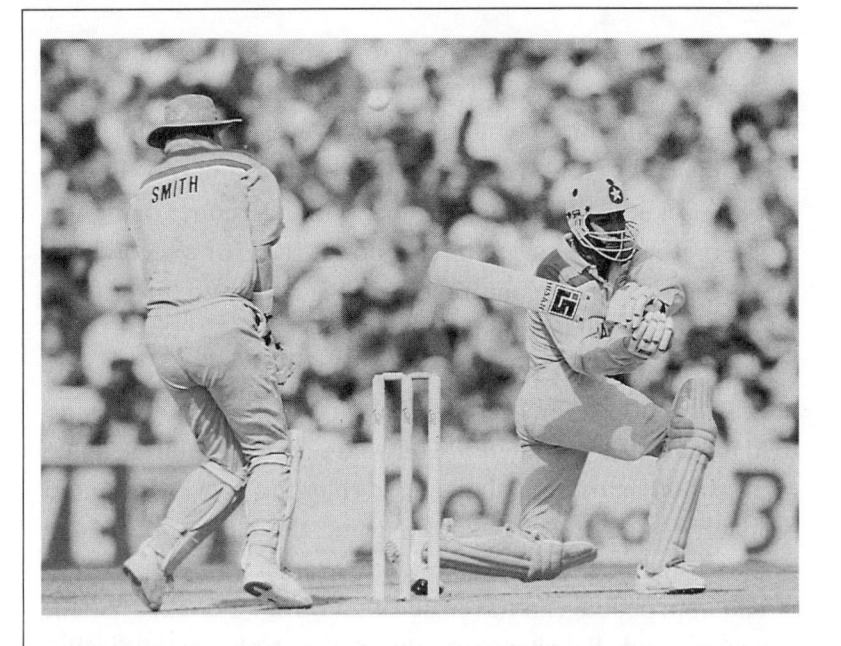

Under the competition rules, New Zealand, in first place, played Pakistan, who were fourth, in Auckland, on Saturday, March 21, while England and South Africa, second and third, met in Sydney in a day-night match on Sunday.

While the South Africans built up towards their match, I flew to Auckland for the third time in five weeks for the first semi-final.

Once again, Eden Park was filled close to capacity with a noisy and exuberant crowd who were treated to dancing girls and pop bands in addition to the cricket. New Zealand, to the delight of the crowd, went on a batting rampage and raced to 262 for 7 in 50 overs after winning the toss. The tone was set by the remarkable Greatbatch who swung and missed perhaps half a dozen times before opening his score with a slashed six off Wasim Akram. There were two sixes in Greatbatch's 17, taking his tournament total to 12 sixes, double the number of his nearest rival, his captain, Martin Crowe.

Crowe played another majestic innings, hitting 91 off 83 balls and proving that classy and correct strokeplay can be as effective a one-day weapon as a Greatbatch whirlwind. Before the match Crowe was named World Cup Champion for his performances in the preliminary games.

Sadly for New Zealand, Crowe tore a hamstring while going for his 80th run and he had to call for Greatbatch as a runner. Despite his mobility being affected Crowe continued to play splendid strokes and had just hooked Imran for six when he lost his wicket in nightmare fashion, with his runner being run out. Greatbatch was slow to respond to a call for a second run by Ian Smith and was comprehensively beaten by a throw from Rameez Raja on the boundary.

Quite apart from robbing the New Zealand captain of a probable century, the injury meant Crowe could not take the field to lead his team's defence of what seemed an unreachable total, although to the jubilant crowd chanting 'Kiwi, Kiwi', and probably to the New Zealand players, the chance of a New Zealand defeat seemed remote.

The improbable can never be ruled out in a cricket match, however, and Pakistan set about the task methodically. Rameez Raja, having hit a century against the Kiwis only three days earlier, played well for 44 off 55 balls, but Imran Khan seemed to be batting too slowly as he and Javed Miandad took the total to 134 in the 34th over. With Salim Malik being caught in the next over, Pakistan's quest seemed hopeless.

In walked a young man from Multan touted by Imran as one of the most talented young batsmen in the world. Inzamam-ul-Haq could not have picked a better occasion to prove his captain right. He swatted Larsen imperiously to the midwicket boundary to open his score and launched an extraordinary innings. Seven fours flowed from the young champion's bat, as well as a stunningly executed drive for six over extra cover. He hit 60 runs off 37 balls and changed the course of the match. Although he was run out by a direct hit from Chris Harris at cover, he had taken his team to within 36 runs of victory with five overs and one ball left.

All the while, the veteran Javed Miandad was quietly accumulating runs, never looking like getting out. Akram came and went but Moin Khan, who according to Imran was one of several players picked for his fighting qualities as much as for his natural talent, sealed a sensational win with a flurry of hitting which culminated in a soaring six into the once-noisy

Javed Miandad ... overjoyed in Auckland.

popular stands in the south-east corner followed by a four to complete the match with an over to spare.

The batsmen raced off in triumph, to be greeted by jubilant teammates running on to the field to hug them. Javed did a somersault and kissed the ground. The New Zealand players looked dazed and shattered but gathered themselves to make a lap of the ground and wave to a crowd who had given them tremendous support throughout the tournament. They were accompanied by their captain, a sad, limping figure in a white tracksuit. Perhaps Inzamam would have produced his magic in any circumstances, but the vice-captain John Wright did not appear to control the game with anything approaching the deft touch of Crowe.

They were remarkable events but a sober analysis had to conclude that finally New Zealand's mediocre bowling had been found out. Pakistan's uneven brilliance was more likely to succeed in a final in Melbourne than a New Zealand team who had played above themselves for most of the World Cup and for whom the final would have been their first match outside their own country.

World Cup Semi-final, NEW ZEALAND v PAKISTAN
Eden Park, Auckland, March 21
Toss won by Martin Crowe

NEW ZEALAND	Runs	4	6	Min	Balls
M Greatbatch b Aaqib Javed	17	–	2	41	22
(fooled by slow ball)					
J Wright c Rameez Raja b Mushtaq	13	1	–	57	44
(hit to deep midwicket)					
A Jones lbw b Mushtaq	21	2	–	60	53
(beaten by top-spinner)					
M Crowe run out (Raja/Moin)	91	7	3	132	83
(runner slow to respond to call)					
K Rutherford c Moin Khan b Wasim Akram	50	5	1	68	68
(skied hook to wicketkeeper)					
C Harris st Moin Khan b Sikander	13	1	–	15	12
(going for big hit)					
I Smith not out	18	3	–	21	10
D Patel lbw b Wasim Akram	8	1	–	10	6
(hitting across line)					
G Larsen not out	8	1	–	7	6
Extras (4b, 7lb, 4nb, 8w)	23				
Total (7 wickets, 50 overs)	262				

Falls: 1/35 (Greatbatch), 2/39 (Wright), 3/87 (Jones), 4/194 (Rutherford), 5/214 (Harris), 6/221 (Crowe), 7/244 (Patel).
Bowling: Wasim Akram 10-0-40-2 (4nb, 2w), Aaqib Javed 10-2-45-1 (2w), Mushtaq Ahmed 10-0-40-2, Imran Khan 10-0-59-0 (3w), Iqbal Sikander 9-0-56-1 (1w), Aamir Sohail 1-0-11-0.

PAKISTAN	Runs	4	6	Min	Balls
Aamir Sohail c Jones b Patel	14	1	–	26	20
(sweeping, caught at leg gully)					

Top: The South African players celebrate the fall of a West Indian wicket in Christchurch.

Above: Triumphant. Allan Donald, after taking the last West Indian wicket in Christchurch.

Right: West Indian captain Richie Richardson and Kepler Wessels meet before the crucial match at Lancaster Park, Christchurch.

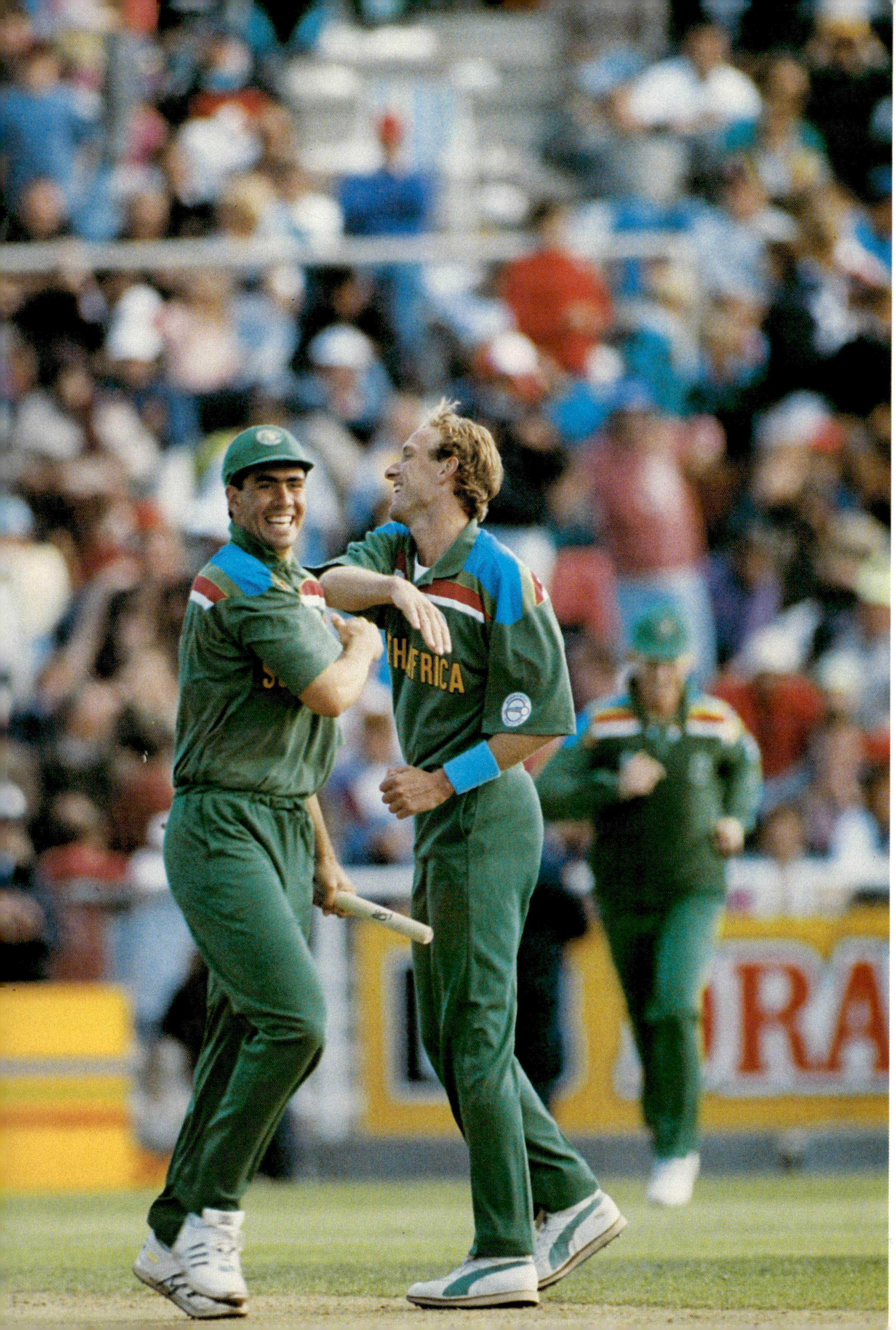
AFRICA

Left: Hansie Cronje and Allan Donald celebrate victory over the West Indies in Christchurch.

Right: Brian McMillan and Malcolm Marshall share a joke during the match in Christchurch.

Below: Jonty Rhodes hits out while scoring 22 off 27 balls against the West Indies in Christchurch.

Left: Teammates. Robin Smith and Allan Lamb, both former SA Schools players, during an England net practice.

Below: The new face of cricket. One of the hundreds of supporters who followed England's matches during the World Cup.

Right: Adrian Kuiper cools off during a net practice in Melbourne.

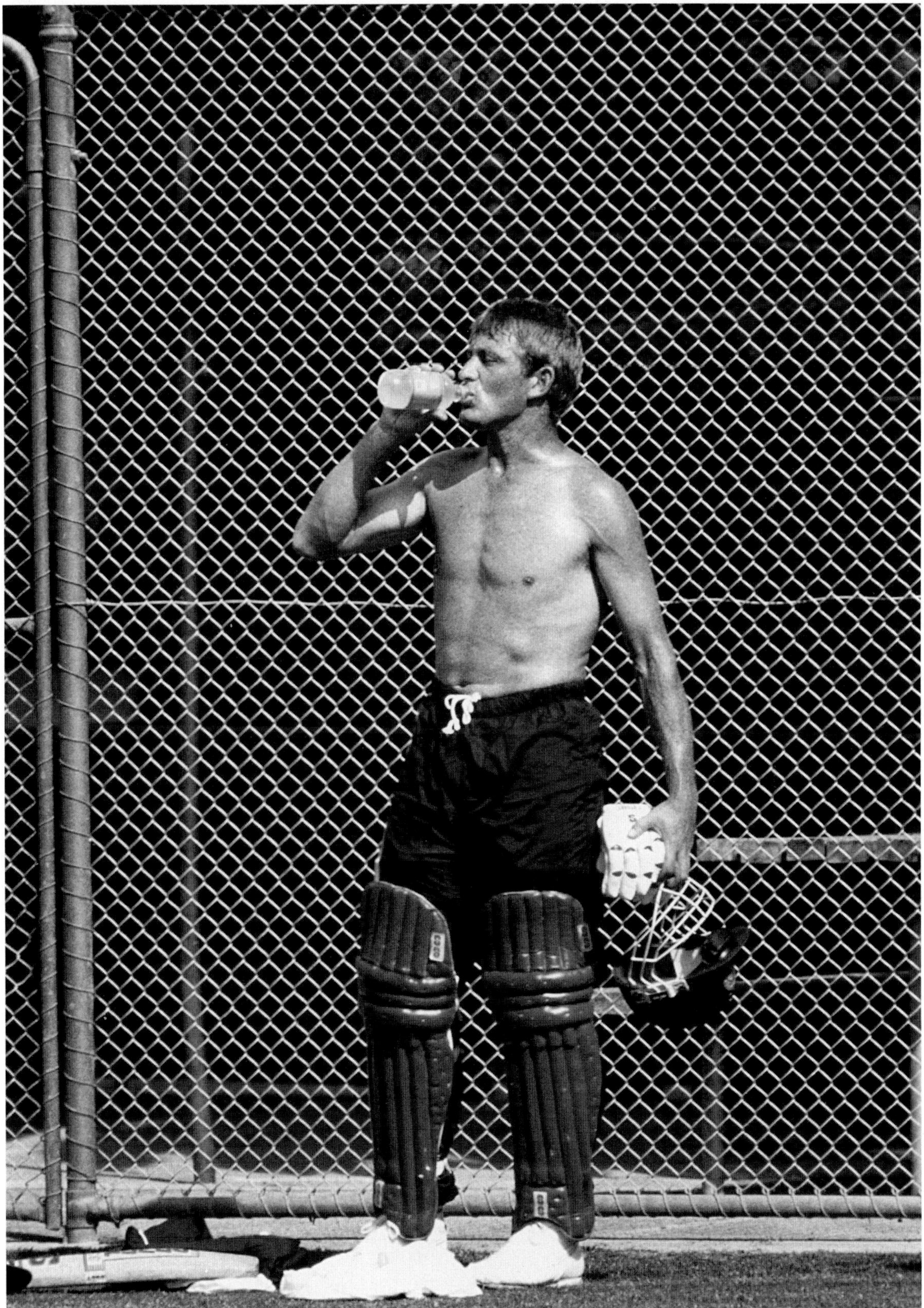

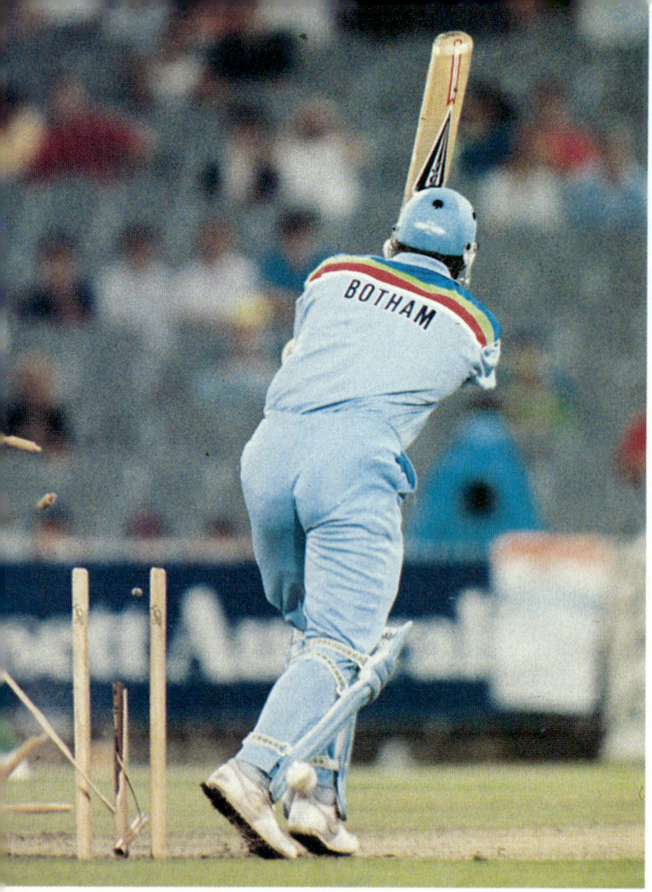
BOTHAM

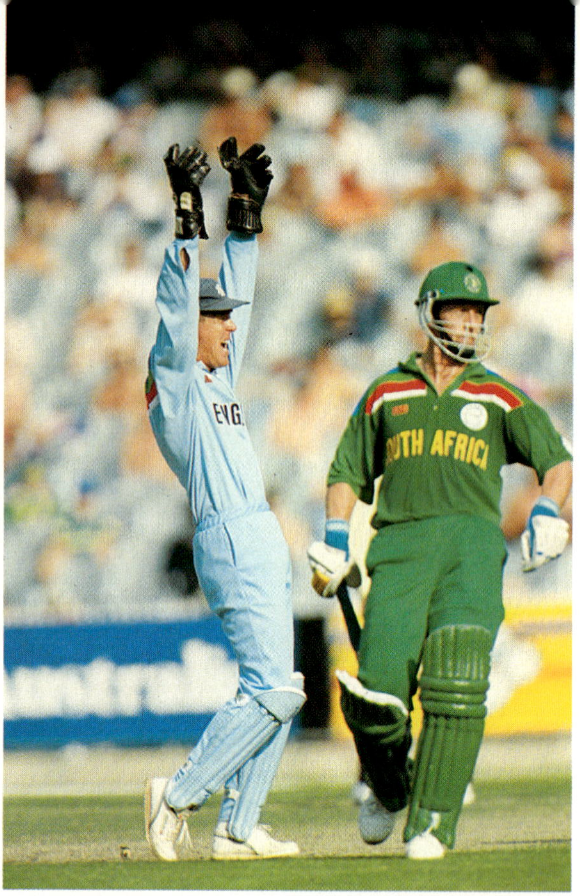
UTH AFRICA

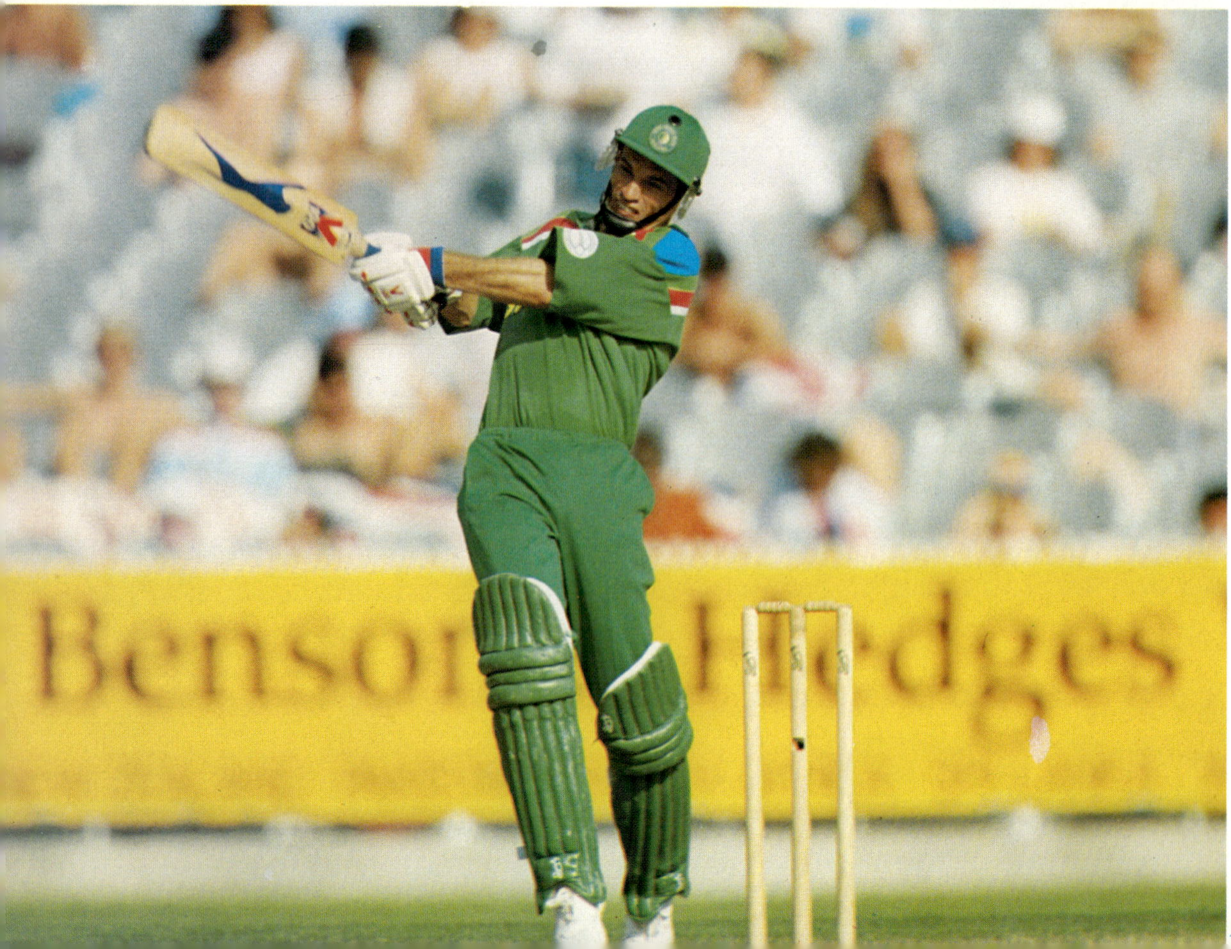

Far left: England's Ian Botham bowled by Brian McMillan for 22 soon after the re-start of the rain-interrupted match in Melbourne.

Left: England wicketkeeper Alec Stewart raises his arms after running out Jonty Rhodes during the match against South Africa in Melbourne.

Left bottom: Kepler Wessels pulls the ball to leg during his innings of 85 against England in Melbourne.

Right: Dave Richardson watches Alec Stewart hit the ball to the offside during his man-of-the-match innings of 77 for England in Melbourne.

Below: Celebrations. Jonty Rhodes and teammates after Rhodes ran out Chris Lewis during the match against England in Melbourne.

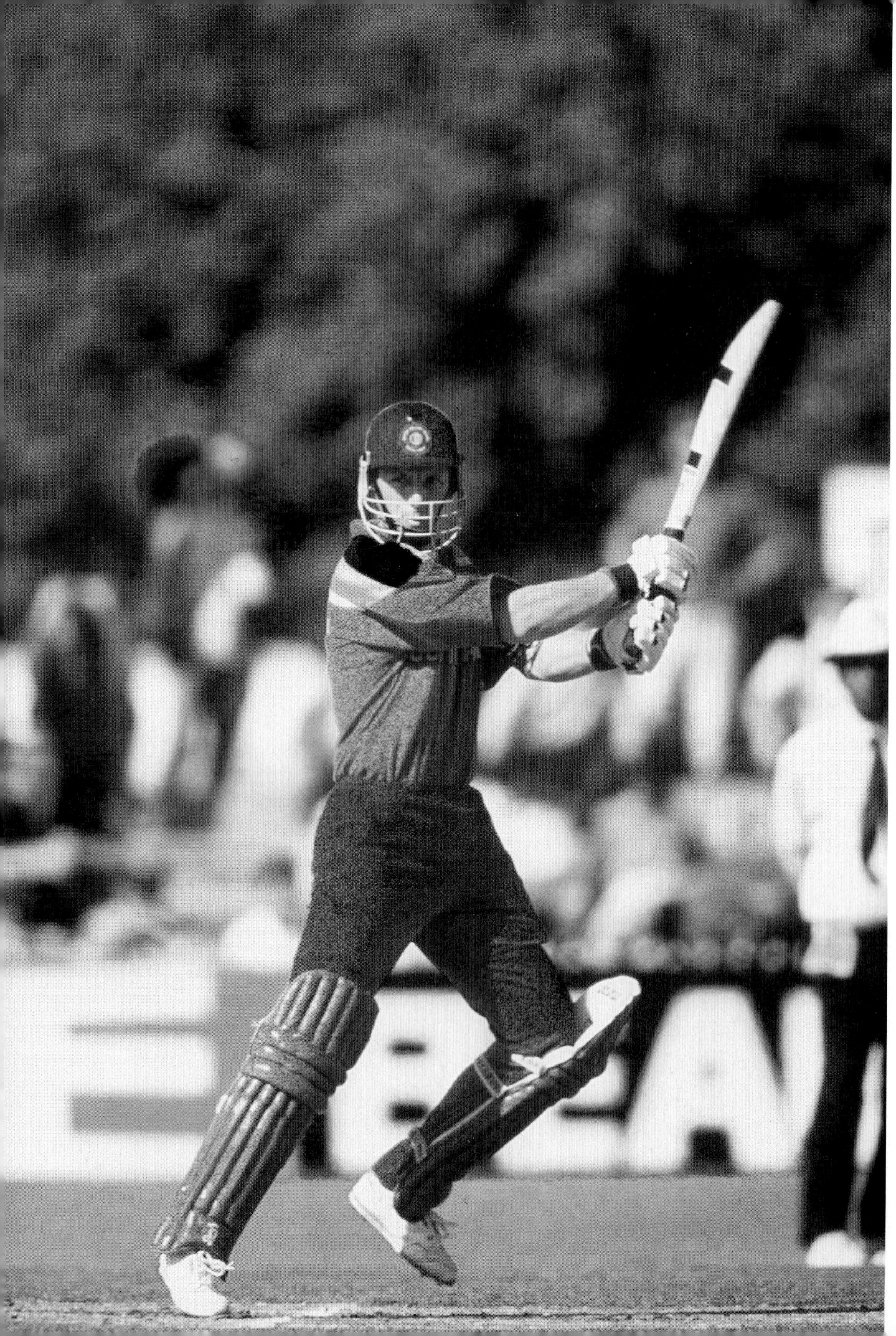

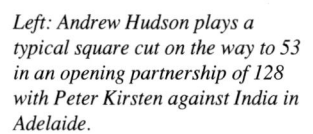

Left: Andrew Hudson plays a typical square cut on the way to 53 in an opening partnership of 128 with Peter Kirsten against India in Adelaide.

Top: Peter Kirsten raises his arms in triumph after reaching his 50 against India in Adelaide.

Above: Kepler Wessels during a net practice in Sydney.

Right top: England matchwinners Alec Stewart and Neil Fairbrother after the match against South Africa in Melbourne.

Right: Peter Kirsten during his match-winning 84 for South Africa against India in Adelaide.

Left: Serious business. SA coach Mike Procter and manager Alan Jordaan confer with their England counterparts Mickey Stewart and Bob Bennett after rain interrupted play during the closing stages of the semi-final in Sydney.

Below: The scoreboard tells the sorry tale. The target was actually 21, but one run didn't really matter.

Right top: Allan Donald and Jonty Rhodes after Donald had Graham Gooch caught behind in the semi-final in Sydney.

Right middle: Kepler Wessels after the controversial defeat by England in the semi-final in Sydney.

Far right: Graeme Hick of England drives Brian McMillan during his innings of 83 in the semi-final in Sydney.

Right bottom: Lap of honour for the losers after the drama in Sydney.

SWINDON TOWN
ADRENALIN IN THE LAND OF OZ
WORLD CUP
AUSSIE
HEREFORD
Coca-Cola

Left: Pakistan captain Imran Khan appeals against England's Allan Lamb during the final.

Below: Jonty Rhodes welcomed at Jan Smuts.

Bottom: The floodlit stage for the final drama of the World Cup: the Melbourne Cricket Ground.

Right: Javed Miandad plays a reverse sweep. He scored 58 in the final.

Right bottom: To the victor the spoils. Imran Khan and cup.

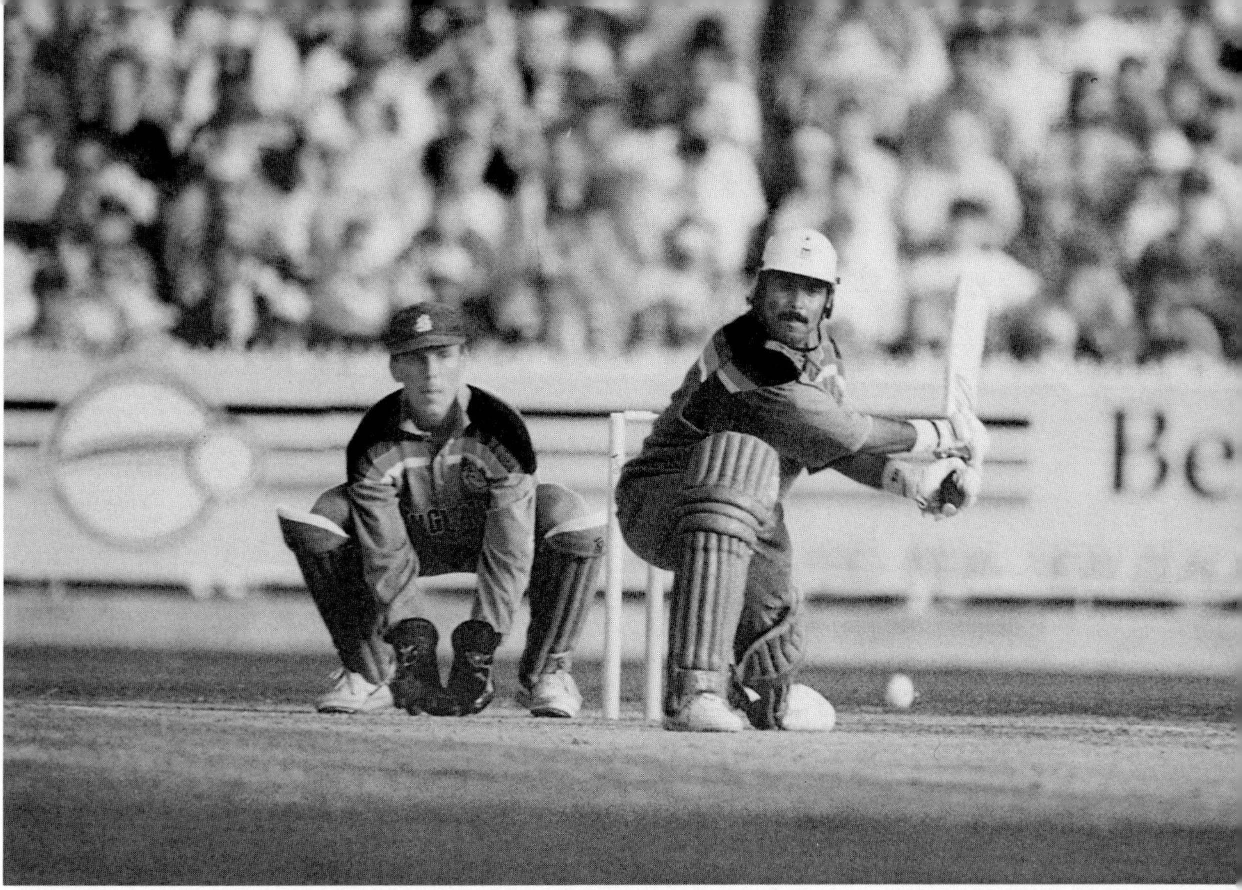

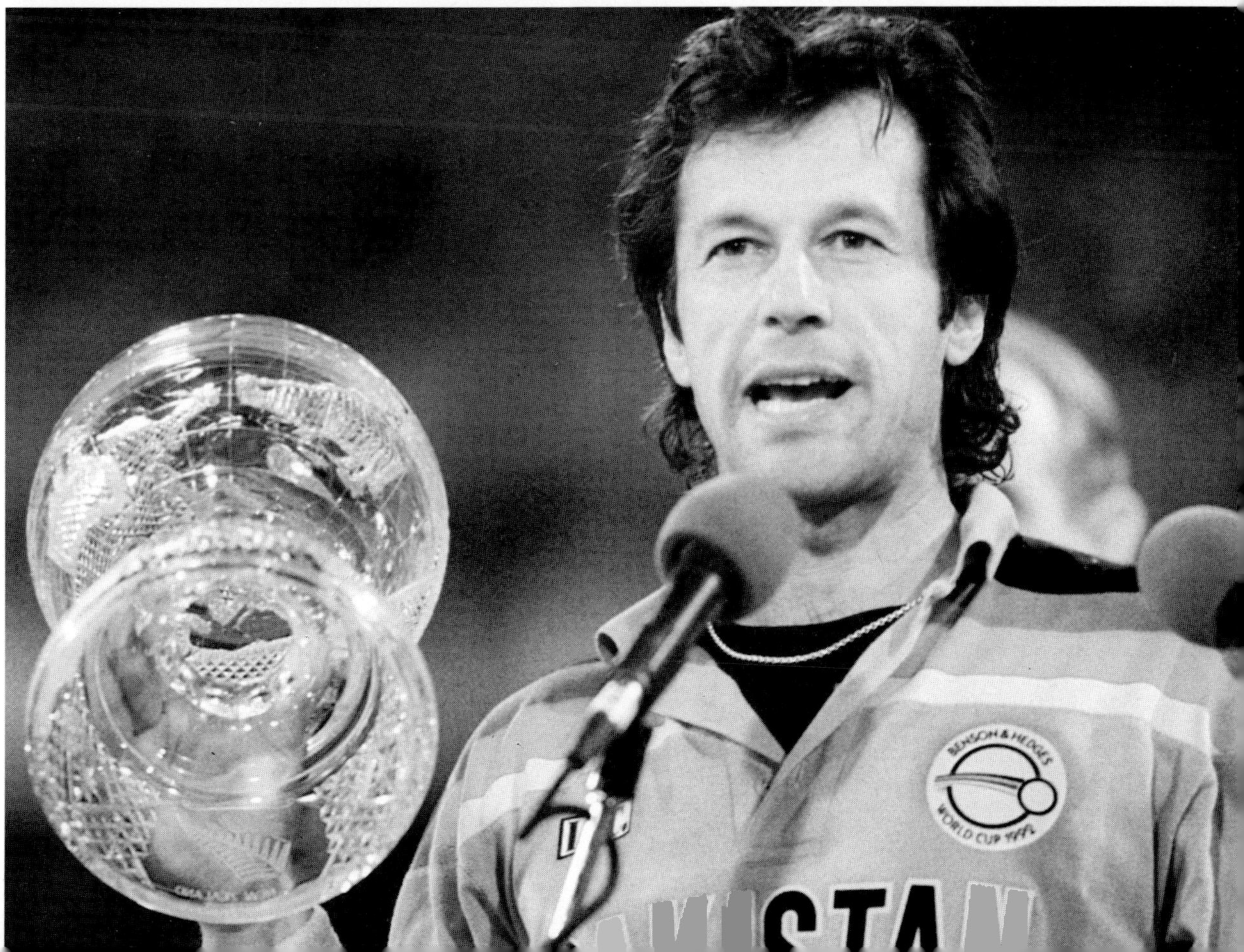
BENSON & HEDGES
WORLD CUP 1992

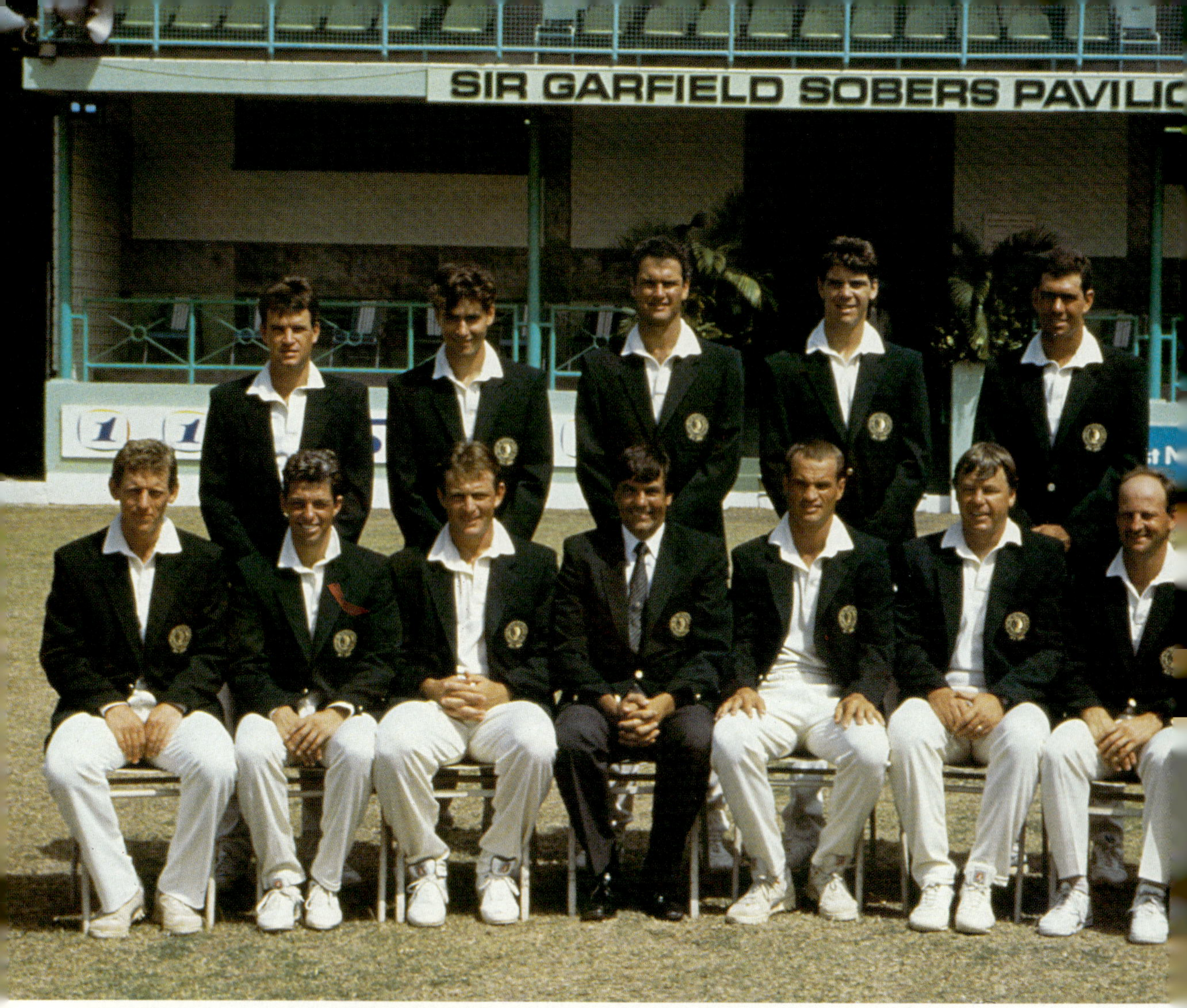
SIR GARFIELD SOBERS

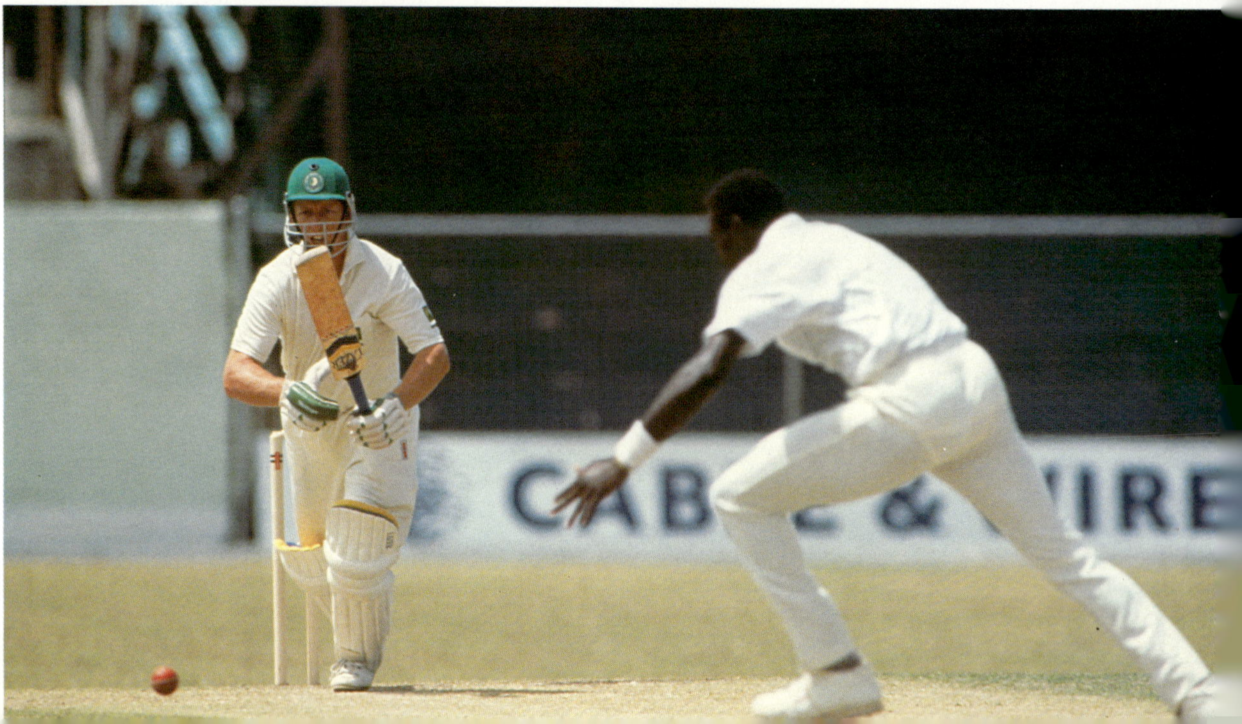

Top: The Test team in Bridgetown. Standing, from left: Mark Rushmere, Richard Snell, Tertius Bosch, Meyrick Pringle, Hansie Cronje, Jonty Rhodes (12th man). Sitting: Andrew Hudson, Dave Richardson, Adrian Kuiper (vice-captain), Alan Jordaan (manager), Kepler Wessels (captain), Mike Procter (coach), Peter Kirsten, Allan Donald.

Left: Andrew Hudson, century-bound.

Right top: Mark Rushmere, bowled by Curtly Ambrose.

Right: Kepler Wessels out on the final day.

Left: Congratulations. Curtly Ambrose, David Williams, Richie Richardson and Kenneth Benjamin.

Below: Jimmy Adams during his valiant second innings.

Above: West Indian manager David Holford hugs a triumphant Courtney Walsh.

Rameez Raja c Morrison b Watson *(caught at long-on)*	44	6	–	81	55
Imran Khan c Larsen b Harris *(skied sweep to square leg)*	44	1	2	98	93
Javed Miandad not out	57	4	–	125	69
Salim Malik c sub (Latham) b Larsen *(square cut to point)*	1	–	–	4	2
Inzamam-ul-Haq run out (Harris) *(direct hit from cover)*	60	7	1	48	37
Wasim Akram b Watson *(going for big hit)*	9	–	–	12	8
Moin Khan not out	20	2	1	14	11

Iqbal Sikander, Mushtaq Ahmed and Aaqib Javed did not bat
Extras (4b, 10lb, 1w)   15
Total (6 wickets, 49 overs)   264
Falls: 1/30 (Sohail), 2/84 (Raja), 3/134 (Imran), 4/140 (Malik), 5/227 (Inzamam), 6/238 (Akram).
Bowling: Patel 10-1-50-1, Morrison 9-0-55-0 (1w), Watson 10-2-39-2, Larsen 10-1-34-1, Harris 10-0-72-1.

Pakistan won by four wickets.
Man of the Match: Inzamam-ul-Haq. Crowd: 32 000.

South Africa, were in rather better shape than England for the second semi-final at the Sydney Cricket Ground. Despite suffering from an Achilles tendon injury Brian McMillan was determined to play. England, though, had numerous problems. Derek Pringle was ruled out with a rib injury and Robin Smith hurt his back during fielding practice on the day before the match. In the circumstances, Chris Lewis and Dermot Reeve, and the recently recovered Allan Lamb and Graham Gooch – simply had to play. The midweek defeat against Zimbabwe was by no means a disaster but it must have created doubts in English minds about the solidity of the batting.

The morning had been grey and gloomy. Rain fell shortly before play was due to start, causing a 30-minute delay. In the circumstances, Kepler Wessels' decision to send England in was not easily made. He reasoned, though, that if the forecast of clearing conditions was accurate, it was worth the gamble, especially as South Africa had established themselves as a better team chasing targets than setting them. If rain were to fall during the England innings South Africa would have the advantage in the event of overs being reduced equally. Another factor was that in the heavy atmosphere there was likely to be plenty of assistance for the seam bowlers.

The floodlights were already switched on when play eventually began.

The first two overs were a nightmare for South Africa. Gooch was off the mark with an edge off Donald, who then bowled a wide. Botham also edged the ball and received four runs. Donald bowled two more wides.

Pringle was no-balled three times in his first over and also bowled a wide. His 10th delivery of the over was over-pitched and Botham drove it for four.

Gooch was out in controversial circumstances, adjudged caught behind off a ball which cut back at him and seemed to brush the thigh pad rather than the bat, but South Africa's problems were far from over.

Pringle settled down and bowled an excellent maiden over in which he beat Stewart three times. He also beat Botham, who edged the ball just above the reach of the slips. Runs were coming when it could so easily have been wickets falling.

It was a match that might have been devised by a scriptwriter with a savage sense of irony. Having been lucky to survive a succession of edgy strokes, Botham was unlucky to drag an attempted square cut onto his stumps. Graeme Hick, having failed in the round robin match against South Africa, was totally beaten by his first ball from Pringle and an examination of the television replay could uncover no reason why umpire Aldridge might have given the batsman the benefit of any doubt in turning down an impassioned appeal for lbw. Three balls later, Hick lunged at an away-swinger and edged a catch to

IAN BOTHAM, born in Heswall, Cheshire, on November 24, 1955, may have been past his best when he played in the World Cup but he bowled steadily and was always a threat as a hard-hitting opening batsman.

Botham made his first-class debut for Somerset at the age of 18 and was a Test player at 21. In his early years he was a devastating fast-medium bowler, swinging the ball prodigiously and gaining numerous five-wicket hauls. He also achieved near-legendary status with his hard-hitting batting when he hit 149 not out against Australia at Leeds in 1981 to enable England to win a Test they had seemed certain to lose.

By the end of the 1991/92 season he had played in 100 Tests, scoring 5 192 runs with 14 centuries and taking 383 wickets.

Surprisingly, his limited overs international record is less impressive with fewer than 2 000 runs at an average in the low 20s and 140 wickets at 28,03 in 111 matches.

Wessels at slip but umpire Aldridge called no-ball. An outstanding over by Pringle was to prove the turning point in England's favour as Hick started what was virtually his third innings.

Snell pitched short and Hick struck a square cut that flew to the boundary before even Jonty Rhodes could react. Snell was short again and Hick produced a carbon copy stroke of such consummate power and elegance that there could be no doubt that the pendulum had swung England's way.

Stewart played the standard English one-day nudge towards third man once too often and Richardson held a fine diving catch far to his right. Fairbrother, as in Melbourne, was off the mark with an edged stroke.

Hick, tall and graceful, was gathering momentum, scoring off almost every ball. McMillan was whipped away to the square leg boundary and so was Kuiper when the ball dropped short. Donald, in his second spell, gave up 14 runs in an over including successive boundaries by Hick, one to square leg and the other through extra cover.

Pringle returned and bowled an outstanding over to Fairbrother, turning the left-hander almost inside out with his late swing before bowling him.

Hick edged one more boundary, his ninth, off Snell before hitting a square cut which flew to Rhodes at backward point to end a spectacular innings. His 83 had been scored off only 90 balls.

With two new batsmen in at 187 for 5 in the 37th over there was the chance of South Africa applying the brakes and slowing down the English avalanche of runs.

A new factor had entered the equation. South Africa had been bowling their overs at an unacceptably slow rate, although the wet conditions were a mitigating factor. With England scoring so quickly from the start it would have made tactical sense to try to shorten the game, but both Wessels and coach Procter denied afterwards this was the case.

In any event, when Chris Lewis joined Allan Lamb, there was not much more than half an hour available for the innings. Both batsmen launched into the bowling to reap the maximum runs possible and they hammered 34 off five overs before Lamb chased a wide ball from Donald and was caught behind.

Dermot Reeve brought the innings to a riotous end by smashing 17 off five balls from his Warwickshire teammate Donald. Whatever the length of the ball, Reeve swung lustily to midwicket and kept making contact.

South Africa had bowled only 45 overs in three and a half hours and they left the field to boos. They needed 253 to win off the same number of overs at a run rate above 5,6 an over.

South Africa went on the attack from the start. Although Hudson hit the first boundary, a square cut off Lewis, in the second over, it was Wessels who took the fight to England. He hooked Botham for four, square cut the next ball for two and off-drove for three in an over which yielded 11 runs and took the total to 21 off three overs.

Wessels was looking in commanding form but a searing square cut was snapped up at point by Lewis.

Hudson and Kirsten kept the scoring rate at around five an over before Kirsten was bowled at 61. Hudson had scored 46 off only 52 balls when he was trapped leg before by a ball from the slow left-armer Richard Illingworth which straightened on him.

Once again South Africa looked to Kuiper to produce a match-winning contribution. It had not been a happy tournament for the big-hitter from the Western Cape, although his efforts in preparation could not be faulted. In nets before the game he hit the ball over the stone wall surrounding the SCG and a Sydney newspaper published a photograph of him peering over the wall. 'It only happens in practice,' he said ruefully to a bystander.

After playing himself in watchfully, Kuiper went down the pitch to Illingworth twice in successive overs and lofted the ball over the bowler's head into the small sightscreen inside the playing area. If the ball rolls into the screen it counts four, although the boundary is a few metres away. Was it six if hit on the full? Umpire Aldridge was not sure. He had to consult his Australian colleague Steve Randell before awarding four.

Despite Kuiper's aggression, Illingworth's slow deliveries

kept the South African batsmen in check. Going into the last 20 overs, South Africa had scored 116 off 25, and needed 137 more.

Kuiper pounded Gladstone Small for three successive boundaries, a clip to square leg, a lofted offdrive and a hook. It was starting to look as though it could be Kuiper's night, but in the next over he went down the wicket once more to Illingworth and was bowled.

South Africa's two youngest players, Cronje and Rhodes, found themselves together with the hopes of a nation on their shoulders. Rhodes immediately danced out to Illingworth and lofted him to the long-on boundary.

The two 22-year-olds, responding to the challenge, kept the score moving. Boundaries were difficult to come by against lithe Englishmen well-placed in the outfield, but the youngsters ran superbly between wickets until Cronje mistimed a hook against Small and was caught at square leg. Now 77 were needed in just under 10 overs.

Botham bowled a good over to the new batsman McMillan, bowling two successive 'dot balls' – with no runs scored – and forcing McMillan to play a desperation stroke, edging a chance to wicketkeeper Stewart who dropped it.

Rhodes hooked Botham for four and, in the 40th over, launched into what had to be the final assault, slashing Small to the backward point boundary. Gooch shuffled his field, moving his best fielder Lewis to deep point in place of the more cumbersome Illingworth. Rhodes tried to repeat his successful shot but it flew high and fast to the safe Lewis. It had been an excellent innings by Rhodes, with 43 scored off 38 balls. McMillan took a single and 46 were needed off the last five overs, just 30 balls.

The match was slipping away from South Africa, but McMillan and Richardson scored off 11 of the next 12 balls to reduce the target to 32 off 18 balls.

Rain was already falling when Lewis started the 43rd over. McMillan took a single, Richardson hit a square cut as if he were a tennis player executing a smash and the ball raced for four. He hit straight and took two more, followed by a single.

McMillan scored two. Ten already off five balls, just 22 more needed off 13.

But the rain was so persistent that the umpires had to consult the players. The batsmen, well aware of the rules, wanted to play on. Gooch threw the question back at the men in charge. Are the conditions fit for play? No, the umpires ruled. The players left the field. South Africa's World Cup was effectively over. The ritual return to bowl one last ball only intensified the irony. It is possible that South Africa might have scored the runs if the match had gone its full distance, although the odds favoured England. It had, nevertheless, been a wonderful World Cup for South Africa.

World Cup Semi-final ENGLAND v SOUTH AFRICA
Sydney Cricket Ground, March 22
Toss won by Kepler Wessels

ENGLAND	Runs	4	6	Min	Balls
G Gooch c Richardson b Donald	2	–	–	15	9
(inside edge, dubious decision)					
I Botham b Pringle	21	3	–	35	23
(edged attempted square cut into stumps)					
A Stewart c Richardson b McMillan	33	4	–	87	54
(wicketkeeper diving to right)					
G Hick c Rhodes b Snell	83	9	–	133	90
(square cut to backward point)					
N Fairbrother b Pringle	28	1	–	64	50
(ball swung in to left-hander)					
A Lamb c Richardson b Donald	19	1	–	27	22
(flashing at wide ball)					
C Lewis not out	18	2	–	37	16
D Reeve not out	25	4	–	13	14
P DeFreitas, R Illingworth and G Small did not bat					
Extras (1b, 7lb, 6nb, 9w)	23				
Total (6 wickets, 45 overs)	252				

Falls: 1/20 (Gooch), 2/39 (Botham), 3/110 (Stewart),
4/183 (Fairbrother), 5/187 (Hick), 6/221 (Lamb)
Bowling: Donald 10-0-69-2 (2nb, 5w),
Pringle 9-2-36-2 (4nb, 2w), Snell 8-0-52-1 (2w),
McMillan 9-0-47-1, Kuiper 5-0-26-0, Cronje 4-0-14-0.

SOUTH AFRICA	Runs	4	6	Min	Balls
K Wessels c Lewis b Botham	17	1	–	17	21
(square cut to point)					
A Hudson lbw b Illingworth	46	6	–	78	52
(beaten by ball that straightened)					
P Kirsten b DeFreitas	11	–	–	30	26
(ball seamed past outside edge)					
A Kuiper b Illingworth	36	5	–	62	44
(went down wicket, missed)					
H Cronje c Hick b Small	24	1	–	72	46
(mistimed hook to square leg)					
J Rhodes c Lewis b Small	43	3	–	61	38
(slashed to deep backward point)					
B McMillan not out	21	–	–	41	22
D Richardson not out	13	1	–	13	10

R Snell, M Pringle,
A Donald did not bat
Extras (17lb, 4w) 21
Total (6 wickets, 43 overs) 232
Falls: 1/26 (Wessels), 2/61 (Kirsten), 3/90 (Hudson),
4/131 (Kuiper), 5/176 (Cronje), 6/206 (Rhodes)
Bowling: Botham 10-0-52-1 (3w), Lewis 5-0-38-0,
DeFreitas 8-1-28-1 (1w), Illingworth 10-1-46-2,
Small 10-1-51-2.

England won by 19 runs (reduced target 252).
Man of the Match: Graeme Hick. Crowd: 28 410.

The Pakistan team celebrate in the dressing room after the final.

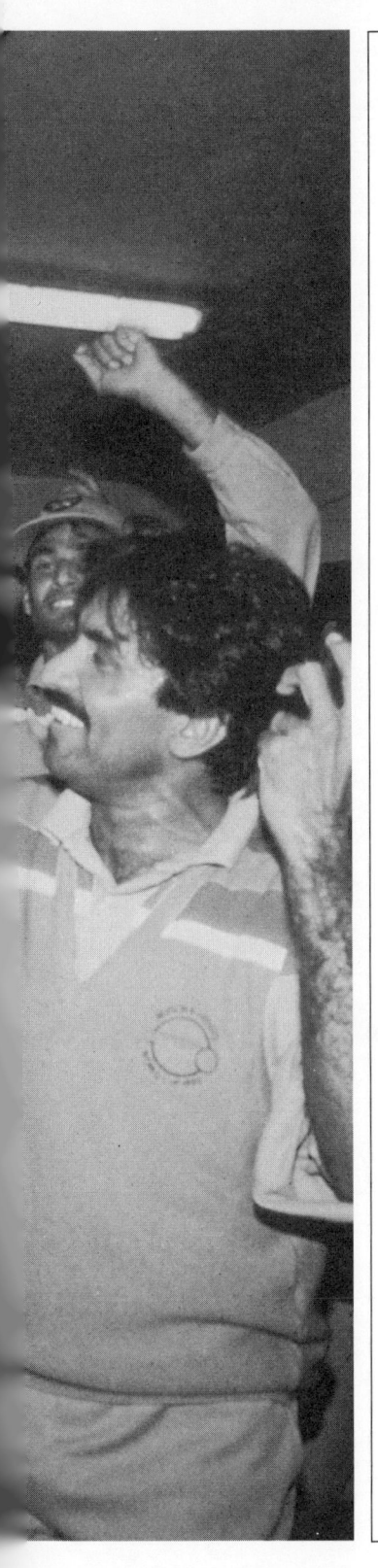

CHAPTER ELEVEN

REFLECTIONS...
AND THE FINAL

Reaching the semi-finals was a remarkable achievement for a team that entered the World Cup with no real idea of how good they were, particularly with such cricket powers as Australia, the West Indies and India failing to qualify.

Such was the nature of the semi-final defeat that there would always be an element of doubt. Would South Africa have made it or not? No-one will ever know. The team had every reason to be proud as they prepared to travel to Melbourne for the final, not as players but as spectators. Because of the scarcity of flights between Australia and South Africa, they could not return home before Thursday, the morning after the final.

The World Cup campaign over, there was a tour of the West Indies to plan, with the departure date only 11 days away.

The selectors announced on the Monday after the World Cup semi-final that the same 14 players would go to the West Indies. A case could certainly have been made for the Transvaal spin bowler Clive Eksteen, whose ability to gain genuine turn could have made him a threat in South Africa's first Test match in 22 years. But it was hardly surprising that the selectors decided to stay with the players who had done so well and matured so quickly in their first sustained venture into official international cricket.

The four-pronged seam attack of Donald, Pringle, Snell and McMillan served the team well, although towards the end of the tournament the bowling was less controlled and disciplined than in earlier games.

The fielding was uniformly excellent, with Jonty Rhodes

living up to expectations as an exceptional fielder at cover-point, with an infectious ability to exhort older teammates to emulate his own levels of concentration and enthusiasm.

The batting initially relied greatly on the experience of Kepler Wessels and Peter Kirsten, but Andrew Hudson emerged as a world-class batsman, while Hansie Cronje and Brian McMillan both responded well to pressure situations and Rhodes took the same positive approach to the batting crease as he displayed in the field.

The result was that a team whose batting was labelled stodgy and conservative became more confident and daring as the tournament progressed.

As an introduction to world cricket, it could hardly have been better, with the South Africans coming up against teams from all the other Test nations. Although obviously individuals within those teams will change, the players have first-hand knowledge of the characteristics, strengths and weaknesses of key players from all their opponents of the near future.

Although clearly it would be unwise to try to pass judgements on other teams on the basis of one or two limited overs matches, it was interesting to find that many teams appeared to have a lack of depth, particularly in bowling. As Andrew Hudson noted after facing – successfully for the most part – a variety of international bowlers, there were only a handful of bowlers of awesome standard. He felt there were bowlers unable to make the South African team, including Rudi Bryson and Craig Matthews, who were better than several of those he had faced in the World Cup.

South Africa's performance, then, was a tribute to the competitiveness and quality of the country's domestic cricket and to the efforts that have gone into maintaining that standard through years of isolation. If there has been a benefit of isolation, apart from hastening the process of political change and social justice within sport, it has been that so much attention has been paid to domestic cricket. It has been the focus of players' efforts and sponsorship rands.

With the heady delights of international cricket at hand, it would be a shame if domestic cricket were allowed to become an irrelevance except as a stepping stone to Tests and limited overs internationals.

Before concluding an account of South Africa's participation in the World Cup it is worth examining the contribution made by each member of the squad.

KEPLER WESSELS. The South African captain may appear to be dour and inflexible in his methods but his record of success is formidable. He has relentless concentration, sets an unparalleled standard of dedication and has the ability to absorb copious knowledge on the game and its players. All of these qualities were evident in the World Cup, as was his stubborn streak when he failed to lift the tempo of the South African innings against Sri Lanka. Overall, though, he could be hugely proud of his achievements both as a solid and consistent batsman and as a captain who guided a young and inexperienced team through a testing seven weeks.

Wessels played in all his team's nine World Cup matches, scoring 313 runs off 585 balls at an average of 44,71. His scoring strike rate was 53,54 runs per 100 balls, with a highest score of 85 against England. He held seven catches, which made him the most successful fieldsman of the tournament.

ANDREW HUDSON. With confidence came splendid strokes and calm assurance. The Natal opening batsman looked a player of genuine international quality. His driving and square cutting were of the highest standard and he showed he had the ability to prosper against the best attacks in the tournament, always seeming to have time to play his strokes.

Eight matches, 296 runs (37,00), strike rate 62,98, highest score 79 v England.

PETER KIRSTEN. Given the opportunity to shine at the age of 36, he was masterful against all types of bowling. His exquisite footwork and timing against slow bowling was just one reason why most experts picked Kirsten in their World Cup XIs. The leading scorer in the round robin stages, he finished third highest overall, behind Martin Crowe and Javed Miandad.

Eight matches, 410 runs (68,25), strike rate 66,13, highest score 90 v New Zealand, five wickets (17,40), 4,83 runs an over, best bowling 3 for 31 v Zimbabwe.

HANSIE CRONJE. Mature and confident, he batted well when he had the opportunity, fielded with ferocious concentration and did well as an accurate bowler of medium-pace in-swingers. Although one of the youngest players in the team he showed the type of leadership qualities which make him a likely South African captain of the future.

Eight matches, 102 runs (34,00), strike rate 68,92, highest score 47 not out v Pakistan, two wickets (42,50), 4,25 runs an over, best bowling 2 for 17 v Zimbabwe.

ADRIAN KUIPER. He did not live up to his reputation as a big hitter but was showing some of his best form in the semi-final. His bowling was erratic but he picked up important wickets.

Nine matches, 113 runs (16,16), strike rate 71,97, highest score 36 v England, nine wickets (26,11), 5,73 runs an over, best bowling 3 for 40 v Pakistan.

JONTY RHODES. Not even the unfailingly positive Natalian could have expected to attract the amount of attention he did for his spectacular fielding at cover point. He approached batting with similar self-belief in a succession of situations when he was expected to perform at close to a run-a-ball.

Nine matches, 132 runs (18,86), strike rate 89,79, highest score 43 v England. He held four catches and was involved in four run-outs.

BRIAN McMILLAN. Intensely competitive, McMillan looked a world-class allrounder. He batted well, usually in difficult circumstances, and bowled aggressively despite a painful ankle injury which troubled him through the second half of the programme, requiring pain-killing injections.

Nine matches, 125 runs (62,50), strike rate 79,62, highest score 33 not out v New Zealand, 11 wickets (27,82), 4,33 runs an over, best bowling 3 for 30 v Zimbabwe.

DAVE RICHARDSON. Overcoming an ankle injury scare shortly before the World Cup, he kept wicket well and his quota of 14 catches and a stumping was the highest of any wicketkeeper in the competition. He did not often get a chance to shine with the bat but always looked capable at the crease.

Nine matches, 66 runs (22,00), strike rate 66,67, highest score 28 v New Zealand.

RICHARD SNELL. At his best, Snell was one of the most economical bowlers of the World Cup, able to bowl at a lively pace on or outside the offstump and giving the batsmen almost nothing to score from. On other days he struggled to find the right length and occasionally his deliveries strayed down the leg side but overall he could be proud of his performances, usually being called on to bowl as first change when the brakes needed to be applied with the batsmen already set.

Nine matches, 24 runs (12,00), strike rate 126,32, highest score 11 not out v New Zealand, eight wickets (38,75), 4,25 runs an over, best bowling 3 for 42 v England.

MEYRICK PRINGLE. One of the discoveries of the World Cup, Pringle's outswing always spelt danger for opposing batsmen. Reliable fielder in the deep with an excellent throwing arm. An inspired selection from outside the original short list of 20, Pringle proved to have a big match temperament, revelling in the challenge of the occasion.

Seven matches, eight wickets (29,50), 4,14 runs an over, best bowling 4 for 11 v West Indies.

ALLAN DONALD. Donald was the fastest bowler at the World Cup, although this was not always an advantage in a competition in which containment is an essential element. Donald, like other strike bowlers, struggled to control the white ball which swung unpredictably in the early overs and bowled 32 no-balls, second only to Pakistan's Wasim Akram. He was among the leading wicket-takers in the World Cup and one of the better boundary fielders.

Nine matches, 13 wickets (25,32), 4,22 runs an over, best bowling 3 for 34 v Australia.

MARK RUSHMERE. Once Andrew Hudson became established as Kepler Wessels' opening partner, Rushmere was doomed to playing a stand-in role which he did effectively when Peter Kirsten could not play against Pakistan. Fielding several times as 12th man, Rushmere put in maximum effort and although his results were modest he made a worthwhile contribution to the team cause.

Three matches, 49 runs (16,33), strike rate 47,57, highest score 35 v Pakistan.

TERTIUS BOSCH. The powerfully built fast bowler could not have chosen worse circumstances in which to make his only appearance of the tournament, bowling just 15 balls against the rampant New Zealand batsmen in conditions which were totally unsuited to a style of bowling which is enhanced by bounce and pace off the pitch. Although unlikely to play in any other matches unless one of the other bowlers was injured, Bosch continued to make a big effort in the nets.

One match, 0 for 19 in 2,3 overs.

OMAR HENRY. After the drubbing he took in the warm-up match against the Academy XI in Adelaide, Henry was doomed to play a minor role in the World Cup, becoming a victim of a selection policy of a four-pronged pace attack. The left-arm spinner might have been useful in the match against New Zealand, but was picked instead against Sri Lanka. Although achieving respectable figures he did not bowl impressively and did not figure in the selector's plans again.

One match, 11 runs, strike rate 84,62. One wicket (31,00), 3,10 runs an over.

ALAN JORDAAN. The manager, an advocate from Pretoria, proved to be a good choice. As a former captain of Northern Transvaal and current president of the Northern Transvaal Cricket Union, he was able to put to good use his varied experience in the sport. Although he had prepared himself for a political grilling, he found instead that he had to handle mainly cricketing queries from the media. He was always accessible and cooperative. He put the interests of his players first and it is a tribute to all concerned in the team management that at the end of seven hectic, stressful weeks which involved an enormous amount of travelling, it remained a happy and united party. He handled the speech-making at official functions and did so with panache, a broad South African accent and a sense of humour.

MIKE PROCTER. The coach had been one of South Africa's greatest players and he found himself singled out by the international media for opinions and information on the South African team, thereby reducing the pressure on his captain. Procter also handled his primary task well. Practices were

GRAHAM GOOCH, born in Leytonstone on July 23, 1953, ruefully remarked after the World Cup that he had probably set a record that would never be broken by playing on the losing side in three finals, in 1979, 1987 and 1992.

Another record likely to last for a long time is that of scoring a triple century and a century (333 and 123) in a Test against India at Lord's in 1990.

The strongly built Essex opening batsman made his Test debut in 1975 and despite serving a three-year ban for joining the 1982 rebel tour of South Africa he had played in 94 Tests by the end of the 1991/92 season, scoring 7 189 runs at an average of 43,57 with 16 centuries. He had captained his country 23 times.

In 107 limited overs internationals he had scored 3 960 runs (40,00).

slickly organised, the fielding exercises were fast-moving and purposeful and he was able to get the bowlers well-drilled. He insisted on a large supply of new white balls and his 'channel school' in which the fast bowlers operated in the nets at full pace with new balls was a major reason for the team's success. His vast knowledge of top-class cricket and his many years of experience of limited overs cricket were priceless assets.

The South African players had already switched their attention to the West Indies tour and had a net practice with red balls on the morning of the World Cup final. Although they were all invited to the final, several players – including Wessels – chose not to go, which is not an uncommon trait in sportsmen, who prefer to be part of the action rather than to be spectators.

Pakistan's late flourish and four-match winning streak had sounded warning bells but England were the overwhelming favourites of most experts. Their team had great depth in batting and impressive experience in limited overs matches. It was Pakistan's first appearance in a World Cup final, but it was England's third final. They had, however, failed to negotiate the last step on both previous occasions, against the West Indies in 1979 and Australia in 1987.

The final was given some extra spice for Australians on the night before the match when Graham Gooch and Ian Botham walked out of the pre-final banquet in protest at what they considered an insulting cabaret performance by a local comedian who lampooned the Queen.

With republican sentiment running high in Australia, Botham had already unleashed the jingoistic excesses of the British tabloid newspapers when he had played a starring role in England's round robin win over Australia. Always a showman, Botham had claimed this earlier victory for Queen and Country following alleged breaches of protocol by Australian Prime Minister Paul Keating during a visit by the queen to Australia shortly before the World Cup. This latest demonstration of offended patriotism would do no harm to his already high standing with the painted hordes of England supporters in their pale blue replica England shirts.

Following the controversy of the semi-final in Sydney the World Cup needed to finish on a high note. There had been some concern that there might be showers on the night of the final, but the weather could not have been kinder, with clear blue skies being followed by a perfect sunset and balmy evening. With most of the tickets pre-sold, a big crowd in the huge stadium was guaranteed.

England brought back Derek Pringle – recovered from the rib injury that kept him out of the semi-final – into their team to strengthen the bowling. This meant no place for Gladstone Small, while Robin Smith was bitterly disappointed not to be picked despite believing he had recovered from the back injury which had sidelined him the previous weekend.

Pakistan made one change from their winning semi-final team, with allrounder Ijaz Ahmed replacing legspinner Iqbal Sikander who had been expensive against New Zealand.

Steve Bucknor, the tall Jamaican representing the West Indies, and Brian Aldridge of New Zealand were selected to stand in the final. Bucknor, amiable yet imposing, had stood out as the most impressive umpire of the World Cup but South Africans were less impressed by Aldridge, who had made mistakes in the games he had handled involving them.

Imran Khan won the toss and decided to bat in perfect conditions. The early stages of the Pakistan innings were far from impressive with Derek Pringle keeping a tight rein on the batsmen and dismissing both openers, Aamir Sohail and Rameez Raja.

Imran and Javed Miandad then batted as though they were playing in a five-day Test. Only 10 runs came in the first eight overs of their partnership, of which seven were extras.

Imran finally signified more aggressive intentions when he lofted Botham over mid-off for four but soon afterwards he was dropped by Gooch, running from square leg to midwicket and failing to hold what would have been a magnificent catch off DeFreitas. Gradually the two most experienced players in the Pakistan team – and the only two men from any country to have played in all five World Cups – lifted the tempo. After 20 overs of the innings the total was only 49 and although this was

IMRAN KHAN, born in Lahore on November 25, 1952, attended Oxford University after completing his schooling in Pakistan, winning three 'blues'. He had already made his first-class debut for Lahore at the age of 17 and had toured England with the Pakistan team as an 18-year-old.

Imran, who played county cricket for Worcestershire and Sussex, developed from an allrounder who bowled medium-pace into a genuine fast bowler who was especially feared for his fast yorker before his bowling was slowed by advancing age.

It was as a captain that Imran made the biggest impact at the World Cup, hand-picking his young team and nurturing them through a discouraging start to their campaign.

By the end of the 1991/92 season he had scored 3 807 runs in 88 Tests at an average of 37,69 and taken 362 wickets (22,81).

In 175 limited overs internationals he had scored 3 709 runs (33,41) and taken 182 wickets (26,63).

increased to 96 after 30 Pakistan did not seem likely to set any sort of challenging target.

Imran lifted Illingworth imperiously for six over long-on, and there was a profitable 12-run over against Reeve in which Javed pulled a short ball for four and Imran leg-glanced a boundary.

Both batsmen drove Lewis for boundaries in the 39th over, which yielded 13 runs before Javed, not for the first time, assayed a reverse sweep against Illingworth and popped the ball gently to point, or what was square leg to the left-hander that Javed's stroke turned him into.

The tall Inzamam came in and was on the attack immediately, slashing Illingworth for four, then hammering Botham away to square leg followed by a cut wide of the wicketkeeper, both strokes being worth four runs.

Imran, having batted for almost 40 of the 50 overs, was finally out for 72, hitting high to long-on, but Inzamam and Wasim Akram launched into a late assault. Altogether 153 runs were scored in the last 20 overs, and England had a fight on their hands.

Wasim Akram, having scored his 33 runs off only 19 balls, came charging in to bowl as fast and as aggressively as he could. The big left-hander had already set a tournament high of 32 wides, and he bowled two more in his first over as well as conceding three runs to a Gooch square cut.

Aaqib Javed bowled a tight maiden over to Gooch, Wasim bowled another wide, and then produced a superb delivery which lifted and seamed away from Botham. The England allrounder was given out caught behind for a duck by umpire Aldridge, which delighted many of the Australians in the huge crowd. Botham was less pleased, clearly believing he had not touched the ball, and television replays showed he may have had a point.

Wasim led an appeal that was more of a wild celebration than a query about a caught behind decision, but Stewart survived, only to fall in the same way in the next over to the steady Aaqib, only 19 but a mature and accurate bowler.

Gooch and Hick tried to dig their team out of trouble and

back into contention and had taken the total to 59 before Hick was deceived by a classic googly from the legspinner Mushtaq Ahmed and trapped palpably leg before wicket.

In Mushtaq's next over Gooch went on the sweep against the spin and skied the ball to deep square leg where Aaqib held the catch. At 69 for 4 in the 21st over England were in disarray.

Mushtaq, a short, jaunty figure, was one of Imran's personal selections. Imran has always been a supporter of legspinners, with Abdul Qadir having been one of his principal lieutenants for many seasons, and Mushtaq fits Imran's requirements by having a fighting spirit.

Imran, who portrayed himself as a man of almost visionary powers of talent-spotting, selection and strategy, was adamant after the match that old-fashioned cricket virtues are still the most effective. The best way of stopping a man from scoring is to bowl him out.

'Wasim is, I've always maintained, the most talented cricketer in the world. Waqar Younis might even be a shade quicker, a shade more consistent, but Wasim, when he is on song, there is no bowler like him,' said Imran. 'And, really, to make him bowl medium-pace would be stupid. We only had two bowlers to play with, Mushtaq and Wasim, and Mushtaq, when we first came here, was bowling so badly we almost sent him back. So we never wanted Wasim to bowl medium-pace line and length. And Mushtaq is a tenacious little fighter, and that's why I adore him. I know whenever I give him the ball, he never rates anyone, he just puts it there.'

Wasim came back in mid-innings to rip out the heart of the rest of England's resistance. Allan Lamb was bowled by an inswinger which straightened past the outside edge of the bat, and Chris Lewis went next ball to one which snaked back from outside the offstrump.

Fairbrother found himself virtually a man alone. He scored 62 off 70 balls but had to keep charging. He mistimed a pull and wicketkeeper Moin Khan scampered to square leg to take the catch.

Such was Imran's confidence that Mushtaq, after taking 2 for 29 in eight overs, came back in the 44th over and undid yet

Disappointed England players wait to receive their runners-up medals.

another Englishman, Dermot Reeve, skying the ball to cover.

Although England batted down to number 11 their chance had gone. The eventual margin of 22 runs may look relatively close in the record books but in truth they were never in the match after Mushtaq's double strike against Hick and Gooch.

Wasim Akram, though, had been the dominant performer and he deservedly won the Man of the Match award.

For Pakistan there was joyful celebration. Unlike England they only had a handful of supporters at the game, but they all seemed to find their way across the road to the Hilton hotel afterwards, waving flags and chanting delightedly in the driveway and cramming the foyer, waiting for a glimpse of their returning heroes.

It was a remarkable triumph for a team that revolved around their aristocratic and autocratic captain. The 39-year-old Imran claimed the credit for the victory and probably deserved it. As he explained it, Pakistani domestic cricket is in a mess. There is no strong regional competition and first-class cricket revolves around teams representing banks or other commercial organisations. Without his intervention, he believes, fighters like Moin Khan and Mushtaq Ahmed would not be playing first-class cricket, let alone representing their country.

He blamed their poor form in the warm-up phase and the early World Cup matches on the lack of competitive cricket at home. 'These boys can only learn how to play good cricket when they are on an international tour.' On the evidence of the World Cup final, they had learnt their lessons well.

World Cup Final ENGLAND v PAKISTAN
Melbourne Cricket Ground, March 25
Toss won by Imran Khan

PAKISTAN	Runs	4	6	Min	Balls
Aamir Sohail c Stewart b Pringle	4	–	–	20	19
(beaten outside offstump)					
Rameez Raja lbw b Pringle	8	1	–	36	26
(played across line)					
Imran Khan c Illingworth b Botham	72	5	1	169	115
(lofted to long-on)					
Javed Miandad c Botham b Illingworth	58	4	–	125	98
(skied reverse sweep to point)					
Inzamam-ul-Haq b Pringle	42	4	–	46	35
(going for big hit)					
Wasim Akram run out	33	4	–	31	19
(going for run off last ball)					
Salim Malik not out	0	–	–	1	1

Ijaz Ahmed, Moin Khan, Mushtaq Ahmed and Aaqib Javed did not bat

Extras (19lb, 7nb, 6w) 32
Total (6 wickets, 50 overs) 249

Falls: 1/20 (Sohail), 2/24 (Raja), 3/163 (Miandad), 4/197 (Imran), 5/249 (Inzamam), 6/249 (Wasim)

Bowling: Pringle 10-2-22-3 (5nb, 3w), Lewis 10-2-52-0 (2nb, 1w), Botham 7-0-42-0 (1w), DeFreitas 10-1-42-0, Illingworth 10-0-50-1, Reeve 3-0-22-0 (1w).

ENGLAND	Runs	4	6	Min	Balls
G Gooch c Aaqib b Mushtaq Ahmed	29	1	–	93	66
(skied sweep to deep square leg)					
I Botham c Moin Khan b Aaqib Javed	0	–	–	12	6
(ball lifted and seamed)					

A Stewart c Moin Khan b Wasim Akram *(playing outside offstump)*	7	1	–	22	16
G Hick lbw b Mushtaq Ahmed *(trapped by googly)*	17	1	–	41	36
N Fairbrother c Moin Khan b Aaqib Javed *(mistimed pull, wicketkeeper to square leg)*	62	3	–	97	70
A Lamb b Wasim Akram *(ball swung in, straightened off seam)*	31	2	–	54	41
C Lewis b Wasim Akram *(ball cut back off seam)*	0	–	–	1	1
D Reeve c Rameez Raja b Mushtaq Ahmed *(running back at deep cover)*	15	–	–	38	32
D Pringle not out	19	1	–	29	16
P DeFreitas run out (Malik/Moin Khan) *(throw from deep square leg)*	10	–	–	13	8
R Illingworth c Rameez Raja b Imran *(drove to mid-off)*	13	2	–	9	11
Extras (5lb, 6nb, 13w)	24				
Total (all out, 49,2 overs)	227				

Falls: 1/6 (Botham), 2/21 (Stewart), 3/59 (Hick), 4/69 (Gooch), 5/141 (Lamb), 6/141 (Lewis), 7/180 (Fairbrother), 8/183 (Reeve), 9/208 (DeFreitas).
Bowling: Wasim Akram 10-0-49-3 (4nb, 6w), Aaqib Javed 10-2-27-2 (1nb, 3w), Mushtaq Ahmed 10-1-41-3 (1w), Ijaz Ahmed 3-0-13-0 (2w), Imran Khan 6,2-0-43-1 (1nb), Aamir Sohail 10-0-49-0 (1w).

Pakistan won by 22 runs.
Man of the Match: Wasim Akram. Crowd: 87 182.

West Indian elation and 'high fives' as a South African wicket falls in the Test in Bridgetown.

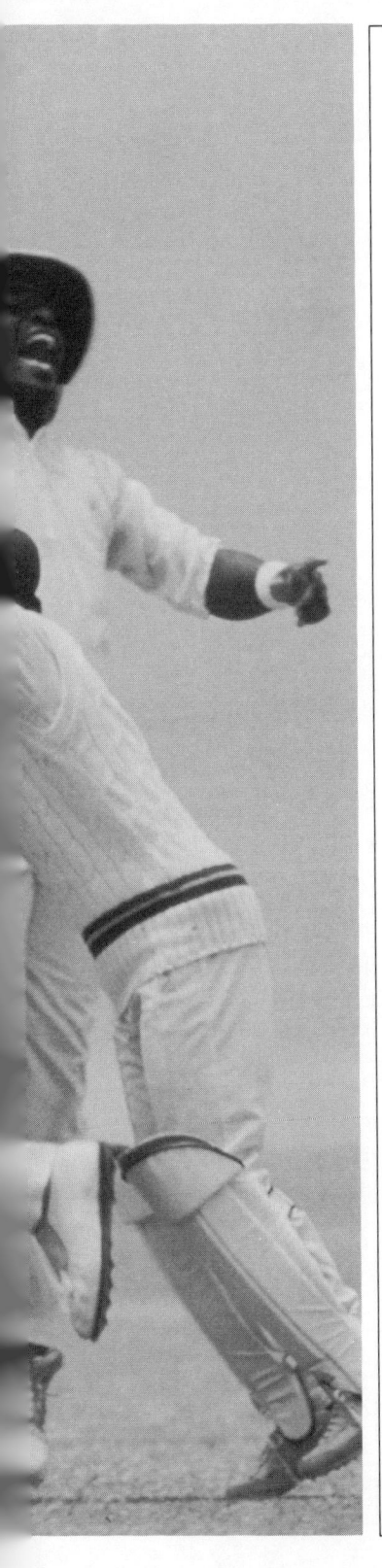

CHAPTER TWELVE

CARIBBEAN SUNSET

The West Indies Cricket Board of Control had been the only ICC full member to abstain from voting in favour of South Africa's admission to the world body in July 1991, and had opposed South Africa's participation in the World Cup. This was despite a conference of Caribbean heads of state signifying their approval of cricket contacts because of the positive view of the African National Congress.

The cricket situation was more complicated than a simple matter of getting political approval. The board comprises six member associations spread over a vast area of the Caribbean Sea – Barbados, Guyana, Jamaica, Trinidad and Tobago, the Windward Islands and the Leeward Islands, the latter two each representing a number of islands.

The board only meets twice a year and Clyde Walcott, the WICBC president who headed their delegation to the ICC, told the South Africans he could not commit his board without a proper mandate. The contacts between the South Africans and the former great West Indian batsman were to prove valuable in the near future, however, as were meetings with the executive secretary of the WICBC, Steve Camacho.

Deryck Murray, the former West Indian wicketkeeper who managed the team at the World Cup, explained to Ali Bacher: 'West Indians identify very strongly with the struggle against apartheid. It is a major issue in the Caribbean.' It was therefore of paramount importance that the United Cricket Board of South Africa establish a working relationship with the West Indians as soon as possible.

Walcott and Camacho were invited to visit South Africa in

January 1992 and gained the approval of their board to negotiate 'future contacts at all levels' between the WICBC and the UCB. The West Indian pair visited black townships, as had many other international cricketing figures, most of whom had been gushingly enthusiastic about the development programme. Walcott, though, made possibly the most realistic assessment of the situation. 'I am very impressed with the genuine efforts that are being made,' he said, 'but you are going to need a lot of help. We in the West Indies produce cricketers from similar environments but cricket is the sport that most youngsters want to play, whereas soccer is the most popular sport here and these youngsters have to be introduced to the game.'

Walcott and Camacho met the executive of the UCB in Johannesburg and extended an invitation for South Africa to make a short tour of the Caribbean within a week of the end of the World Cup. In addition to the national side, an under-19 team representing the development programme would play matches against West Indian youngsters. South Africa would undertake to find sponsorship for the venture and in return the West Indies would visit South Africa in February 1993 for a series of one-day internationals.

Finding sponsorship was no easy task. Live television coverage was essential to attract a sponsor but the West Indian islands did not have the facilities. A television crew would have to be imported from Miami in the United States with all their equipment. It pushed the total cost of the venture to R5 million, a huge amount for a four-match tour. Without sponsorship the tour would not take place.

Dr Bacher regarded early playing links with the West Indies as a vital piece in completing the jigsaw of South Africa's return to international cricket. Interest in cricket among black South Africans, he reasoned, would receive a huge impetus from exposure to the skills of the West Indian stars, many of whom had risen from humble beginnings to become international celebrities. In the townships, he reasoned, there must be hundreds if not thousands of potential Curtly Ambroses and Richie Richardsons.

Sabina Park in Kingston, scene of the first one-day international.

The South African team left for the World Cup with no finality having been reached on a West Indian tour and it was only midway through the tournament that Dr Bacher announced that a deal had been done with BP Southern Africa who would 'support' the tour.

South Africa would play a one-day international in Jamaica, two one-day games in Trinidad and, the cherry on the top, a five-day official Test at the Kensington Oval in Bridgetown, Barbados.

For the cricketers, the timing was far from ideal, especially as no warm-up matches were scheduled, but it was an exciting challenge.

Although the selectors named an unchanged squad, the team suffered a serious blow just three days before departure when Brian McMillan, who appeared to be the only man with the qualities of a genuine Test-class allrounder, withdrew because of the Achilles tendon injury which had plagued him through the second half of the World Cup.

Corrie van Zyl of Free State was selected in McMillan's place, but despite having hit a maiden first-class century during

Brian Lara, who continued his World Cup form in the series against South Africa.

the domestic season, he could not be regarded as anything more than a steady seam bowler who could bat reasonably well. Would the selectors have picked Clive Rice if he had been playing until the end of the season? Despite his controversial public statements, Rice would have been the most logical replacement for an allrounder, but having missed selection for the World Cup, the former captain had joined the Australian Channel Nine television commentary team and had therefore disqualified himself from selection by not having played cricket for more than six weeks.

Ever resourceful, Dr Bacher persuaded South African Airways to reschedule a flight to New York to stop in

Kingston, Jamaica, and for an inward flight from New York to collect the touring party in Barbados.

Barely a week after returning from Australia and two days after the domestic Benson and Hedges Series final, in which both Kepler Wessels and Adrian Kuiper had hit centuries, the South African cricket circus gathered again at Jan Smuts airport. Because of a bomb scare, presumably initiated by the Pan Africanist Congress, which remained opposed to any relaxation of sanctions against South Africa, all luggage had to be searched before a check-in which was so chaotic that couples were told they could not sit together because the flight was full, only to find numerous empty seats on board. SAA did not appear to have catered for the extra stop, because even light eaters arrived hungry in Kingston, and the unhelpful attitude of the cabin staff indicated they were not happy with having to work a longer than usual shift from the mid-Atlantic stop in Ilha do Sal. The passengers in the row behind me were headed for New York and had only been told about the diversion to Kingston a week earlier although the extra touch-down had been planned for more than a month. The flight would eventually arrive in New York some six hours later than usual.

The irritations of the flight were quickly forgotten in Kingston, where local officials were on the tarmac to meet the first South African cricket party to arrive in the West Indies. The weather was warm and in the terminal building a television screen was showing a recording of the World Cup match between South Africa and the West Indies.

Players, officials, supporters and media were loaded on to buses and escorted by police motorcycles to two adjoining hotels in uptown Kingston, an area of relative modernity in a city dominated by decaying buildings, shanties, narrow streets and ancient vehicles. Although the air of poverty was not as depressingly pervasive as in Calcutta, the general appearance of the poorer areas, and in particular the way in which people gathered on the streets and traded from makeshift stalls, was reminiscent of the Indian city – or a South African township such as Alexandra. Although Kingston, on the southern coast of Jamaica, has been immortalised in song by Harry Belafonte and was the home of reggae king Bob Marley, it is essentially a port and commercial centre. Such tourist areas as exist in the vicinity – for example Port Royal, once the headquarters of Henry Morgan and known as 'the wickedest city on earth' – are neglected and run-down. The north coast boasts white-sanded beaches and tourist resorts such as Montego Bay, Ocho Rios and the wondrous Dunn's River Falls, 200 metres of natural limestone steps which climbers can ascend from the beach to the top through cascading water.

There were no such diversions for the players, however. Within hours of arrival they had their first look at the famed Sabina Park, where Gary Sobers made a world record Test score of 365 against Pakistan in 1958 and was partnered in a West Indian record stand of 446 by Conrad Hunte, who made 260. Hunte was now travelling with the South African development squad, having spent the previous six months assisting in the township development programme. The second highest Test score for the West Indies, 302, had been made in Bridgetown by Lawrence Rowe against New Zealand in 1972. Rowe led the West Indian rebel teams in South Africa in 1982/83 and 1983/84.

Sabina Park, in a built-up area between uptown and the slums of Trench Town, is behind drab concrete walls. It has been enlarged and upgraded since the feats of Sobers and Hunte. The relatively new George Headley stand at the southern end of the ground and a stately though faded Kingston Cricket Club pavilion on the western side provide spectators with comfortable accommodation. High fencing surrounds the playing area, giving the low grandstand on the eastern side the appearance of a cage, while spectators stand amid piles of rubble at the northern end. Lord's or the Sydney Cricket Ground it is not. The pitch must have revived memories of India for the bowlers as they contemplated a surface of hard, bare earth – although the time-honoured test of throwing a ball against the surface revealed reasonable bounce. The outfield was hard and bumpy.

Back at the team's comfortable Pegasus hotel, the first press conference of the tour provided early confirmation that apart-

Queens Park Oval in Port of Spain, Trinidad.

heid was an important issue in the West Indies. Several questions related to the political situation, but the UCB had done its homework. In attendance was Tebogo Mafole, the ANC representative at the United Nations, who had flown from New York to join the touring party. He assured journalists that the ANC backed the tour, as indeed had the former Prime Minister Michael Manley, who was a guest at the opening one-day international on Tuesday, April 7.

Surprisingly, South Africa omitted Meyrick Pringle, who had taken 4 for 11 and was Man of the Match in the win over the West Indies in Christchurch, from the team for the first match.

All three one-day games were to be depressingly one-sided from a South African viewpoint, but South Africa enjoyed an early success after Wessels had sent the West Indies in. Desmond Haynes, the only man to have scored 7 000 runs in limited overs international matches, clipped Donald off his toes and Omar Henry picked up a smart catch at square leg.

The left-handed Brian Lara played delightfully to score a half-century before becoming frustrated after losing the strike and not scoring for two overs, going down the wicket to Henry and lofting a catch to Wessels at mid-on. This brought the West Indian captain Richie Richardson to the crease amid an astonishing chorus of boos which continued throughout his innings. The poor performance of the West Indies in the World Cup had been the subject of much criticism in the Caribbean and some reaction was inevitable, but experienced West Indian commentators said they had never heard such antagonism towards a home captain. When I asked spectators why they were so vehement, I was told that Richardson had to take the blame for the West Indies going to the World Cup without Vivian Richards and Gordon Greenidge, and in particular for the omission of the Jamaican wicketkeeper and strokeplayer Jeffrey Dujon.

To his credit Richardson played a sound innings of 30 after surviving an early and confident appeal for lbw by Donald, who had the rare experience of being loudly supported by thousands of Jamaicans. The match, however, belonged to the tall right-hander Phil Simmons, who ripped into the South African bowlers. After reaching 30 in relatively sedate style, Simmons lashed a huge six over long-on off Henry. The ball bounced on the roof of the media centre, which is some five storeys high, and bounced into the street where it was retrieved by a small boy. Seizing his opportunity, the youth demanded to be allowed into the ground in exchange for the ball. The gateman refused this quite reasonable request and the boy decided to take his trophy, disappearing into the back streets pursued by security men. Simmons had no more mercy on the replacement ball as he reached 50 off 67 balls with another six over long-on off Henry, and then raced to his second 50 off only 31 deliveries, hitting blows of such power that it seemed Sabina Park had suddenly shrunk in size. Corrie van Zyl, who earlier had bowled tidily, went for 17 in one over including an awesome drive over long-off for six.

West Indies, who had scored a respectable 107 runs off the first 25 overs of the innings, added another 180 off the next 25 to set South Africa a target of 288, the same as they had needed against India in New Delhi, but against bowlers of far greater quality. The early run out of Kepler Wessels started South

RICHIE RICHARDSON, born in Antigua on January 12, 1962, played in his first Test a year after making his debut for the Leeward Islands in 1982. He took over the captaincy of Leeward Islands from his fellow Antiguan Viv Richards in 1990 before being appointed West Indian captain for the World Cup in 1992.

Having inherited the legacy of successful captains such as Clive Lloyd and Richards he always faced a difficult task. With West Indies having failed to reach the semi-finals he was booed when he led the team in the one-day international against South Africa in Kingston, Jamaica, although crowds in Trinidad and Barbados applauded.

Richardson is a free-scoring top-order batsman who took his Test total to 4 693 runs (47,40) during the match against South Africa, his 63rd Test. This included 14 centuries with a highest score of 194 against India in Georgetown in 1989. His limited overs record stood at 4 016 runs (34,90) from 160 matches.

Africa on a slide from which they were never likely to recover despite a polished 50 by Andrew Hudson and a fighting 42 by Hansie Cronje.

Victory by 107 runs was pleasing for the Jamaican fans, but they nevertheless booed both Richardson and the tiny wicket-keeper David Williams, who had replaced their own man Dujon, at every opportunity. Afterwards Richardson was philosophical. 'It just makes me stronger,' he said. 'Even though they boo me, I will do my best for them (the crowd) and for West Indies cricket.'

FIRST ONE-DAY INTERNATIONAL
Sabina Park, Kingston, Jamaica, April 7
Toss won by Kepler Wessels

WEST INDIES	Runs	4	6	Min	Balls
D Haynes c Henry b Donald	9	–	–	30	27
(clipped to backward square leg)					
B Lara c Wessels b Henry	50	4	–	97	68
(down wicket, mistimed to mid-on)					
P Simmons c Wessels b Kuiper	122	12	5	148	109
(hit wide ball to extra cover)					
R Richardson lbw b Kuiper	30	–	–	66	46
(cutting at ball which seamed in)					
K Arthurton c Wessels b Donald	27	1	–	27	26
(lofted to mid-on)					
C Hooper not out	19	–	–	32	18
W Benjamin c Wessels b Kuiper	8	1	–	3	5
(mistimed to midwicket)					
C Ambrose not out	0	–	–	1	0

A Cummins, P Patterson did not bat
Extras (1b, 5lb, 4nb, 12w)   22
Total (6 wickets, 50 overs)   287
Falls: 1/32 (Haynes), 2/104 (Lara), 3/209 (Richardson), 4/238 (Simmons), 5/277 (Arthurton), 6/286 (Benjamin)
Bowling: Donald 10-1-47-2 (3nb, 5w), Snell 10-1-56-0 (1nb, 3w), Van Zyl 8-2-53-0 (3w), Henry 10-0-53-1, Cronje 3-0-18-0, Kirsten 4-0-21-0, Kuiper 5-0-33-3 (1w).

SOUTH AFRICA	Runs	4	6	Min	Balls
A Hudson c and b Patterson	50	5	–	91	69
(driving, right-handed catch)					
K Wessels run out	8	1	–	24	17
(Lara/Williams)					
(Hudson played to cover)					
P Kirsten c Lara b Patterson	15	2	–	71	38
(drove to cover)					
A Kuiper st Williams b Hooper	15	–	–	39	26
(lost balance, playing forward)					
H Cronje b Cummins	42	–	1	81	54
(stepping away to cut)					
J Rhodes b Cummins	17	1	–	23	16
(played on, driving)					
R Snell run out	1	–	–	2	2
(Hooper)					
(direct hit from gully)					
D Richardson c Arthurton b Benjamin	5	–	–	6	8
(hooked to deep square leg)					
C van Zyl c Ambrose b Benjamin	0	–	–	9	9
(mistimed pull, looped to mid-off)					
O Henry b Benjamin	1	–	–	7	3
(missed pull)					
A Donald not out	5	–	1	2	3
Extras (8lb, 3nb, 10w)	21				
Total (all out, 42,2 overs)	180				

Falls: 1/10 (Wessels), 2/79 (Hudson), 3/82 (Kirsten), 4/121 (Kuiper), 5/153 (Rhodes), 6/155 (Snell), 7/161 (Richardson), 8/169 (Van Zyl), 9/174 (Cronje).
Bowling: Ambrose 7-1-20-0 (1nb), Patterson 7-2-17-2 (1nb, 2w), Benjamin 9,2-0-45-3 (1w), Cummins 9-0-34-2 (1nb, 2w), Hooper 8-0-44-1 (1w), Simmons 2-0-12-0 (4w).

West Indies won by 107 runs.
Man of the Match: Phil Simmons. Crowd: 10 000.

Both teams embarked the next day for Port of Spain, Trinidad. The British West Indian airways flight was due to land at three islands on a cross-Caribbean haul that would last almost six hours. Almost immediately after taking off, an hour late, the aircraft lost height and banked right as the captain announced that a heat warning light had come on and it was therefore necessary to return to Kingston. This done, the flight was delayed by another two hours. All ended well as the flight was re-scheduled direct to Port of Spain and landed safely two-and-a-half hours after passengers had anxiously held their breath while the aircraft took off for the second time. Because the intermediate stops had been cancelled the flight actually landed slightly ahead of schedule in Port of Spain.

Trinidad is a lively and friendly melting pot of nationalities. Roads and other infrastructures are well-developed because Trinidad is an oil exporter and enjoyed a boom when the oil price was high in the 1970s. The focal point of Port of Spain is the Savannah, a vast expanse of open parkland, on the edge of which the Hilton hotel sprawls around a hillside. Beyond the far end of the Savannah is the Queens Park Oval, venue of successive matches on Saturday and Sunday.

Queens Park Oval is a vibrant cricket venue. With a capacity of 25 000, it is the largest cricket stadium in the Caribbean and its two- and three-tiered grandstands were packed long before the first ball was bowled on Saturday. Underneath the popular stands next to the Press box a virtual village of activities had sprung up, with food stalls, ice-cream vendors and gambling tables. Strong-lunged men blew into conch shells to keep up a constant level of noise, while a drummer somewhere in the stand beat out a steady rhythm. For all its charm, however, Queens Park was not to be a happy venue for South Africa.

The Saturday match was embarrassingly one-sided despite Ambrose's opening over yielding 13 runs, including four leg byes, four wides, a single by Wessels and finally a sweetly timed on-drive for four by Hudson. But Wessels was caught, cutting rashly at Ambrose and Hudson was run out by a brilliant piece of fielding by Simmons, fielding at deep gully, who stopped a flashing cut and threw down the stumps with Hudson having ventured out of his ground.

Kirsten cut at Anderson Cummins and the ball flew high but straight into the hands of Winston Benjamin on the third man boundary. Hansie Cronje looked promising but was needlessly run out, while Adrian Kuiper struggled to score 19 singles off 64 balls. The only highlight for South Africa was a valiant innings of 45 by Jonty Rhodes before he was run out by a direct hit from Keith Arthurton, who achieved a level of fielding at coverpoint that Rhodes himself could not better.

A target of 153 was no challenge to the West Indians, but in the best Caribbean tradition Lara and Haynes took their team to a 10-wicket victory with rollicking strokeplay rather than measured caution. Lara, a member of the Queens Park club and playing his first international match in front of his own supporters, was in magnificent form and fully justified the slogan 'Lara the Best' printed on cards waved by joyful spectators around the ground.

SECOND ONE-DAY INTERNATIONAL
Queens Park Oval, Port of Spain, Trinidad, April 11
Toss won by Richie Richardson

SOUTH AFRICA	Runs	4	6	Min	Balls
A Hudson run out	6	1	–	36	26
(Simmons)					
(direct hit from deep gully)					
K Wessels c Williams b Ambrose	1	–	–	14	9
(flashing at short ball)					
P Kirsten c Benjamin b Cummins	9	1	–	39	23
(cut to deep third man)					
A Kuiper c Lara b Harper	19	–	–	94	64
(off toes to square leg)					
H Cronje run out	22	4	–	34	30
(Richardson/Harper)					
(midwicket to bowler's end)					
J Rhodes run out	45	5	–	85	71
(Arthurton)					
(direct hit from cover)					

D Richardson c Arthurton b Cummins	6	–	–	18	15
(drove to cover)					
R Snell c Arthurton b Cummins	8	–	–	16	10
(drove to cover)					
O Henry not out	8	1	–	22	10
M Pringle b Ambrose	1	–	–	6	4
(yorked)					
A Donald b Ambrose	0	–	–	2	2
(beaten by pace)					
Extras (10lb, 2nb, 15w)	27				
Total (all out, 43.4 overs)	152				

Falls: 1/17 (Wessels), 2/24 (Hudson), 3/36 (Kirsten), 4/67 (Cronje), 5/98 (Kuiper), 6/118 (Richardson), 7/138 (Snell), 8/146 (Rhodes), 9/152 (Pringle).
Bowling: Ambrose 7.4-0-24-3 (7w), Patterson 9-2-30-0 (3w), Cummins 9-0-40-3 (3w), Benjamin 8-1-21-0 (2nb, 2w), Harper 10-0-28-1.

WEST INDIES	Runs	4	6	Min	Balls
D Haynes not out	59	7	1	115	71
B Lara not out	86	13	2	115	91
P Simmons, R Richardson,					
K Arthurton, R Harper,					
D Williams, W Benjamin,					
C Ambrose, A Cummins and					
P Patterson did not bat					
Extras (1b, 1lb, 5nb, 2w)	9				
Total (no wickets, 25.5 overs)	154				

Bowling: Donald 8-1-49-0 (3nb), Pringle 7-0-32-0 (1nb), Henry 4.5-0-41-0, Snell 6-0-30-0 (1nb, 2w)

West Indies won by 10 wickets.
Man of the Match: Brian Lara. Crowd: 22 000.

Richardson won the toss for the second time on Sunday and sent South Africa in. Although the tourists performed better, scoring 189 for 6 off 50 overs, they were clearly more intent on preparing for the next week's Test match than on making a major effort to prevent a West Indian clean sweep. Allan Donald was given a much-needed rest, Jonty Rhodes did not play because of a thigh strain and Mark Rushmere and Tertius Bosch were both brought into the side in anticipation of their selection for the Test.

There was a rare moment of delight for the South Africans when Haynes was beaten and bowled by the first ball of the West Indian innings, a Meyrick Pringle away-swinger. But the home town favourites, Lara and Simmons, both surviving confident lbw appeals early on, put the team back on target for victory. Lara was out for 35 but Simmons, after a much slower start, re-found his Jamaican form. After reaching 50 from 103 balls, he needed only 32 more for his second 50 as he launched into a repeat of his big-hitting feats at Sabina Park. The major sufferer was Bosch, caned for 21 in one over and 9 in his next.

Apart from suffering three humiliating defeats, South Africa had a major injury worry. Pringle had been unable to bowl again because of a rib cartilage injury suffered in a collision with his teammate Richard Snell while swimming.

THIRD ONE-DAY INTERNATIONAL
Queens Park Oval, Port of Spain, April 12
Toss won by Richie Richardson

SOUTH AFRICA	Runs	4	6	Min	Balls
A Hudson c Williams b Harper *(flashing at off-spinner)*	30	4	–	72	54
M Rushmere c and b Harper *(down wicket, mistimed drive)*	29	2	–	94	71
K Wessels b Benjamin *(trying to force off back foot)*	45	3	–	101	77
P Kirsten c Harper b Benjamin *(drove to cover)*	28	2	–	66	50
A Kuiper c Richardson b Patterson *(skied to mid-on)*	2	–	–	7	5

H Cronje run out (Benjamin)	23	–	1	31	23
(bowler following up, direct hit)					
D Richardson not out	17	–	–	28	18
C van Zyl not out	3	–	–	3	2

M Pringle and T Bosch did not bat
Extras (8lb, 1nb, 3w) 12
Total (6 wickets, 50 overs) 189
Falls: 1/54 (Hudson), 2/67 (Rushmere), 3/135 (Kirsten), 4/139 (Kuiper), 5/142 (Wessels), 6/185 (Cronje).
Bowling: Ambrose 10-1-39-0 (1w), Patterson 10-2-35-1 (1nb), Benjamin 10-1-37-2 (2w), Cummins 10-0-39-0, Harper 10-0-31-2.

WEST INDIES	Runs	4	6	Min	Balls
D Haynes b Pringle	0	–	–	1	1
(beaten by away-swinger)					
B Lara c Pringle b Kuiper	35	4	–	105	73
(drove to mid-off)					
P Simmons c Cronje b Snell	104	10	2	173	139
(lofted to deep mid wicket)					
R Richardson not out	37	2	–	72	44
K Arthurton not out	1	–	–	3	4

R Harper, D Williams, W Benjamin, C Ambrose, A Cummins and P Patterson did not bat
Extras (7lb, 2nb, 4w) 13
Total (3 wickets, 43 overs) 190
Falls: 1/0 (Haynes), 2/78 (Lara), 3/182 (Simmons).
Bowling: Pringle 5-3-6-1 (1w), Bosch 6-0-47-0 (2nb), Snell 10-2-45-1 (2w), Van Zyl 10-0-40-0, Kuiper 7-0-28-1 (1w), Kirsten 5-0-17-0.

West Indies won by seven wickets.
Man of the match: Phil Simmons. Crowd: 13 000.

Mark Rushmere and Andrew Hudson walk out to start their first innings in Test cricket.

CHAPTER THIRTEEN

THE ULTIMATE CHALLENGE

There is a special magic about Barbados for anyone with a sense of cricket history. For a start, there is an extra sense of anticipation flying in to Grantley Adams international airport, on an island so small that passengers can see the sea surrounding all sides of what is one of the most remarkable breeding grounds for cricket players in the world.

This tiny speck of land, just 33 km by 23 km, has produced some of the greatest cricketers of all time, from the Three Ws, Everton Weekes, Clyde Walcott and Sir Frank Worrell, through Sir Garfield Sobers, Conrad Hunte and Wesley Hall, to the modern greats such as Malcolm Marshall, Gordon Greenidge and Desmond Haynes.

Every bit as impressive as the great cricketers produced by Barbados is the Test record of the West Indies at Kensington Oval in the small capital of Bridgetown. The West Indies had last tasted defeat at the Oval in 1935, and had won all their previous 10 Tests there, dating back to 1978.

It was no wonder, then, that the South African cricketers ignored the temptations of the coral-sanded beaches that have made Barbados a popular tourist destination and headed instead for the Kensington Oval and the excellent but frighteningly fast-paced practice pitches.

The South African team arrived at a time of bitter controversy. The West Indies Test team had been announced two days earlier and to the dismay of Bajan cricket lovers there was no place in the 13-man squad for Anderson Cummins, a promising 25-year-old fast bowler who had performed adequately, although not exceptionally, in the World Cup and in the one-day internationals against South Africa.

There was already unhappiness about the way in which Gordon Greenidge and Malcolm Marshall, both from Barbados, had so easily been allowed to slip out of the West Indies team, and the omission of Cummins unleashed a tidal wave of emotion. Radio talk shows were dominated by angry callers demanding a boycott of the Test.

Surprisingly, the boycott call was to prove highly effective, with no more than 6 000 spectators watching the five days of the Test. Having heard about the atmosphere created when the Kensington Oval is filled to its capacity of 12 000, it was a highly disappointing aspect of a historic occasion. Officials and journalists said the boycott was fuelled by a general political unhappiness in the island which had manifested itself in a march by 20 000 protesters some weeks earlier.

For an outsider, the cricket argument seemed to have been blown out of all logical proportion. Cummins had played in 19 one-day internationals, taking 29 wickets at an average of 23,79, which provided a solid enough argument for keeping him in the side. But he had yet to play in a Test and on the evidence of the limited overs matches did not appear to be an unusually dangerous bowler.

Another player left out of the squad that had played in the one-day games was Roger Harper, the tall off-spinner from Guyana who had given the South African batsmen plenty of problems during his two appearances.

Into the team came the Jamaican captain, Courtney Walsh, a proven Test strike bowler, and a newcomer, Kenneth Benjamin, a 24-year-old from Antigua who rejoiced in the middle names Charlie Griffith after the famous fast bowler.

As a cynical observer remarked, it would have been easy enough for the selectors, Jackie Hendriks, Irving Shillingford and David Holford, to keep Cummins in a 13-man squad and leave him out on the day of the match without provoking the ire of the public. Only one player from Barbados remained in the squad, veteran opening batsman Desmond Haynes.

S K Reddy, the only South African selector on the tour, must have enjoyed a wry chuckle if he was aware of the extent of the West Indian selection furore.

Allan Donald rips through the defences of Keith Arthurton in the second innings.

Gordon Greenidge, who had scored a double century in Barbados in the previous year's Test against Australia, had missed the subsequent tour of England because of a knee injury and had been left out of the West Indian team for the World Cup. He announced his retirement in November 1991. Viv Richards, the former captain from Antigua, whose batting genius appears to have transcended inter-island rivalries, had also been left out of the World Cup team after failing to play in the domestic first-class season, while Malcolm Marshall had played in the World Cup but had been left out of the team towards the end of the tournament ostensibly because of injury. (He denied he was injured, maintaining that he had been dropped.) He announced his retirement after the World Cup.

Without knowing the personalities involved, or the detailed background, the way in which three such senior players had been treated seemed to have parallels with the omission of Clive Rice and Jimmy Cook from the South African team and the exclusion of Peter Kirsten from the original World Cup squad of 20.

Such West Indian domestic matters were not the concern of the South African players, however. They had just three days in which to prepare for a Test match, the first of their careers for all except Wessels. Pringle's injury was a major worry and he was unable to bowl on Wednesday at the first practice. But the other fast bowlers worked at full pace and gave the top order batsmen a grilling, aided by some young local bowlers, including Victor Walcott, a Barbados senior player who looked a fine bowler. The batsmen looked far from comfortable as the ball whipped past their noses but Charlie Griffith, looking decidedly less menacing than when he was Wes Hall's new ball partner, chuckled. 'These practice pitches are much faster than the one in the middle. The bowlers won't get so much help in the Test match.'

The players attended a spectacular welcome party on a spit of land jutting into the sea, hosted by Wesley Hall in his capacity as Minister of Tourism. Cabinet ministers attended the function in addition to a galaxy of former cricket stars including Clyde Walcott, the president of the West Indies board, and the other surviving member of the Three Ws, Everton Weekes. 'I saw this elderly gentleman standing on his own, so I went up and introduced myself,' said Bradley Bing, the outgoing son of UCB board member Fritz. 'I felt embarrassed but honoured when he told me he was Everton Weekes.'

The players were back at the Kensington Oval for another intensive practice on Thursday. Pringle turned his arm over. Although the next day was Good Friday, the players had a light workout before the tour selectors announced a team which included Pringle. Left out were Omar Henry (which left the team with Peter Kirsten as the only slow bowler), Corrie van Zyl and Jonty Rhodes, whose batting was adjudged to be not yet up to the standards of discipline and concentration required for five-day cricket.

And so to the Test match on a clear, sunny day.

Any doubts about the effectiveness of the planned boycott were dispelled instantly when it was possible to park within metres of the main entrance of the Oval less than an hour before the start. Instead of an excited buzz, there were the forlorn echoes that characterise sparsely populated sports stadia.

By the time the teams were introduced to Erskine Sandiford, the Prime Minister of Barbados, there were probably

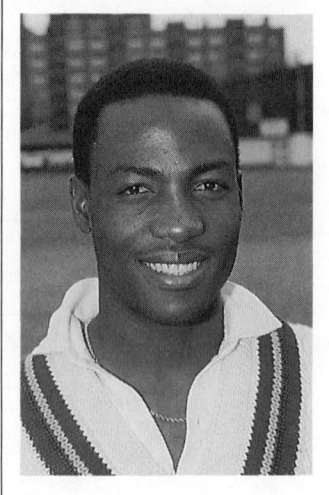

BRIAN LARA, born in Santa Cruz, Trinidad, on May 2, 1969, showed during the World Cup and the series against South Africa that he is one of the most talented young batsmen in the world. The experiment of using him as an opener worked well in the World Cup in which he scored 333 runs at an average of 47,57.

A slightly built left-hander who is quick on his feet and able to play strokes to almost any part of the ground, Lara made his first-class debut for Trinidad in 1988. A year later he made his highest score, 182, for a West Indies under 23 XI against India in St Kitts.

By the end of the series against South Africa he had already played in 27 one-day internationals, but only two Tests, despite touring Pakistan and England. The cheerful, outgoing Lara has shown leadership qualities, captaining West Indies youth to Australia in 1988 and West Indies B to Zimbabwe in 1989, although he was unsuccessful when appointed as captain of Trinidad and Tobago for one season in 1990.

1 000 spectators in the ground. By mid-afternoon the Barbados Cricket Association made what seemed an optimistic estimate that there was a crowd of 3 000.

It was nevertheless a Test match, with all the tensions that such occasions engender. In view of the reputation of the Kensington Oval pitch – lively on the first day, and then less so on the second and third days, there was relief throughout the South African camp when Wessels won the toss and sent the West Indies in. The pitch was hard and lightly grassed. A breeze blew briskly from the south and from his back as Allan Donald raced in to bowl the first ball.

Donald's opener was over-pitched and Haynes, in his 103rd Test, played it easily away to the on-side for two. The next ball was also over-pitched and Haynes despatched it briskly to the midwicket boundary across a rock-hard outfield. Athough Donald produced four better deliveries and had Haynes sparring at the last ball, it was not a good first over for South Africa.

Bosch, so often wayward, started his Test career with a maiden.

Donald produced a sharp lifter which had Haynes taking evasive action, but a ball pitched too short was hooked for four as Donald's first two overs cost 13 runs.

Bosch bowled a no-ball and was then punched through the covers for four by Haynes. After five overs the West Indies had scored 22.

The sixth over brought back nightmare memories for Bosch of his treatment in Port of Spain as Simmons, quiet until then, square cut for four, then pounded a straight drive past the bowler for another four, before tucking a loose delivery to the leg-side for three.

Pringle and Snell came into the attack and Snell was dealt with harshly in only his third over as Haynes nudged the ball past the slips for four and off-drove a no-ball for another boundary in an over which cost 12 runs.

Snell was regularly bowling too full a length and the batsmen took advantage, with Haynes cover-driving for four to raise 50 for the 53rd time in his Test career (16 half-centuries having

Kepler Wessels pulls Patrick Patterson to midwicket in the second innings.

been converted into hundreds). In the same over Simmons hit another over-pitched ball to the cover boundary. The West Indies had raced to 99 in only the 22nd over at better than a run a minute, but Simmons went on the drive again and hit a catch straight to Kirsten at wide mid-off. It had been a fine opening partnership, full of bold strokes which would not have been out of place in a limited overs game.

Snell, lifted by his success, produced a superb first delivery to the left-handed Lara, who edged it straight to Wessels at first slip. The chance went down.

Donald came back for a pre-lunch burst but was hooked for four by Haynes, who fell victim to Snell two overs later, caught by Wessels as he edged a drive.

At lunch West Indies were 114 for 2. It had been a rollicking start but both openers had been dismissed and the home team did not have a great deal of batting in their lower order.

Bosch was brought back after lunch and had Richie Richardson edging the ball short of Wessels at slip, before Lara tried to leg glance a delivery which lifted higher than expected and succeeded only in providing Dave Richardson with a spectacular catch, diving to his right.

Richie Richardson and the left-handed Arthurton settled in as the match evolved into a more cautious Test mode.

Richardson lifted the tempo again with a straight drive for four off Snell, and Arthurton, a dapper player from the small island of Nevis, unleashed two stunning cover-drives off Snell before dishing out the same treatment to Pringle.

Once again the West Indies strokeplay was in the ascendancy as Arthurton thrashed Bosch to midwicket and cover for boundaries, but the adventurous left-hander survived a difficult low chance to Andrew Hudson at point before Snell struck again. Snell's attacking full-length bowling had been expensive, but he was giving the ball the maximum opportunity to swing and it was late movement that undid Richardson, who edged a chance to his namesake behind the stumps.

From tea at 226 for 4 the West Indies subsided suddenly. Arthurton, having hit most of his 10 boundaries through the covers, tried one cover-drive too many and hit the ball hard to Kuiper to provide Pringle with his first wicket.

Wessels immediately brought Donald on from the southern end. Donald's first 16 overs had cost 62 runs without reward, but his pace was just what was needed to dislodge the tail. The tiny wicketkeeper Williams could only jab a sharply lifting ball to gully while the left-handed Jimmy Adams, making his Test debut because Carl Hooper had been injured in the nets the day before, was beaten for pace and bowled by a fierce yorker.

Benjamin was beaten and bowled by Snell before Walsh took a wild swing to be bowled by Pringle, and Patterson was run out in a mix-up with Ambrose. Seven wickets had fallen for 43 runs and Wessels had made the right decision. Snell, about to embark on a season in English county cricket, had gone, in the cynical words of an English tabloid journalist, from 'taking a hammering on his Test debut' to being 'Somerset's sensational new signing'.

Under the rules which require 90 overs to be bowled in a day, less allowances for wickets, drinks breaks and changes of innings, nine overs remained to be bowled. Mark Rushmere and Andrew Hudson could not have chosen a tougher way to launch their Test careers, but they survived to the end. Hudson was lucky to get off the mark with an awkward top edge over gully off Patterson for two but otherwise both batsmen played competently and courageously. Much more of the same would be required the next day.

First day: West Indies 262 all out. South Africa 13 for 0 in 9 overs (Rushmere 2, Hudson 9).

Light rain fell early in the morning but the second day started on time under an overcast sky.

Rushmere was out in only the second over of the day, edging a lifting ball from Ambrose to Lara at first slip.

Hudson played the first aggressive strokes of the morning, off-driving Patterson for two and then hooking a short ball for four with effortless timing. A thick edge off Ambrose flew to the boundary with no third man in place in an attacking field setting.

Courtney Walsh replaced Patterson, bowling into the wind, and took a hammering from Wessels, who pulled two fours in Walsh's first over and hit three boundaries in the lanky Jamaican's next over, with a hook, a cover-drive and a nudge to third man which took the total to 52.

Hudson had an escape on 22 when he hooked Ambrose and the luckless Walsh, making ground to his left at long-leg, allowed the chance to slip through his fingers and cross the boundary.

Wessels was in excellent form and rare attacking mood, pulling a short ball from Ambrose for four and then hooking the tall Antiguan for the only six of the match. After conceding only 10 runs in his first 10 overs, Ambrose was rested with figures of 1 for 24 from 12 overs.

With Benjamin proving to be awkward, cutting the ball in from an open-chested action, and Walsh settling into a better rhythm replacing Ambrose downwind, there were no more boundaries for almost an hour. Then Wessels reached his 50 by pulling a short ball from Arthurton, tried as a left-arm spinner, to midwicket three overs before the lunch break, which was taken at 109 for 1.

Both Wessels and Hudson hit boundaries in the same over from Patterson, with Hudson's four through the covers bring-

RICHARD SNELL, born in Durban on September 12, 1968, was singled out as an outstanding fast bowling prospect at Durban High School, playing for SA Schools in his last two years. Although he made his debut for Natal B as a 19-year-old he has played most of his first-class cricket for Transvaal since enrolling as a student at Wits University.

An amiable, seemingly casual air gives little indication of the menace of his bowling. A high arm action gains him maximum benefit from any bounce in the pitch and he is able to make the ball swing both ways.

At the age of 21 he was selected for South Africa against Mike Gatting's English team at the Wanderers and returned match figures of 6 for 66 on a pitch which helped the bowlers.

Snell's performance in his Test debut against the West Indies showed him at his best and worst. He took eight wickets by producing some excellent deliveries but the West Indies batsmen scored quickly against him because he bowled too many loose balls, in particular through over-pitching.

ing up his 50, as the partnership continued to prosper. But Ambrose made the breakthrough when Wessels steered a short ball firmly to Adams, who held the catch at deep gully. Wessels, who had made 162 on his debut for Australia against England in Brisbane nine seasons earlier, had scored 59 in his first Test innings for his country of birth.

In the next over the West Indies fluffed a chance to put the pressure firmly back on South Africa when Hudson, on 66, edged a chance to Williams' right off Patterson. Lara at first slip dived but failed to hold the rebound from the wicket-keeper's gloves.

Having survived two chances, Hudson proceeded to play almost flawlessly until tea. But there were two more blows for South Africa. Kirsten, having waited so many years for his first Test innings, seemed to have settled in when he punched Walsh through the covers off the back foot, but he tried to cut a ball too close to his body and presented Benjamin with a maiden Test wicket and Lara with his second catch. Lara was in action again shortly before tea when Cronje cut at Adams, bowling an innocuous first over of left-arm spin, and hit the ball straight to the slip fielder. Adams was so overjoyed that he raced to his captain in the covers and hugged him.

From tea at 188 for 4, with Hudson on 93, Hudson and Kuiper resolved to play out the day – which would involve facing the second new ball.

For Hudson there was the delight of becoming the first South African to score a century on his Test debut, achieved when he on-drove Adams for four to reach 99 and then scampered a single to midwicket.

In all of South Africa's 172 Tests between 1888/89 and 1969/70, Louis Tancred's 97 against Australia at the old Wanderers in 1902/03 had been the highest innings by a newcomer.

Hudson, though, was only vaguely aware of the historical significance as he waved his bat in triumph. He was not four years old when South Africa had played their previous Test match. 'People always talked about 1970, and Pollock and Richards, but it always seemed a bit unreal to me,' the modest Natalian said the next day. 'It's only starting to dawn on me now what it means, although I don't think I'm in the same league as players like that.'

He said he had not dwelt on the significance of batting in a Test match. 'I was too busy thinking specifically about the bowlers and getting myself organised. I had played against people like Ambrose before and after getting to 50 several times in one-day games, I was aware that I needed to play a long innings. Luckily I got into a groove and eventually felt I knew exactly what to do, but it was tiring because the bowling was good and there were hardly any loose balls.'

The last two hours were a grim struggle as Hudson and Kuiper saw off Ambrose's post-tea spell and then survived the second new ball for 13 overs before the close. Only 66 runs were scored off 36 overs in a period of play which ran more than 20 minutes past the scheduled close as the West Indies struggled to complete their quota of overs for the day.

Second day: West Indies 262. South Africa 254 for 4 in 99 overs (Hudson 135, Kuiper 19).

The pattern of attrition continued on a sunny third day as South Africa set out to achieve a substantial lead. In an uncharacteristic innings, Kuiper batted for more than three hours for his 34, with just one brief burst of aggression when he hooked Walsh and then cracked him over mid-wicket for fours.

With Hudson struggling to find the 'groove' of the previous day, the scoring was slow before Kuiper edged Patterson to wicketkeeper Williams. Adams again proved an unexpected trump card for Richie Richardson when Dave Richardson lost patience and lofted a catch to mid-on. Hudson reached 150 and seemed to be settling into a comfortable scoring pattern when he square cut Benjamin and hooked a four, but Benjamin produced a faster ball which yorked Hudson after more than eight-and-a-half hours at the crease.

He had become the first foreigner to score a debut century in Bridgetown and it was the highest Test debut innings in history against the West Indies. His 50 had come off 135 balls,

Courtney Walsh strikes a critical blow as Peter Kirsten is bowled on the last day.

his 100 off 223 and 150 off 365. Altogether he had faced 384 balls in a monumental triumph of concentration and technique.

Apart from a few daring blows by Pringle, the South African innings folded quickly with the unlikely Adams, having bowled only four overs for Jamaica all season, finishing with 4 for 43. South Africa's lead was 83, smaller than they might have liked, but a worthwhile advantage.

The rest of the afternoon belonged mainly to South Africa. Bosch made a ball lift sharply, looping off the shoulder of Simmons' bat to Kirsten at gully, and Snell again produced a telling ball when Haynes played forward defensively and was beaten by late swing to edge a catch to Richardson.

Richie Richardson was trapped leg before by a ball which kept low as the pitch started to show signs of wear and the West Indies were 68 for 3.

The left-handers Lara and Arthurton played positively but the South Africans were infuriated and astonished when Lara, playing Bosch to fine leg, failed to walk after dislodging a bail when his left foot slipped into the stumps. The square leg umpire David Archer had seen nothing, however, and Lara, on 52, survived, only to be given out to a catch behind off

Donald 12 runs later when there was doubt as to whether the ball had brushed his bat or his thigh pad.

With Donald firing at full speed, Arthurton had his off-stump uprooted by a swinging yorker. Williams and Ambrose were both out before the close as Donald and Snell finished the day with three wickets apiece.

With West Indies only 101 runs ahead and with only three wickets standing it seemed South Africa were well on the way to victory after Tuesday's rest day. Not surprisingly it was the South Africans who danced most joyously during an evening cruise party for both teams after the day's play.

Third day: West Indies 262 and 184 for 7 in 49 overs (Adams 23, Benjamin 6). South Africa 345.

The rest day was filled with discussion about the possibility of South Africa pulling off a sensational victory, but Mike Procter and Kepler Wessels warned that it was not over yet, while Richie Richardson predicted boldly that the West Indies could still win.

The general consensus was that South Africa needed to wrap up the West Indian innings quickly. Although the pitch remained fast and largely true, several deliveries had kept low towards the end of the third day and this was likely to occur more regularly as the match progressed. Any target in the region of 160 could be difficult against high-quality bowling.

All seemed well for South Africa on the fourth morning as Donald trapped Benjamin leg before in the sixth over with just 12 runs added. The tall Walsh looked ungainly with a bat in his hands, but he survived. The left-handed Adams, showing superb temperament in his first Test, played calmly.

Snell came on and with his second ball had Walsh caught behind. West Indies were 221 for 9, only 138 ahead.

The next 86 minutes were a nightmare for South Africa as Adams and Patterson not only held out but prospered as the visiting attack again offered enough loose balls to keep the scoreboard moving.

Adams went on the attack against Snell and reached his 50

CURTLY AMBROSE, born in Antigua on September 21, 1963, was widely expected to be the biggest threat to the South African batsmen and so it proved. A fast bowler with a basketball player's build, the lean, two metre tall Ambrose bowls at a lively pace with relentless accuracy. His height enables him to gain awkward lift and he is a worthy successor to Joel Garner in the West Indian team.

A relatively late starter in cricket, he made his first-class debut for the Leeward Islands in 1986 and played in his first Test against Pakistan two years later. He has played county cricket for Northamptonshire since 1988.

His eight wickets in the Test against South Africa took his total to 148 in 34 Tests at an average of 22,42. He took 8 for 45 in an innings against England in Bridgetown in 1990. He bats left-handed with occasional success, scoring 53 against Australia in Port of Spain in 1991.

with his third four in a single over, one of them all run from a lofted hit over mid-on.

Patterson survived a sharp chance to Hudson in the gully off Pringle when the total was 250, and Pringle himself then twisted acrobatically but could not hold a lofted straight drive from Adams five runs later.

The second new ball had to be taken and it took another 39 deliveries before Bosch yorked Patterson. The last wicket had added 62 precious runs. South Africa's task was no longer easy.

Time was not a factor with some nine hours of play remaining in which to score 201. A good start was essential but Hudson, having resisted temptations outside the off-stump so resolutely in the first innings, pushed at the second ball from Ambrose and was caught at slip. His long international season had turned full circle, from his duck in Calcutta to a duck in Barbados, with much excellence in between.

Wessels relieved immediate anxieties as he took advantage of loose bowling from Patterson, hitting 14 runs off the fourth over, including boundaries to mid-off, midwicket and point.

Rushmere, though, was unable to do anything more than survive as he struggled for 40 minutes before going neither forward nor back and being bowled by a ball which skidded through low.

At 27 for 2, South Africa needed their most experienced batsmen to play soundly. Wessels and Kirsten did exactly that.

It was tense cricket. Kirsten was off the mark with a neatly clipped four through midwicket off Benjamin but boundaries were difficult to score. Haynes earned the applause of his teammates as he dived to stop a searing square cut from Wessels. There was a moment of near catastrophe after tea when Wessels played a no-ball to cover and called for a single. Kirsten was slow to respond but Arthurton was unable to get his throw in quickly enough.

Patterson had to leave the field with a toe injury and gradually South Africa seemed to be gaining control. Richardson was forced to resort to Adams, but against these experienced campaigners Adams was unlikely to succeed.

Simmons was tried with his medium-pace as Richardson ran out of options with Patterson still off the field.

By the close, Wessels and Kirsten had added 95 in 42 overs of watchful, sensible batting. Only 79 needed to be scored on the final day with eight wickets in hand.

Fourth day: West Indies 262 and 283. South Africa 345 and 122 for 2 in 51 overs (Wessels 74, Kirsten 36).

The final day was overcast and a brisk breeze was blowing across the ground from the east. South African supporters went to the ground in a buoyant mood, expecting to enjoy one of the great moments in the country's cricket history. But Professor Bruce Murray, a stalwart of Wits University cricket, confessed he had not slept all night worrying about the outcome.

Walsh bowled from the pavilion, northern end. A leg bye came off his first over. Ambrose bowled a maiden to Kirsten. Wessels played defensively to Walsh. In the pavilion named after him, Sir Garfield Sobers turned to former South African captain Jackie McGlew and warned: 'Your players are batting too cautiously. They will lose unless they are more positive.' McGlew privately thought Sobers could not possibly be right but kept his counsel.

The sixth ball of the day's third over was temptingly wide of the stumps and Wessels drove. The ball seamed away from him and Lara lunged to his left to hold an excellent catch at first slip. Only one run had been added off three overs and South Africa had lost their most likely match-winner.

Ambrose and Walsh settled into a relentless rhythm. Both tall and menacing, they seemed to bowl faster and better with every over.

Cronje could only score two runs as South Africa eked out one run an over. There were no loose deliveries, no no-balls to relieve the tension.

A ball from Ambrose hurried through low, Cronje jabbed his bat into the turf and the ball carried low to the wicket-keeper. Cronje was given out and looked unhappy with the de-

Curtly Ambrose and Mike Procter in the dressing room after the Test.

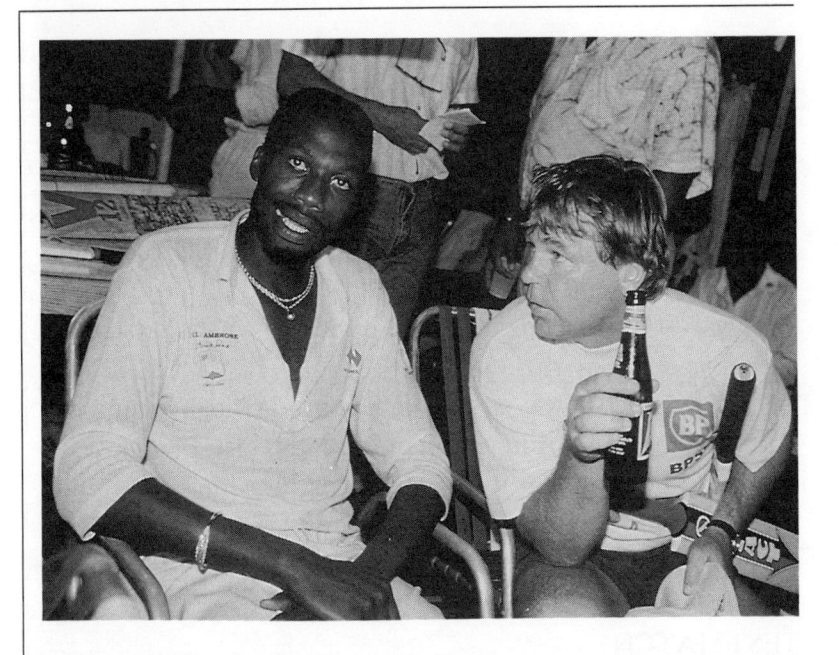

cision, but a television replay indicated he had touched the ball.

Kuiper was unable to score before Walsh, who was making the ball seam prodigiously, induced an inside edge. At 131 for 5 Kirsten was South Africa's last remaining recognised batsman.

Kirsten batted on grittily and reached his 50 with a firm cut backward of point off Ambrose. He needed to break the pattern of domination achieved by the bowlers and tried to force Walsh away to the offside in the next over. Once again Walsh, aided by the cross breeze, was able to make the 66-over-old ball deviate sharply and Kirsten was able only to deflect it into his stumps.

The match was all but over after just an hour of this fateful fifth day. Against lesser bowlers, Souch Africa might have been able to score 59 more runs with four wickets in hand, but Walsh and Ambrose relentlessly mowed down the remaining batsmen.

Donald was the last man out and Ambrose and his teammates started a wild victory dance, ripping out the stumps in triumph before linking arms in a lap of honour. Sadly, the boycott had persisted and there were only a few hundred spectators to witness a remarkable West Indian victory.

Afterwards Wessels reflected on what might have been. 'Test matches are about playing well for five days,' he said.

Wessels said the match had been lost on the fourth day when the last three West Indian wickets had cost 99 runs, while inexperience and superb bowling had been South Africa's downfall on the final morning.

Richardson was delighted with a victory which he said he had never doubted was possible.

That evening it was a subdued South African team that boarded the first SAA flight out of Barbados. They had lost, as many had before them, to a magnificent bowling attack, but they had gained immeasurably in experience in South African cricket's longest summer.

TEST MATCH
Kensington Oval, Bridgetown, Barbados, April 18–23
Toss won by Kepler Wessels

WEST INDIES first innings	Runs	4	6	Min	Balls
D Haynes c Wessels b Snell	58	9	–	109	82
(edged to first slip)					
P Simmons c Kirsten b Snell	35	4	–	93	65
(drove to wide mid-off)					
B Lara c Richardson b Bosch	17	3	–	46	33
(leg glance, diving catch to right)					
R Richardson c Richardson b Snell	44	4	–	122	78
(driving, edged to wicketkeeper)					
K Arthurton c Kuiper b Pringle	59	10	–	124	97
(drove to cover)					
J Adams b Donald	11	1	–	60	30
(fast yorker)					
D Williams c Hudson b Donald	1	–	–	4	4
(edged to gully)					
C Ambrose not out	6	–	–	47	29
K Benjamin b Snell	1	–	–	19	9
(played down wrong line)					

C Walsh b Pringle	6	1	–	5	6
(missed wild swing)					
P Patterson run out	0	–	–	1	1
(sub Rhodes/Pringle)					
(throw from cover to bowler's end)					
Extras (7lb, 17nb)	24				
Total (all out, 71,4 overs)	262				

Falls: 1/99 (Simmons), 2/106 (Haynes), 3/137 (Lara), 4/219 (Richardson), 5/240 (Arthurton), 6/241 (Williams), 7/250 (Adams), 8/255 (Benjamin), 9/262 (Walsh).

Bowling: Donald 20-1-67-2 (6nb), Bosch 15-2-43-1 (3nb), Pringle 18,4-2-62-2 (5nb), Snell 18-3-83-4 (3nb).

SOUTH AFRICA first innings	Runs	4	6	Min	Balls
M Rushmere c Lara b Ambrose	3	–	–	37	30
(edged lifted to first slip)					
A Hudson b Benjamin	163	20	–	519	384
(yorked)					
K Wessels c Adams b Ambrose	59	8	1	147	102
(chopped to deep gully)					
P Kirsten c Lara b Benjamin	11	1	–	49	31
(edged cut to first slip)					
H Cronje c Lara b Adams	5	–	–	28	20
(edged cut to slip)					
A Kuiper c Williams b Benjamin	34	4	–	195	168
(edged to wicketkeeper)					
D Richardson c Ambrose b Adams	8	1	–	31	27
(down wicket, skied to mid-off)					
R Snell run out (Benjamin)	6	1	–	28	20
(Pringle's drive deflected, backing up)					
M Pringle c Walsh b Adams	15	–	–	38	33
(lofted to mid-on)					
A Donald st Williams b Adams	0	–	–	23	21
(going for big hit)					
T Bosch not out	5	1	–	8	7

Extras (4b, 6lb, 25nb, 1w)   36
Total (all out, 135.4 overs)   345
Falls: 1/14 (Rushmere), 2/139 (Wessels), 3/168 (Kirsten),
4/187 (Cronje), 5/279 (Kuiper), 6/293 (Richardson),
7/311 (Hudson), 8/316 (Snell), 9/336 (Donald).
Bowling: Ambrose 36-19-47-2 (1nb),
Patterson 23-4-79-1 (11nb), Walsh 27-7-71-0 (1nb),
Benjamin 25-3-87-2 (12nb, 1w), Arthurton 3-0-8-0,
Adams 21.4-5-43-4.

WEST INDIES second innings	Runs	4	6	Min	Balls
D Haynes c Richardson b Snell	23	4	–	72	39
(playing forward, outside edge)					
P Simmons c Kirsten b Bosch	3	–	–	13	12
(edged lifter to gully)					
B Lara c Richardson b Donald	64	11	–	150	102
(ball lifted and seamed away)					
R Richardson lbw b Snell	2	–	–	6	2
(ball kept low)					
K Arthurton b Donald	22	2	–	66	55
(swinging yorker hit off-stump)					
J Adams not out	79	11	–	221	169
D Williams lbw b Snell	5	1	–	28	27
(went back on stumps)					
C Ambrose c Richardson b Donald	6	–	–	18	12
(prodding forward, edged)					
K Benjamin lbw b Donald	7	1	–	32	18
(ball kept low)					
C Walsh c Richardson b Snell	13	–	–	46	30
(jabbing outside off-stump)					
P Patterson b Bosch	11	–	–	86	47
(yorked)					
Extras (17b, 11lb, 20nb)	48				
Total (all out, 81.3 overs)	283				

Falls: 1/10 (Simmons), 2/66 (Haynes), 3/68 (Richardson),
4/120 (Arthurton), 5/139 (Lara), 6/164 (Williams),
7/174 (Ambrose), 8/196 (Benjamin), 9/221 (Walsh).

Bowling: Donald 25-3-77-4 (6nb), Bosch 24,3-7-61-2 (4nb), Snell 16-1-74-4 (2nb), Pringle 16-0-43-0 (8nb).

SOUTH AFRICA second innings	Runs	4	6	Min	Balls
A Hudson c Lara b Ambrose	0	–	–	2	2
(edged cut to first slip)					
M Rushmere b Ambrose	3	–	–	40	26
(ball kept low)					
K Wessels c Lara b Walsh	74	7	–	215	174
(driving, thick edge to first slip)					
P Kirsten b Walsh	52	5	–	223	168
(inside edge, trying to force to off)					
H Cronje c Williams b Ambrose	2	–	–	19	14
(edged ball that kept low)					
A Kuiper c Williams b Walsh	0	–	–	10	7
(inside edge, off-cutter)					
D Richardson c Williams b Ambrose	2	–	–	50	25
(driving, edged to wicketkeeper)					
R Snell c Adams b Walsh	0	–	–	9	8
(turned to short leg)					
M Pringle b Ambrose	4	–	–	12	7
(yorked)					
T Bosch not out	0	–	–	10	3
A Donald b Ambrose	0	–	–	1	1
(fast ball, kept low)					
Extras (4b, 3lb, 4nb)	11				
Total (all out, 72,4 overs)	148				

Falls: 1/0 (Hudson), 2/27 (Rushmere), 3/123 (Wessels), 4/130 (Cronje), 5/131 (Kuiper), 6/142 (Kirsten), 7/142 (Snell), 8/147 (Pringle), 9/148 (Richardson).
Bowling: Ambrose 24,4-7-34-6, Patterson 7-0-26-0 (1nb), Benjamin 9-2-21-0, Walsh 22-10-31-4 (3nb), Adams 5-0-16-0, Simmons 5-1-13-0.

West Indies won by 52 runs.
Man of the Match: Curtly Ambrose and Andrew Hudson (shared). Crowd 6 000.

SOUTH AFRICAN INTERNATIONAL CRICKET RECORDS

TEST MATCHES

Opponents	First Match	Total	Won	Lost	Drawn
England	1888/89	102	18	46	38
Australia	1902/03	53	11	29	13
New Zealand	1931/32	17	9	2	6
West Indies	1991/92	1	0	1	0
Total		173	38	78	57

Most appearances	50 John Waite (1951–65)
Highest total for	622/9 v Australia, Durban 1969/70
Highest total against	654/5 by England, Durban 1938/39
Lowest total for	30 v England, Port Elizabeth, 1895/96
	30 v England, Birmingham, 1924
Lowest total against	75 by Australia, Durban, 1949/50
Highest score for	274 Graeme Pollock v Australia, Durban, 1969/70
Highest score against	299 not out, Donald Bradman, Adelaide, 1931/32
Most runs for SA	3 471 (average 48,89) Bruce Mitchell (1929–49)
Most centuries	9 Dudley Nourse (1935–51)
Century on debut	163 Andrew Hudson v West Indies, Bridgetown, 1991/92
Best bowling for	9/113 Hugh Tayfield v England, Johannesburg, 1956/57
(match)	13/165 Hugh Tayfield v Australia, Melbourne, 1952/53
Best bowling against	9/28 George Lohmann (England), Johannesburg, 1895/96
(match)	17/159 Sydney Barnes (England), Johannesburg, 1913/14
Most wickets for SA	170 (average 25,91) Hugh Tayfield (1949–60)

Partnership records

1st	260	IJ Siedle/B Mitchell v England, Cape Town, 1930/31
2nd	198	EAB Rowan/CB van Ryneveld v England, Leeds, 1951
3rd	341	EJ Barlow/RG Pollock v Australia, Adelaide, 1963/64
4th	214	HW Taylor/HG Deane v England, The Oval, 1929
5th	157	AJ Pithey/JHB Waite v England, Johannesburg, 1964/65
6th	200	RG Pollock/HR Lance v Australia, Durban, 1969/70
7th	246	DJ McGlew/ARA Murray v New Zealand, Wellington, 1952/53
8th	124	AW Nourse/EA Halliwell v Australia, Johannesburg 1902/03
9th	137	EL Dalton/ACB Langton v England, The Oval, 1935
10th	103	HG Owen-Smith/AJ Bell v England, Leeds 1929

LIMITED OVERS INTERNATIONALS

Opponents	First Match	Total	Won	Lost
India	1991/92	4	2	2
Australia	1991/92	1	1	0
New Zealand	1991/92	1	0	1
Sri Lanka	1991/92	1	0	1
West Indies	1991/92	4	1	3
Pakistan	1991/92	1	1	0
Zimbabwe	1991/92	1	1	0
England	1991/92	2	0	2
Total		15	6	9

Most appearances	15 Kepler Wessels, Adrian Kuiper, Dave Richardson, Richard Snell
Highest total for	288/2 in 46,4 overs v India, New Delhi
Highest total against	287/4 in 50 overs by India, New Delhi
	287/6 in 50 overs by West Indies, Kingston
Lowest total for	152 in 43,4 overs v West Indies, Port of Spain
Lowest total against	163 in 48,3 overs by Zimbabwe, Canberra
Highest score for	90 Kepler Wessels v India, New Delhi
	90 Peter Kirsten v New Zealand, Auckland
Highest score against	122 Phil Simmons (West Indies), Kingston
Most runs for SA	578 (44,46) Kepler Wessels
Most fifties for SA	6 Kepler Wessels
Best bowling for	5/29 Allan Donald v India, Calcutta
Best bowling against	3/24 Curtly Ambrose (West Indies), Port of Spain
Most wickets for SA	24 (22,71) Allan Donald

Partnership records

1st	151	KC Wessels/AC Hudson v England, Melbourne
2nd	112	KC Wessels/PN Kirsten v Zimbabwe, Canberra
3rd	105*	PN Kirsten/AP Kuiper v India, New Delhi
4th	79	PN Kirsten/DJ Richardson v New Zealand, Auckland
5th	45	WJ Cronje/JN Rhodes v England, Sydney
6th	71	WJ Cronje/BM McMillan v Pakistan, Brisbane
7th	41	PN Kirsten/BM McMillan v New Zealand, Auckland
8th	28*	BM McMillan/RP Snell v New Zealand, Auckland
9th	21	BM McMillan/O Henry v Sri Lanka, Wellington
10th	9	BM McMillan/AA Donald v Sri Lanka, Wellington

* *Denotes unbroken partnership*

Individual limited overs international records

	M	I	NO	R	HS	Av	50	Ct/St	R	W	Av	R/over
T Bosch	2	0	–	–	–	–	–	–	66	0	–	7,76
SJ Cook	3	3	0	53	35	17,33	–	1				
WJ Cronje	11	9	3	189	47*	31,50	–	4	103	2	51,50	4,48
AA Donald	14	3	1	8	5*	4,00	–	1	545	24	22,71	4,41
CE Eksteen	1	1	1	7	7*	–	–	–	18	0	–	9,00
O Henry	3	3	1	20	11	10,00	–	1	125	2	62,50	5,03
AC Hudson	13	12	0	382	79	31,83	4	–				
PN Kirsten	14	14	3	557	90	50,64	5	4	148	6	24,67	4,93
AP Kuiper	15	14	2	276	63*	23,00	1	3	356	14	25,43	5,48
CR Matthews	2	1	1	9	9*	–	–	–	91	1	91,00	4,79
BM McMillan	11	6	3	127	33*	42,33	–	5	376	11	34,18	4,32
MW Pringle	9	2	1	6	5*	6,00	–	2	274	9	30,44	3,97
JN Rhodes	11	10	1	196	45	21,78	–	4				
CEB Rice	3	2	0	26	14	13,00	–	–	114	2	57,00	4,96
DJ Richardson	15	10	4	103	28	17,17	–	15/3				
MW Rushmere	4	4	0	78	35	19,50	–	1				
TG Shaw	1	1	1	0	0*	–	–	–	46	1	46,00	4,60
RP Snell	15	8	2	51	16	8,50	–	2	575	10	57,50	4,64
CJPG van Zyl	2	2	1	3	3*	3,00	–	–	93	0	–	5,17
KC Wessels	15	15	2	578	90	44,46	6	11				
M Yachad	1	1	0	31	31	31,00	–	1				

Note: Kepler Wessels played in 54 one-day internationals for Australia, scoring 1 740 runs (average 36,25), highest score 107.

INDEX

Please note:
Page numbers in **bold** type refer to photographs.
Photographic illustration sections are not included in this index.

Ackerman, Hylton 22
Adams, Jimmy 189–93, 195–6
Adelaide 78–9, 133
African National Congress 15, 25, 35
Ahmed, Ijaz 80, 116, 119, 160
Ahmed, Mushtaq 114, 116, 162–3
Akram, Wasim 80, 116, 142, 161–3
Alderman, Terry 76–7
Aldridge, Brian 90–1, 146–8, 161
Ambrose, Curtly 109, 111, 177, 189–190, 192, **194–197**
Amiss, Dennis **22**
Amre, Praveen 53, 55
Andrews, Wayne 77
Anurasiri, Don 103
Archer, David 193
Arthurton, Keith 110, 178, **185**, 188–90, 193–5
Ashoka Hotel 57
Australia
  cancelled South African tour 1971/2 18–19
  one-day match against South Africa 76–8
  rebel tours 1985/6, 1986/7 23
  World Cup opening match 85
  World Cup match against South Africa 87–95
Australian Cricket Academy, South African match against 78–9
Azharuddin, Mohammed 49–50, 53, 134–5

Bacher, Ali **14**, 16, **26**–9, 32–9, 41–2, 45–6, 55–6, 61, 66, 90, 167–70
Barlow, Eddie 65
Begg, Yasien 69
Bellerive Oval 82
Benjamin, Kenneth 184, 189–92, 194–5
Benjamin, W 109, 178
Bevan, Michael 84
Biggs, Anthony (Dassie) 22
Bing, Bradley 186
Bland, Colin 71
Boon, David 85, **86**, 90–2
Border, Alan 89, 91–4
Bosch, Tertius 65, 68–9, 73, 83, 89, 98, 158, 180, 187–9, 193, 195
Botham, Ian 127–8, **146**, 148–9, 159–61
Bowral 83
Boycott, Geoffrey 21, **22**
Bradman, Donald, Sir 19, 83
Brandes, Eddo 73, 123
Bryson, Rudi 65, 69, 154
Bucknor, Steve 160
Burger, Chris 62

Cairns, Chris 85, 98–9
Calcutta, arrival of South African team 46–53
Callaghan, James 18
Camacho, Steve 167–8
Campbell, Alastair 72

Channel Nine, cricket broadcast 12
Chappell, Greg 21
Chappell, Ian 21
Chesterfield, Trevor 64
Cook, Jimmy 16, **40**, 43–4, 50–1, 55, 58–9, **62**–5, **67**–9, 185
Cooke, Peter 21
Cowdrey, Colin 15, 39
Cronje, Hansie 44, 59, 65, 68, 73, 77, 79, 90, 91, 98, 108, 116, 118, 128, 137, 149, 154, 156, 175, 178, 191, 196
Crookes, Derek 44
Crowe, Martin **84**, 85, **99**, 100, 141–3
Cullinan, Daryll 43, 59, 65
Cummins, Anderson 109, 111, 178, 183–4

Dakin, Geoff **14**, **16**, 32, 37–9, 46, 49, 56, 66, 68
Dalmiya, Jagmohan 41–2, 46
Davids, Faiek 44, 68, 83
Day, Chris 47
De Beers Country Club, Kimberley, demonstrations 27–30
De Freitas, P 126–7, 130, 160
De Klerk, F W, President 31
De Kock, Gerald 49
De Silva, Aravinda 102, 104
De Vaal, Peter 22
Dev, Kapil 51, 55, **134**, 135, 137
declaration of intent, December 1990 36–7
Denness, Mike 21
D'Oliveira, Basil 18–**19**
Donald, Allan 12, 32, 43, **48**, **50**, 52–3, 55, 65, 68, 72–3, 77, 80, 82–3, 90–2, 100, 104–5, 110–11, 116, 127, 129, 134–5, 146–8, 153, 157, 173–4, 180, **185**, 187–9, 194, 197
du Preez, Jackie 71
Dujon, Jeffrey 175–5
Dum Dum airport, Calcutta 46

Ebrahim, Baboo 21
Eden Gardens Stadium, Calcutta 42, 47, 49
Eden Park 97, 141
Egar, Colin 75
Eksteen, Clive 43–4, 55, 65, 153
Emburey, John **22**
England
  World Cup 1975 20–1
  World Cup 1992 9–13, 126–31, 159–65

Fairbrother, N 128–30, 147, 162
Farrell, Michael 82
Fazal, Zahid 81, 117
Flower, Andy 72, 122

Gatting, Mike 15, 23, 25–32, **34**, 61–62, 93
Gavaskar, Sunil 38

Gooch, Graham 9, **10**, 11, 21–**22**, 125, 145–6, 149–50, **159**–63
Graveney, David **34**
Greatbatch, Mark 100, 141
Greenidge, Gordon 174, 183–5
Griffith, Charlie 184, 186
Griffiths, Edward 65–6
Gurusinha, Asanka 104
Gwalior, visit to 54–7

Haider, Wasim 115
Hall, Wesley 183, 186
Halt All Racist Tours organisation (HART) 97
Harare Sports Club 70, 72
Harper, Roger 184
Harris, Chris 85, 98–9, 142
Hathurusinghe, Asanka 104
Hayat, Khizar 98
Haynes, Desmond 109, **110**, 111, 173, 178, 180, 183–4, 187–8, 193, 195
Healy, Ian 91
Hendriks, Jackie 184
Henry, Omar 65, 68, 73, 79, 83, 89, 97, 102, 158, 173–4, 186
Hick, Graeme 127–8, 146–7, 161–3
Hills, Dene 82
Hobart 82
Holford, David 184
Hooper, C 110
Houghton, David 74, 122
Howa, Hassan 19–20
Hudson, Andrew **40**, 43, 50–2, 59, 65, 68, 73, 79–80, 89, 92, 98, 108–9, **116**, 119, 126–7, 135–7, 148, 154–5, 175, 177, **182**, 189–92, 195
Hughes, Kim 23, 62, 75–6, 78
Hunte, Conrad 172, 183

Illingworth, R 127, 148–9, 161
Imperial Cricket Conference, 1909 17
India
  Board of Control for Cricket invitation to South Africa 41
  South African tour 42–59
  World Cup match 133–9
International Cricket conference formation 1965 18
  South African exclusion 20
International Cricket Council 37–9
International Wanderers XI 1975/76 21
Inzamam-ul-Haq **2**–**3**, 81, 118–19, 142–3, 161
Irvine, Lee 63

Jackson, John 30
James, Wayne 72–3, 122
Jardine, Bill 27
Jarvis, Malcolm 73, 123
Javed, Aaqib 80, 116–17, 161–2
Jawaharlal Nehru Stadium, New Delhi 57
Jayasuriya, Sanath 104–5
Jennings, Ray 65
Jones, Andrew 85
Jones, Dean 91
Jordaan, Alan 66, 74, 158
Julian, Brendon 77–8

Kalpage, R 105

Kensington Oval, Bridgetown 183, 187
Khan, Imram 80, **81**, 82, 115–9, 142, **160**–3
Khan, Moin 81, 116–17, 142, 162–3
Kingston 171
Kirsten, Peter 43, 51, 55, 58–9, 62, 64–6, 68–9, 73–4, 77, 79–80, 93–4, 98, 100, 103, 105, 109, 111, 122–3, 127, 129, 134–7, 148, 154–5, 178, 185–7, 191, **193**, 195–7
Knott, Alan **22**
Koornhof, Piet 20
Kuiper, Adrian 34, 43, 52, 55, 59, 65, 68, 72, 74, 77, 79, 83, 91, 98–100, 102, 108–9, 111, 118, 127–30, 134, 137, 147–9, 171, 178, 191–2, 197

Lamb, Allan 125, 145, 147–8, 162
Lancaster Park, Christchurch 108
Lara, Brian 109–10, **170**, 173, 178, 180, **186**, 188, 191, 193, 196
Latham, Rod 85, 100
Lavender, Mark 77
Lever, John **22**
Lewis, Chris 9, 125, 129–30, 145, 147–9, 161–2
Lillee, Dennis 21
Lloyd, Clive 174
Logie, Gus 110–11

Mackay-Coghill, Don 75, 78
Mackerdhuj, Krish **14**, 16, 36–9, 71
Mafole, Tebogo 173
Mahanama, Roshan 104–5
Majiet, Rushdie 63
Majola, Kaya 15–16
Malik, Salim 18, 142
Manack, Hoosain 44
Mandela, Nelson 39
Manjrekar, Sanjay 52, 54, 58, 134
Manley, Michael 173
Manuka Oval, Pakistan 80
Marsh, Geoff 77, **78**, 90–1
Marsh, Rodney 79
Marshall, Malcolm 109–10, 183–5
Martyn, Damian 77
Masemola, Walter **38**
Mashishi, Moss 15
Matthews, Craig 43, 65, 154
Mbeki, Thabo 37
MCC, cancelled tour of South Africa 1968/69 18
McCague, Martin 77
McDermott, Craig 85, 92–3
McEwan, Kenny 62
McGlew, Jackie 196
McMillan, Brian 9–10, 13, 43, 53, 65, 68, 77, 81–2, 91, 100, 103, 105, 109–11, 116–17, 119, **122**, 128–9, 145, 147, 149–50, 153–4, 156, 169
Medworth, C 17
Melbourne Cricket Ground 125–6
Miandad, Javed 80, 115, 142, **143**, 160
Moody, Tom 76–7, 91
moratorium on international sports contacts 35–6, 39
More, Kiran 55
Moyo, Dan 15
Murray, Bruce 196
Murray, Deryck 167

Naidoo, Krish 25, 27–8, 32
National Olympic and Sports Congress (NOSC) 15, 25–32, 39
New Zealand, World Cup matches 85, 97–100, 141–5
Nosarka, Liq 25, 45

Oberoi Grand Hotel, Calcutta 46–7

Pakistan
　anti-South Africa sentiment 17, 39
　cancellation of Indian tour 41
　match against South Africa 80–2
　World Cup match against England 159–65
　World Cup match against South Africa 115–21
　World Cup, victory in final match 13
Pamensky, Joe 19, **20**
Pan Africanist Congress, bomb scare 171
Panasonic (company sponsorship) 45
Partridge, Joe 71
Patel, Dipak 85, 98
Patterson, Patrick **188**, 189–92, 195–6
Perth, cricket match in 74–8
Pienaar, Roy 43
Pietmaritzburg, anti-tour demonstration 31
Pithey, Tony 63
Pollock, Peter 63
Port of Spain, Trinidad 177
Prabhakar, Manoj 51, 55, 135, 137
Pringle, Derek 145, 160
Pringle, Meyrick 13, 68–9, 73, **75**, 77–8, 90–1, 98, **108**–11, 116, 118, 127, 129–30, 134, 146–7, 153, 157, 173, 180, 185–7, 189, 193, 195
Procter, Mike 13, **46**, 63, 68, 74, 79, 139, 158–9, 194, **197**
Pycroft, Andrew 122

Qadir, Abdul 162
Queens Park Oval, Port of Spain **173**, 177
Queensland, cancellation of match 83

Raja, Rameez 81, 115, 142, 160
Raju, Venkatapathy 52, 55, 58, 136
Ramanayake, Champeke 102, 105
Ramasamy, Sam 71
Ranatunga, Arjuna **103**, 105
Randell, Steve 148
rebel test matches 21–3
Reddie, Syd 63
Reddy, S K 184
Reeve, Dermot 127, 145, 148, 161, 163
Reid, Bruce 76, 85, 92–3
Rhodes, Jonathan (Jonty) **2**–**3**, 59, 65, 68, 74, **76**, 92, **96**, 103–4, 110, 119, 129–30, **132**, 137, 147, 149, 154, 156, 178, 180, 186
Rhodesia, participation in South African cricket 71
　see also Zimbabwe
Rice, Clive 22, **42**, 43, 46, 48–50, 52–3, 55, 59–66, 68, 84–5, 170, 185
Richards, Barry 84
Richards, David 38
Richards, Viv 174, 185
Richardson, Dave 10, 13, 43, 52, 55, 65, 68, 82–3, 90–1, 98, 109, 116, 128, 147, 149, 156, 188, 192
Richardson, Richie 108–11, **174**–5, 179, 188–9, 192–3, 195, 198
Rindel, Mike 65
Robins, Derrik 21
Rowe, Lawrence 23, 62, 172
Rushmere, Mark 43, 65, 68, 76, 78–9, 89, 102, 104, 108, 116, 157, 180, **182**, 189–190, 195
Rutherford, Ken 85

Sabina Park, Kingston **169**, 172
Sandiford, Erskine 186
Sandton Hotel, press conference, 23 October 1991 15–16
Schultz, Brett 65
Scindia, Madhavrao 54–7
Shah, Ali 73, 122
Sharjah, UCB delegation 16
Shastri, Ravi 52, 58
Shaw, Tim 43, 53, 65, 69
Shillingford, Irving 184
Short, Arthur 22
Sidhu, Navjot 49, 52, 54–5, 58
Sikander, Iqbal 80, 160
Simmons, Phil 174, 177, 180, 187–8, 193, 196
Small, Gladstone 126, 149, 160
Smith, Ian 98, 100, 142
Smith, Robin 127–8, 145, 160
Snell, Richard 13, 32, 43, 52–3, 55, 65, 68, 81, 90–1, 100, 110, 117, 128, 134, 147, 153, 157, 180, 187–90, 193–4
Sobers, Garfield, Sir **38**, 183, 196
Sobers, Gary 172
Sohail, Aamir 81, 117, **141**, 160
Sonn, Percy 16, 39
South Africa
　exclusion from World cricket 17–20
　readmission to World Cup cricket competition 15–16, 87–95
　rebel touring teams 21
　referendum 123
South Africa, cricket tours, 1992
　Australia 76–8
　India 42–59
　Pakistan 80–2
　West Indies 169–201
　Zimbabwe 72
South Africa, World Cup matches, 1992
　Australia 87–95
　England 126–31
　India 133–9
　New Zealand 97–100
　Pakistan 115–121
　Sri Lanka 102–7
　West Indies 108–12
　Zimbabwe 122–5
South African Breweries, sponsorship of rebel tours, 1982 21–3
South African Council on Sport (SACOS) 24
South African Cricket Association 17, 19–20
South African Cricket Board (SACB) 16, 20, 35–7
South African Cricket Board of Control (SACBOC) 19–20
South African Cricket Union (SACU) 16, 20–1, 32–3, 35–7

Sparks, Allister 28
Sri Lanka
  tour of South Africa 22–3
  World Cup match against South Africa 102–7
Srikkanth, K 54, 58, 134
Srinath, Jawagal 51–2, 59, 135, 137
Stewart, A 126–30, 146–7, 161
Sydney Cricket Ground 87

Tasmania, match against 82–3
Taylor, P 92–3
Tancred, Louis 191
Tendulkar, Sachin 52–3, 134, **136**
Taj Majal 54
Teresa, Mother 47–9
Tillekeratne, Hashan 104
townships, cricket promotion 36
Traicos, John 71–2
Tshwete, Steve **14**, 35–6, 38, 93, 97
Turner, Glenn 21
Tyamzashe, Mthobi 29

Underwood, Derek 21–**22**
United Cricket Board of South Africa 37–9, 41–2, 45, 168

van der Bijl, Vincent 22
van der Merwe, Peter 42, 61–**64**, 66
van Zyl, Corrie 65, 69, 169, 174, 186
Varachia, Rashid 20
Veletta, Mike 77
Viljoen, Gerrit 28
Vlok, Adriaan 28
Vorster, John 18

Walcott, Clyde 167–8, 183, 186
Walcott, Victor 186
Walker, Max 21
Waller, Andy 73, 122
Walsh, Courtney 184, 189–90, 192–**193**, 195–7
Wanderers Johannesburg, 'test match' 1990 31–2
Warnapura, Bandula 22
Watson, Gary 22
Watson, W 98

Waugh, Mark 89, 93
Waugh, Steve 91
Weaver, Paul 26–7
Webber, Darren 79
Weekes, Everton 183, 186
Wessels, Kepler 11–12, 43, 49, 51–**53**, 55, 58–9, 62, 64–6, 68–9, **72**–4, 76, 79–80, 82, **86**, 88–9, 92–4, 98, 103, 105, 108, 110–1, 116, 112–3, 126–7, 134, 137, 146, 148, 154–5, 171, 173–7, 185, 187–90, 194–8
West Indies Cricket Board of Control, opposition to South African admission to World Cup 38–9, 167
West Indies, South African tour of 1992
  Barbados 183–201
  Port of Spain, Trinidad 177–80
  Sabina Park 169–75
West Indies
  tour of South Africa, 1982/83 73
  World Cup match 108–12
Western Australia, 1991 match against 76–8
Western Australian Cricket Association 75
Whitney, Mike 89, 92–3
Wickremasinghe, P 102
Williams, David 110, 175, 194
World Cup opening 84
World Cup semi-final, Sydney, 1992 9–13
  South Africa's application for admission 38–9
  team selection 63
Worrell, Frank, Sir 183
Wounis, Waqar 162
Wright, John 143

Yachad, Mandy 43, 55, 65
Younis, Waqar 80, 115

Zimbabwe
  match against South Africa 72
  World Cup Match against South Africa 122–5
Zoehrer, Tim 78